The Business of America

The Business
of America

The Cultural Production
of a Post-War Nation

Graham Thompson

Pluto Press

LONDON • STERLING, VIRGINIA

First published 2004 by
Pluto Press
345 Archway Road, London N6 5AA
and 22883 Quicksilver Drive, Sterling, VA 20166–2012, USA

www.plutobooks.com

British Library Cataloguing in Publication Data
A catalogue record for this book is available from the British Library

ISBN   0 7453 1809 6 hardback
ISBN   0 7453 1808 8 paperback

Library of Congress Cataloging in Publication Data
Thompson, Graham, 1965–
    The business of America : the cultural production of a post-war nation
/ Graham Thompson.
        p. cm.
Includes index.
    ISBN 0–7453–1809–6 — ISBN 0–7453–1808–8 (pbk.)
    1. Business anthropology—United States. 2. Corporate culture—United
States. 3. United States—Civilization. 4. United States—Study and
teaching. I. Title.

    GN450.8.T48 2004
    306.4'0973—dc22

                                                                2003022871

10   9   8   7   6   5   4   3   2   1

Designed and produced for Pluto Press by
Chase Publishing Services, Fortescue, Sidmouth, EX10 9QG, England
Typeset from disk by Stanford DTP Services, Northampton, England
Printed and bound in the European Union by
Antony Rowe Ltd, Chippenham and Eastbourne, England

For Blanche and Karen

Contents

Acknowledgements

Many thanks to Anne Beech at Pluto Press for her patience and support and to Emma for her own brand of 'encouragement' that helped me get there in the end.

Introduction

On 17 January 1925, United States president Calvin Coolidge stood up to address the American Society of Newspaper Editors in Washington, DC. Although his subject was 'The Press Under a Free Government', the speech is best remembered now for an aphorism Coolidge introduced to the cultural imaginary of the nation. 'The chief business of the American people', he told his audience, 'is business.'[1] The repetition of the more familiar paraphrased version of this remark – 'the business of America is business' – has turned Coolidge's observation into a familiar slogan. But it is a slogan whose apparent simplicity disguises a powerful argument about the way that the relationship between business and nationhood has been conceived in the United States; a simplicity that also makes the slogan ideologically malleable. Capable of being used to naturalise and defend the operations of United States business on the one hand, on the other it can also be used to criticise these operations on the grounds that the problem with life in the United States is that everything else is subordinated to the demands of business.

This book argues that these conflicting ideological values can be heard echoing through post-war United States literature. They are most evident wherever writers directly represent and engage the various elements of business culture – its executives, managers and employees, or the physical and mental conditions of employment and entrepreneurship. Here, for example, one might place Arthur Miller's canonical *Death of a Salesman*, Sloan Wilson's best-selling *The Man in the Gray Flannel Suit*, Ayn Rand's impassioned *Atlas Shrugged*, or Douglas Coupland's zeitgeisty *Microserfs*. But such conflicting ideological values also inform other texts at a fundamental level, acting as the narrative unconscious of works traditionally appreciated for qualities other than their treatment of business: books like Norman Mailer's *The Naked and the Dead*, Thomas Pynchon's *The Crying of Lot 49*, Carson McCullers's *The Ballad of the Sad Café* and Kathy Acker's *Empire of the Senseless*. The aim of this book is to try and understand not only what drives this preoccupation with business, but also to

1

study the various strategies that writers have used to negotiate their relationship to the discourses of business.

By the discourses of business I mean three things. First of all, I mean the way that business as a theme has been written and talked about in the United States, by presidents, by social critics, by journalists, and by novelists and playwrights. Secondly, I mean the way that the historical accumulation of this collective input has fashioned a set of rules that govern the way successive generations can think about business. These rules need not be mutually supportive. Coolidge's aphorism is an example of how business might be interpreted positively or negatively in the discourses of business. What matters is that business is conceived within a recognisable historical framework of ideas and themes. Think, for example, of the way that 'industry' as a means of succeeding in business has exercised various commentators. Benjamin Franklin in 'The Way to Wealth' has Poor Richard advise his audience that *'Sloth makes all things difficult, but industry all easy ... drive thy business, let not that drive thee'*,[2] while J. Hector St. Jean de Crèvecoeur suggested that Americans were 'all animated with the spirit of an industry which is unfettered and unrestrained, because each person works for himself'.[3] It is this spirit that one can see embraced in Horatio Alger's self-help stories of the nineteenth century and even in the political rhetoric of black leaders like Booker T. Washington. In *Up From Slavery*, Washington writes about educating black children with practical knowledge of business but also of imbuing in them 'the spirit of industry, thrift, and economy'.[4] This is not to deny, of course, the important difference between the subject positions of each of these writers, but merely to emphasise the way that a discourse of business is created, and enshrined as it is repeated.

Finally, I mean by the discourses of business the way that the specialised and professionalised languages of business become tropes and metaphors capable of being transposed outside of a strictly business environment. When words like industry, trading, investment, expansion, organisation and inflation, for example, are used in non-business contexts they carry with them the legacy of their origins into the new context. It is from within the confines of these discourses of business that many post-war literary texts seek to define their themes and characters.

One possible approach to these acts of definition would be to consider the discourses of business as superstructural manifestations of capitalist organisation. In terms of some of the books mentioned above, this would mean bolting the themes of war, postmodernity, sexuality and gender onto an underpinning capitalist base in order to observe what Richard Godden has described as the 'shards of redundant logic and traditions of resistance littered across the marketplace' as capitalism is transformed by technological innovations in the areas of both production and consumption.[5] Whilst sympathetic to such an approach and willing to draw on the work of critics who have attempted such analyses, the objective I have set myself here is somewhat different. What will coordinate my approach is the link that Coolidge made between business and the 'American people', and which the paraphrased version of his remark makes between business and 'America'. This book will examine, then, the way that post-war United States literature has, throughout its engagement with the discourses of business, imagined the complex signifier 'America'; a signifier that has been, and continues to be, the subject of continual social, cultural and rhetorical reconstruction. The conflicting ideological values that I have suggested are part and parcel of a slogan like 'The business of America is business', suggest that what is at stake ideologically is the configuration of 'America' itself. One way to start thinking about the implications of this for post-war literature is to return Coolidge's aphorism to the largely forgotten speech that was its original context and see just how he performed the construction of 'America' and the 'American people'.

THE BUSINESS OF IDEALISM

From the vantage point of the twenty-first century – when the motivations of national and global newsgathering and media conglomerates increasingly generate popular, governmental and academic scrutiny – there is much in Coolidge's speech that appears prescient. Indeed, it rehearses a contemporary debate about the responsibilities facing newspapers – and, for us, other media forms – in their twin roles as sites of cultural information exchange and as moneymaking enterprises. Coolidge constructed his speech as a riposte against public concern with 'the commercialism of the press' and the impartiality of the information disseminated when 'great newspapers are great business enterprises earning large profits and controlled by men of wealth'. Promptly dismissing these concerns, Coolidge declared 'it is probable that a press which maintains an intimate touch with the business currents of the nation, is likely to be more reliable than it would be if it were a stranger to these influences'. His justification was that only by understanding the 'producing, buying, selling, investing and prospering' in which people were daily engaged could a newspaper hope to fulfil its democratic, civilising role. And in a piece of rhetorical mirroring that places his earlier comments about 'the chief business of the American people' into sharp perspective, in his concluding remarks Coolidge maintained that 'the chief ideal of the American people is idealism ... I could not truly criticize the vast importance of the counting room, but my ultimate faith I would place in the high idealism of the editorial room of the American newspaper.'

Ironically, then, one of the most famous declarations about business in the United States, far from being an endorsement of the primacy of business in the construction of 'America', was actually an attempt to refute this conviction. There are things for Coolidge that should be desired ahead of the creation of wealth. 'It is only those who do not understand our people,' he argued, 'who believe that our national life is entirely absorbed by material motives.' The political and national freedom Coolidge emphasises here he made a corollary of economic freedom more explicitly elsewhere. A year earlier, at a meeting of the Business Organization of the Government of which he was Chief Executive, Coolidge told his fellow members that 'any oppression laid upon the people by excessive taxation, any disregard of their right to hold and enjoy the property which they have rightfully acquired, would be fatal to freedom'. Coolidge's quest for freedom in the service of a civilised 'America' – and he admitted it demanded 'a constant and mighty effort' – makes business only the *means* by which higher goals may be achieved. To paraphrase, then, one could claim that for Coolidge 'The business of business is America.'

Coolidge's emphasis upon business as an enabling force together with the link between economic and political freedom is worth bearing in mind when thinking about the negotiation with business in one particular line of post-war literature. White male literary culture, on first examination at least, seems to have been straightforwardly antagonistic towards business during this period. Emily Stipes Watt has upbraided this group of writers, with only minor exception, for its denigration of business. She notes that 'Most businessmen depicted in post-1945 television and serious literature are still characterized as greedy, unethical, and immoral ... whether they are JR of William Gaddis's *JR: A Novel* or J.R. of "Dallas".'[6] Indeed, it has rarely been the case that the explicit ideological objectives of business or businessmen have been ratified by white male literary culture in the

United States. These writers have often been attracted instead to what, as early as the 1840s, Henry David Thoreau was calling the 'lives of quiet desperation'[7] that men lead in the face of a materialistic market society dominated by business. From the 'exhaustion' that Arthur Miller uses in his very first description of Willy Loman in *Death of a Salesman*,[8] through the self-pitying melancholy of Bob Slocum in Joseph Heller's *Something Happened*, right up to Patrick Bateman's disregard for the human body in *American Psycho* inspired by the depthlessness of contemporary stock trading, there has existed a resentment for the pressures and strains business and its attendant culture imposes on the individual male.

In post-war United States culture, this antagonism has manifested itself most clearly as one aspect of what Timothy Melley has recently described as 'agency panic'. For Melley, this is an 'intense anxiety about an apparent loss of autonomy, the conviction that one's actions are being controlled by someone else or that one has been "constructed" by powerful, external agents … especially government and corporate bureaucracies, control technologies and mass media'.[9] Such an entanglement of big business and government has been a source of fear across a broad spectrum of opinion in the post-war era. Dwight Eisenhower warned that America should 'guard against the acquisition of unwarranted influence, whether sought or unsought, by the military-industrial complex',[10] while Joseph Heller in *Catch-22*, published the same year as Eisenhower made this comment, took the chance to further refine Coolidge's dictum about business and America. Milo Minderbinder, head of the shadowy business syndicate that trades across enemy lines while the world is at war, tries to persuade his colleague Yossarian that the government has no place in business, until he suddenly remembers Coolidge and misquotes him: 'the business of government *is* business'.[11] The substitution of 'America' by 'government' here suggests the way in which the two have become interchangeable. The suspicion in Heller's satirical novel is that government and business are in league with one another and that what is threatened by this alliance are the very qualities that American governments are meant to protect: the individualism, freedom and democracy which should mean that the government has no place in business. In white male literary culture it is here where 'America' – with the government standing in for 'America' – is tainted by its connections with business. Where for Coolidge business was no hindrance to achieving a dazzling, civilised 'America', for many white male writers business, and a certain way of doing business, has actually *betrayed* 'America' or other supposedly 'American' values like the individual, the family, the community and freedom. It is for this reason that it is so difficult to find the positive representations of business or businessmen for which Stipes Watt is looking.

This reaction, while suggesting a hostility towards business, does not, however, suggest a similar hostility towards a certain notion of 'America' as a repository of individualism and freedom. Indeed, as a reaction it presents an ideological paradox, and one that is exquisitely captured in Milo's rapid *volte face*. What Milo wants is a free hand to conduct deals and trades; what he also wants is for the government to guarantee this free hand by creating the conditions in which he can do his deals and trades and at the same time to act both as one of his suppliers and consumers. Freedom and state regulation in the realms of business are not mutually exclusive, then, but mutually dependent forces. This circular logic is mirrored in the disenchantment and antagonism with which white male literary culture has treated business. Writers denouncing business because it threatens 'American' liberties may risk implicitly defending the philosophical values upon which that very business is built. To offer a criticism of the size of large corporate businesses and their monopolistic practices – a phenomenon that has marked out the relationship between government, business and social criticism in the United States at least from the time of Standard Oil through to Microsoft – risks defending the principles of free trade, entrepreneurial freedom and deregulation and the very conditions that facilitated the rise of huge corporations from modest origins in the first place. To ask whether John D. Rockefeller or Bill Gates are pioneering start-up entrepreneurs or monopolistic empire-builders is in the end only to submit to a discourse of American business that allows the reconstitution of 'America' on liberal grounds to pass almost unnoticed. If they are pioneers then what better ratification of the enabling possibilities of 'American' values; if they are monopolists then what better ratification of 'American' social criticism and democratic government than the exposure and outlawing of such practices.

It seems to me that there is an uncomfortable symmetry between much of the antagonism towards business in post-war white male literary culture and Coolidge's rhetoric: the idealism, the importance of raising ideals above business in the constitution of 'America' in its civilising form, and the rejection of materialism. One might also add to this an emphasis upon the aesthetic creativity of the individual liberal subject. Coolidge was nothing if not flexible. In the course of his speech he also managed to praise the American journalist for making out of current events not 'a drab and sordid story, but rather an informing and enlightened epic. His work becomes no longer imitative, but rises to an original art.' This symmetry suggests that the relationship between white male literary culture and the business of 'America' cannot be considered to be so straightforwardly antagonistic. Whilst the political motivations of Coolidge may be completely different from the literary opponents of big business, rhetorical commonalities bring the two parties much closer together. In much the same way that current anti-globalisation movements rely for their organisation and publicity upon global communication networks created by the very multinational corporations they oppose, so the explicit anti-business approach of much white male post-war literature relies for its inspiration upon ideals shared by the very forces it opposes. As Emily Stipes Watt also alertly points out, 'no writer has attacked capitalism for its emphasis upon and celebration of the individual'.[12]

Business, then, is a slippery catch to land and another aim of this book is to reverse the paraphrasing impetus that Coolidge's aphorism has fallen victim to. While useful as a kind of shorthand, it is incapable of encompassing the often conflicting ideological discourses about business and their relationship to 'America' in the United States that I have outlined here. Of course, this introductory sketch has used a broad brush and I hope to fill in, particularly in the first half of this book, the subtlety of the convergences and divergences that occur as literary texts negotiate the ideological paradox governing discourses about business. But my starting point will be that white male literary culture is not simply, nor primarily, hostile towards business; that what appears to be criticism of business may actually be the affirmation of the ideological 'America' that business itself seeks. There may have been more truth than Sinclair Lewis could have imagined when he mischievously has George Babbitt declare that, unlike in other countries where literature was left 'to a lot of shabby bums living in attics', in America 'the successful writer ... is indistinguishable from any other decent business man'.[13]

THE BUSINESS OF DIFFERENT EXPERIENCES

I have been careful to mark out a particular lineage here with the rather ungainly delimiter 'white male literary culture'. Clearly this represents a collection of writers whose interests are not entirely harmonised. Yet it serves the purpose of helping to demarcate a particular argument that this book will pursue: namely that there is an identifiable gap between the way that the discourse of business is negotiated by texts produced by the white male writers I consider in Part I of this book, and the texts considered in the second half of the book that I have grouped together by three main categories: gender, race and ethnicity, and sexuality. The reason for splitting the book in this way is primarily to relativise the narrative I have outlined above. This is in many ways a hegemonic narrative of United States business. While ostensibly hostile to the effects of business, it reconstitutes the importance of the individual as the site upon which the sanctity of 'America' rests and thus corresponds with the ideological interests of business by creating citizens loyal to a myth of the nation rather than politically active class groups.

Clearly this is not a narrative confined to white male culture and it is perhaps important to indicate that this hegemonic narrative works elsewhere, as it does for example in Naomi Klein's recent international bestseller *No Logo*. Notwithstanding this book's eloquent and comprehensive protest against the economic downsides of late twentieth-century globalisation and the political intentions Klein proclaims, there is in *No Logo* a discursive tension that catapults Klein's rhetoric right back to the origins of the nation-building project of 'America'. This historical blindness means Klein ignores the almost perpetual discourse of anti-corporatism that has inflected United States social criticism since the end of the nineteenth century, as railway, oil and steel businesses began to grow so rapidly. Klein argues this attitude is only just emerging. Ignoring the alertness of a company like Disney as early as the 1920s and '30s to the principles of branding in economic success, she also suggests that it is only since the 1980s that corporations switched from the production of goods to the production of brands. Ultimately, by not historicising her project, Klein ends up mimicking a Jeffersonian concept of citizenship. 'When we start looking to corporations to draft our collective labor and human rights codes for us,' she argues, 'we have already lost the most basic principle of citizenship: that people should govern themselves.'[14] Compare this to the words of Donald J. Boudreaux, President of the right-wing Foundation for Economic Education, when he complains that 'Almost all that today's state does offends the idea of self-government.'[15] This passion for self-government from both the politically left and right perpetuates the hegemonic narrative of

United States business by offering up as a goal a particularly 'American' version of national citizenship.

Part of the problem with this hegemonic approach is that it treats business, and particularly large corporations, as abstract and synecdochic phenomena at the same time. So 'corporate America' is turned into an overarching condition that is meant to represent the generalised environment under which people live, whilst each representation of an organisation or corporation is made to embody the principles of 'corporate America'. This is certainly the case in Heller's *Catch-22* or Mailer's *The Naked and the Dead*. What results is a tautological argument that confirms what it assumes to be the case in the first place. What gets left behind under this panoptic vision of 'America' is what Jonathan Freedman has called 'the complex tangle of experiences that is life in an advanced capitalist economy'.[16] What the second part of this book will try to articulate is the way that these 'experiences' have been written about from subject positions that do not have such a vested interest in reproducing a hegemonic narrative of United States business. Again, I do not want to schematise too sharply, since in Chapter 3 I will show how a writer like Douglas Coupland recoils from the prevailing 'corporate America' narratives of his white male predecessors. It does appear to me, though, that the texts I treat in the second part of this book offer a more specialised version of what it is like to coexist with discourses of business that are at once intimately connected to the idea of nationhood, whilst at the same time the 'America' these discourses produce are inimical to the subject positions from which the texts in Part II are written.

Dana Nelson has recently shown how what she calls 'Capitalist Citizenship' was, from its moment of inception in the United States after the Revolution, organised and consolidated by a concept of 'white manhood' that undergirded the quest for national unity. Nascent professional and managerial groups in the business sphere marked their affiliations and group solidarity by establishing identities that emphasised their difference from women, blacks and Indians.[17] It is conditions like this which are responsible for creating different experiences of, and relationships to, the discourse of business in the United States. Although philosophically women, minority groups and immigrants have been interpellated as 'American' citizens by the melting pot myth, their experiences have been quite different, particularly in the realms of business. As Chinese labourers were helping to build the transcontinental railroads that would open up an internal market for United States products, the Chinese Exclusion

Act of 1882 was debarring many of these workers from claiming citizenship rights, and similar legislation would continue discrimination against Asian immigrants until the end of the Second World War. As black slaves worked the cotton fields of the South and helped create the huge wealth of plantation owners, so they were systematically and legally excluded from participating in the freedom and democracy they were told marked out the 'American' nation. Even with abolition the transition for many blacks was one that put them into wage slavery. The 'separate spheres' discourse that helped keep the business world the preserve of 'white manhood' was little disturbed by the growth of office-based employment at the end of the nineteenth and the beginning of twentieth century as the demand for low-paid labour was met by the influx of women into the workplace and the demarcation of jobs along gender lines. In 1870, just 2 per cent of American clerical workers were women. By 1930, this figure had risen to 50 per cent.[18] Most, though, were typists and stenographers (almost exclusively female occupations) while male clerks found themselves beginning to occupy the burgeoning number of lower and middle management positions as well as the executive positions they had always dominated. The perpetuation of the glass ceiling in post-war United States business is testament to the legacy of these kinds of practices. The sexualisation of the working and business environment has perhaps been less well documented, but Nelson's work does prepare the groundwork for explaining the increasing masculinisation of business culture which gathers pace towards the end of the nineteenth century. E. Anthony Rotundo has suggested that the growing importance of work and the workplace is one of the two revolutions in thinking about masculinity in the last two hundred years, while the work of someone like Eve Kosofsky Sedgwick can help us to see how this masculinisation becomes crucial in questions of male homosexual/heterosexual definition.[19] The necessity for both men and women to conform to a predominantly 'straight' business culture has had two effects: it has made this culture one in a series of closeted environments that gay, lesbian and queer people have had to endure; and it has provided the impetus for them to establish alternative business cultures, a process depicted in McCullers's *The Ballad of the Sad Café* and Armistead Maupin's *Tales of the City* series. This separate development is a feature common across all of these groups. And in all of these cases the historical remnants of experiences of marginalisation will inflect the way that business is conceptualised and approached.

All of this is not to deny the marginalisation and exploitation that white men have often experienced in the world of business. My argument is that the response to this process of discrimination and exclusion is articulated by recourse to vastly differing strategies. For the purposes of this book I have separated these into two main types. In general terms, white male culture has resorted to what I will call an 'empire anxiety' in order to negotiate its relationship with business, while the response of women and minority groups has been to follow the example of Thorstein Veblen by separating out 'business' from 'industry' and providing a 'narrative of acculturation' that, by concentrating on work, is more localised and specific and resists the appeals to 'America' that distinguishes the work of white male writers. Again, there will be points where these two modes of response jump across group lines and embarrass the general pattern I have suggested. I want to outline now what I mean by 'empire anxiety' and a 'narrative of acculturation'.

THE BUSINESS OF EMPIRE

It may only be of coincidental value, but Calvin Coolidge delivered his speech to the American Society of Newspaper Editors on the thirty-second anniversary of the deposing of Queen Liliuokalani in Hawaii. This was achieved by the concerted efforts of the country's sugar plantation owners, backed up by 300 men from the USS *Boston* which happened to be anchored in Honolulu at the time. Almost immediately the new provisional government headed to Washington with a petition to the United States government requesting that it annex the Hawaiian Islands. Most of the plantation owners were not, however, native Hawaiians but the sons and grandsons of white United States immigrants who had moved to the islands during the nineteenth century when Hawaii was also the destination for many Christian missionaries. This twin-pronged attack in the names of economic development and civilisation wiped out as much as a third of the native population and led to a situation where the white immigrant dynastic elite who owned much of the land was often in confrontation with the native population whose allegiance was to the monarchy. It was the business of sugar cane which inspired this tension and that, along with Hawaii's strategic position in the Pacific in both military and economic terms, meant that successive United States governments were keen to foster informal relations and to protect Hawaii's independence. A series of reciprocity treaties helped open up the Hawaiian market to United States products and internal United States markets to Hawaiian sugar cane. The problem for the plantation owners, however, was that as long as Hawaii remained independent, its exports to the United States were the subject of tariffs which made their sugar cane less competitive. Even in 1890 when the United States abolished all duties on imported raw sugar it still favoured local rather than foreign producers by giving them a two cents per pound duty and caused Hawaiian plantation owners to press more vigorously for formal annexation.[20] When Queen Liliuokalani attempted to introduce a new, pro-native constitution, the plantation owners organised their rebellion.

This rebellion in the interests of business is significant for my purposes because of the tenor of the debate that it generated in the United States. Even more than the Spanish-American war of 1898 that saw the United States take control of Cuba, the Philippines and Puerto Rico, the annexation of Hawaii can tell us just how important was the issue of business and commerce in the way that the United States constructed itself as an imperial power whilst at the same time trying to resist the accusation of being a colonial nation. Such an accusation was, of course, unwelcome in a political system that had founded itself in an anti-imperial moment by breaking away from Britain. But, as John Carlos Rowe suggests, long before the United States became the global power that it was by the end of the Second World War it had 'developed techniques of colonization in the course of ... establishing its own national identity'.[21] This is evidenced most notably in the doctrine of Manifest Destiny that naturalised what amounted to the internal territorial colonisation of a whole continent. For Rowe, '"Americans" interpretations of themselves as a people are shaped by a powerful imperial desire and a profound anti-colonial temper.'[22] This contradiction was encapsulated in Jefferson's concept of an 'empire for liberty' where the United States conquers – or, in the case of the Louisiana Purchase, buys – land only to bestow freedom.[23] But the idea of conquering territorially outside of what had been perceived to be the nation's natural borders, proved to be a contentious issue in the United States by the end of the nineteenth century and has set the tone for much of the way post-war writers have imagined the place of the United States in the world. It is also an issue intimately connected to the role of business.

In his Farewell Address of 1796, George Washington laid the foundations of an isolationism in foreign affairs at the diplomatic level when he declared, 'It is our true policy to steer clear of permanent alliances with any portion of the foreign world'; but in economic terms Washington spoke about 'diffusing and diversifying by gentle means the streams of commerce, but forcing nothing'.[24] This discourse of 'gentle' commercial expansion overseas has driven a particular mode of United States imperialism. By the end of the nineteenth century Uncle Sam was to be seen on the front cover of *Harper's Weekly* proclaiming 'A fair field and no favor ... I'm out for commerce, not conquest.'[25] And at a commemorative event to celebrate the fiftieth anniversary of the Marshall Plan – perhaps the most direct example of United States 'diffusing ... the streams of commerce' – these words were repeated by Bill Clinton, although this time not just in relation to the United States. The 'we' that Clinton refers to is both the United States and Europe. What are predicated as common aims plainly bear an 'American' heritage:

> Our mission is clear: We must shape the peace, freedom and prosperity ... into a common future where all our people speak the language of democracy; where they have the right to control their lives and a chance to pursue their dreams; where prosperity reaches clear across the continent and states pursue commerce, not conquest; where security is the province of all free nations working together; where no nation in Europe is ever again excluded against its will from joining our alliance of values.[26]

This speech, and the historical ancestry into which it fits, articulate the virtues of free trade, self-government and an 'alliance of values' rather than an alliance of political interests. In 1899, in two articles for the *North American Review*, the industrialist and benefactor Andrew Carnegie outlined just this set of issues. The articles were titled 'Americanism versus Imperialism'.[27] Confident that the United States could become an imperial power in the European mould if it so wished, Carnegie argued against moving in this direction. The economic strength of the nation was such that 'the results of non-exportation' to Europe 'would be more serious than the effects of ordinary war'.[28] Carnegie's economic triumphalism substituted for a military one, yet drew its rhetoric from just such military excursions: United States 'manufactures are invading all lands, commercial expansion proceeds by leaps and bounds ... the industrial supremacy of the world lies at our feet'.[29] His opposition to the use of United States troops abroad was based upon a simple test: if people were prepared to defend their country against the United States then they clearly 'believed in the Declaration of Independence – in Americanism'.[30] For Carnegie, imperialism served nobody's purposes. It was bad for business, it stretched the Republic's resources too thinly to occupy non-contiguous territory, it demoralised the host population, and in the end was bad 'for either soldier or businessman when, in a foreign land, he is bereft of the elevating influences which centre in the home'.[31] It is self-government that leads to civilisation and imperialism that is the antithesis of self-government.

What one finds in this kind of anti-colonial discourse, then, is an implicit argument that the export of supposedly exceptional 'American' values – independence, self-government, democracy – should be accomplished by economic rather than military means; that the circulation of United States 'manufactures' in a *laissez-faire* trading environment can do far more to convert the world to 'Americanism' whilst at the same time protecting the virtues of the 'American' Republic at home. Such an argument is crucial to this book, because what it opens up is a site where anxiety develops about the coherency of the relationship between 'America' and empire: 'American' identity is potentially threatened and diluted in the course of territorial excursions overseas; but at the same time 'American' identity requires constant commercial expansion overseas since it is in the commercial not the territorial domain that 'American' strength is built. This anxiety erupts at the constitutional faultline where the doctrine of Manifest Destiny meets the anti-colonial arguments of people like Carnegie, and others like Carl Schurz who based their opposition to territorial expansion on overtly racist grounds. According to Schurz, if the people of the United States 'yield to the allurement of the tropics ... their "manifest destiny" points ... to a rapid deterioration in the character of the people and their political institutions, and to a future of turbulence, demoralization, and final decay'.[32] The United States could maintain its economic strength by owning plantations and businesses overseas, controlling railroads, purchasing mines, all without the negative effects of territorial acquisition, according to Schurz. When I use the word constitutional, I am suggesting that there was something in the quest for a commercial empire that, by the end of the nineteenth century, because of its increasingly extra-continental nature, was starting to fundamentally destabilise the project of 'America' as it had initially been envisaged by 'founding fathers' like Jefferson and Washington.

Many of these debates were played out in relation to Hawaii. Those in favour of annexation, like Lorrin A. Thurston, ex-prime minister of the Islands, argued that 'the financial effect of the future American policy' was 'of more importance to Americans than it was to Hawaiians'.[33] In the balance sheet that he drew up, the United States had a net gain in trade with the Islands of just over 28 million dollars. For John Stevens, the United States minister to Hawaii who was responsible for calling in the troops from the USS *Boston* to support the rebellion, Hawaii offered 'rich resources and splendid future possibilities', that needed to be carved up amongst the 'American and Christian Caucasian people', in order to prevent 'the islands from being submerged and overrun by Asiatics' and to end Japanese ambitions in the country.[34] For Stevens, Hawaii was a beachhead for future United States commercial power in the Pacific. Others who opposed annexation did so sometimes on explicit constitutional grounds. George Ticknor Curtis argued that there was no precedent for the annexation of non-contiguous territory. The only similar situation was Alaska, but this had been purchased. 'If we acquire Hawaii by a construction of the Constitution which is contrary to the long-settled one,' Curtis wrote, 'there will be no limit to future acquisitions of the same kind.'[35]

What I am suggesting is that the empire project, by disrupting the 'long-settled constitution', would become the source of an anxiety for the white male culture that was meant to carry that project forward in the realms of business and commerce in those very non-contiguous regions over which, it was argued, the constitution should have no power. Ultimately the export of 'Americanism' would be incompatible with the idea of an exceptional 'America', since if the rest of the world was to assume 'American' values – or that 'alliance of values' Bill Clinton referred to – how would it be possible to recognise what made 'America' unique?

In the post-war world with which this book is concerned, empire anxiety is particularly acute once the international field of capital is transformed by the effects of globalisation. These developments have facilitated all kinds of commercial and non-commercial exchanges between cultures that have eroded the solidity of national borders and boundaries and the concept of an isolated or exceptional 'American' nation. This book will argue that the white male literature of 'quiet desperation' marks out in the post-war period an emotional field in which white men have tried to deal with the disturbing and unsettling experience of the increasingly multinational and global nature of business and culture. This approach will help the book to argue that one of the reasons for the continuing antagonism towards business in the literary field is the destabilising effect that the push towards an economic globalisation increasingly dominated by United States capital creates for men who have a vested interest in maintaining traditional models of 'America'.

If this is a modern problem in the literary field it is also one with a literary as well as an economic heritage. Problems of this kind were affecting white male writers from the time of Herman Melville and Mark Twain. Amy Kaplan has written about the way that Twain's concept of 'Americaness' was forged in his travels to Hawaii in the 1860s. An ardent critic of European colonialism, Twain tried to mark out the relative virtues of the United States and offered its frontier and anti-colonial values as evidence. Yet Kaplan shows how the rhetoric of his voyage to the islands 'renders Hawaii both as an arena and as a passive treasure, a reward for the contest between American and European power, as it renders Americanization as liberation'.[36] It is at this juncture that Twain, traditionally noted for his local and regional writing, can also be seen to be dependent upon global shifts in power for his sense of identity. And, for all his criticism of European and American imperialism later in his career, John Carlos Rowe has identified in Twain's writing – particularly in A Connecticut Yankee in King Arthur's Court – a commitment to free trade that, while ostensibly projected as a solution to exploitation and colonialism, forms the basis of the kind of 'free-trade imperialism' supported by men like Carnegie and Schurz.[37] After all, Twain was sent to Hawaii by the Sacramento Union newspaper to promote United States investment in the Hawaiian sugar industry.

In an important addition to the way that we might position the individual author in relation to this notion of empire, Wai Chee Dimock has written about the 'mutuality between self and nation' in the work of Herman Melville.[38] No stranger to the impact that business was having in the United States during the nineteenth century – most particularly in short stories like 'Bartleby, the Scrivener' and 'The Paradise of Bachelors and the Tartarus of Maids' – Melville produced a model of authorship that, according to Dimock, replicated Jefferson's paradoxical 'empire for liberty' at the level of the individual. In seeking to create the freedom and space, or the 'sea-room', required for individualism to flourish, Melville conjoined freedom with dominion. 'Each book invokes, confirms and defends', Dimock argues, 'the principle of imperial freedom, a principle of authorial license embedded in a technology of control. In that regard, Melville dramatizes the very juncture where the logic of freedom dovetails into the logic of empire.' I have tried to show how business has been historically intertwined with the creation of an imperial United States, and I therefore want to build on Dimock's argument by locating the discourses of business as important sites for the playing out of these issues of freedom and empire in post-war white male literary culture. For Dimock, the spirit of Jacksonian individualism and the idea of personal progress were 'formally identical to the narrative of Jacksonian imperialism'.[39] For me this mirroring is lost in post-war white male literary culture. Instead, it is replaced by an empire anxiety: business, the means by which the imperial nation is created, has increasingly become the place where it is impossible for the sovereign white male individual self to exist in the post-war world because of the kind of 'agency panic' described by Timothy Melley. The individual and the interests of business have been seen to be pulling in opposite directions. This is the tenor of the treatments of post-war business culture from the 1950s – by social critics like William H. Whyte, David Riesman, and Vance Packard – to the 1990s.[40]

THE BUSINESS OF WORK

As I mentioned earlier, this is only one line in the development of post-war literary engagements with the discourses of business. The texts that I look at in the second half of this book negotiate with these discourses from different perspectives. This is not to say that they do not share, at some points, the empire anxiety I have outlined above. But their subject positions make their relationship with it more problematic. If one accepts that their association to the brand of 'America' as defined by someone like Calvin Coolidge is necessarily limited by race, ethnicity, gender or sexuality, then the danger of any threat to this brand would seem less likely to produce the kinds of anxiety that are generated in white male literary culture. Take, for instance, Paul Gilroy's influential notion of the Black Atlantic and the way that he quite directly tries to sweep away the nation as the primary focus for discussing issues of race. Where the viability of United States – for which read 'American' – borders occupied late nineteenth-century commentators on territorial aggrandisement and produced an anxiety proportionate to the threat to these borders, for Gilroy the African-American experience of diaspora has been part of a much wider experience of mobility, circulation and influence that has formed black people for several centuries. The international capitalist system that relied upon slavery and colonialism needed to be opposed not just by national organisations but through allegiances that were forged across national boundaries.[41] The sanctity of an 'America' that is under threat is not an important issue here.

In similar terms, it is also worth thinking about the way that feminist and gay, lesbian and queer politicisation has developed very much in international terms in the post-war period. The kinds of individuality posited in these movements are not yoked to the same national models of identity that one historically finds in white male literary culture. This is not to say that they are not connected to globalisation and the economic shifts in the nature of capital, but it is to say that their intra-continental concerns mean that their investment in 'America' is strictly limited.

The second part of this book will therefore think about the ways that these texts question, modify and undermine the attitude towards that relationship between business and 'America' conceived by texts in the first part of the book. They do so, I want to suggest, by relating 'the kinds of emotions, cathexes, rages, desires, fears, complacencies, exaltations, and depressions elicited by capitalist culture'[42] as it is experienced not in the realms of business but in the 'industry' that Thorstein Veblen distinguished from 'exploits' carried out by the leisure class: 'Industry is effort that goes to create a new thing, with a new purpose given it by the fashioning hand of its maker out of passive ... material; while exploit, so far as it results in an outcome useful to the agent, is conversion to his own ends of energies previously directed to some other end by another agent.'[43]

Veblen's division of labour along these lines may seem crude – it basically separates workers from employers – and his anthropological justifications for such a division even cruder. Yet in the context of the discourse of business that has developed in the United States, such a division seems to intervene and reconstitute an important ideological narrative. It is no coincidence that Veblen picked on the word 'industry'. As I showed earlier, this word has an important lineage in attitudes towards work and business. Crucially, what Veblen's distinction brings into play is the idea of social, by way of economic, transition; the movement from 'industry' to 'exploit' is the movement of the self-made man (and it is usually a man) from the world of industrious drudgery to the leisured world of a social elite. So Veblen's division of labour is a peculiarly national intervention, although one that may also help to embarrass the national purpose that the leisure class it defines is working towards.

It is the willingness of women and minority writers to concentrate on the 'industry' – as defined by Veblen – of United States business that suggests to me a corresponding willingness to engage with issues that do not have as their ultimate focus the reconstitution of the nation. This is the 'narrative of acculturation' I mentioned earlier. The noun 'acculturation' has two slightly conflicting definitions and it is the tension between the two that motivates my use of it here. While it can mean the process whereby the culture of a particular society is instilled in a human from infancy onward, it can also mean the modification of the culture of a group or individual as a result of contact with a different culture.[44] It strikes me that women and minority writers, while instilled with the hegemonic narrative of United States business through all sorts of official discourses, also seek to modify it as it intersects with other cultural polarities more resonant to their economic and social position.

In Chang-rae Lee's *Native Speaker*, for example, the traditional Korean business support system of the *gehh* and John Kwang's secretive use of it to garner support for his mayoral campaign, looks uncomfortably like corruption and is treated as such by the institutions of United States law and politics. Yet Lee intertwines this narrative with one addressing Henry Park's cultural assimilation and asks the reader to question just how 'American' national identity is constructed in the hegemonic discourse of United States business when Korean businessmen and workers are made to participate in financial and social systems that preclude forms of organisation that are an essential part of non-'American' business culture. The ambiguity of Lee's title poses questions about the difficult relation of second-generation immigrants to questions of national citizenship. Is Park a native speaker of United States English, since he grows up in the United States, or a native speaker of Korean since that is the tongue of his parents and grandparents? Acculturation in this instance is Henry Park's observation and recognition of how the hegemonic discourse of United States business operates and the ways in which he has to adjust and disguise his performance of identity during the course of his daily work as a spy so as to adjust to the demands of United States citizenship. Gone from this kind of literature about business is the dyadic contrast of corporation and homunculus and the appeal to a liberal notion of the consolidated self that reconstitutes the nation as it simultaneously kicks out at it.

There are other narratives about United States business, then. In the end what detaches much of white male culture from engaging with the process of 'acculturation' as it is defined here is a nostalgic belief that members of this group are spiritually and mythically connected to the leisure class for whom industry is unworthy once they have achieved the social success that is white male destiny. Here Willy Loman is progenitor to successive generations of post-war United States men who are constantly searching for the secret that will lift them from the 'industry' that they endure but which they do not consider to be their rightful role. Willy wants to emulate either his father, who comes to represent in the play the 'unfettered and unalienated labour of mercantile capital', or his brother Ben, who epitomises the 'accumulative process of monopoly capital'.[45] Anything, in fact, but the exhausted salesman he has become. Many of the texts I look at in the second part of this book will look through and past this nostalgia in order to identify just what are the demands of being a working United States citizen in the post-war world that has seen all kinds of business change and transformation.

THE BUSINESS OF AMERICAN STUDIES

With all this discussion of the relationship between 'America' and the discourses of business, it is important to remember that 'America' has been not only the concern of politicians, social critics, and novelists and playwrights in the post-war period, but also the nucleus around which a whole academic discipline has crystallised. While literature about business and work has been busy creating and questioning the notion of 'America', so business – in the form of governmental and independent financial support – has played a key role in the creation and development of the field of American Studies in the United States, Europe, and elsewhere. As Paul Giles suggests, it is now an academic commonplace that 'national ideals, and the "canonical" models of aesthetic expression that support them, should be seen as highly politicized entities'.[46] Yet even so, the circular relationship between American Studies, economic and business institutions, and the national ideal of 'America' can provide the telling detail to flesh out the rather generalised phrase 'highly politicised entities'.

Gene Wise has written about the beginnings of the American Studies movement in the 1920s and '30s as a 'pre-institutional' stage of development where individual scholars like the historians Vernon Parrington and Perry Miller, dissatisfied with traditional academic approaches, tried to 'structure new ways to study and teach about

American experience'.[47] This was part of a more general push to take American culture more seriously and to see American literature not as an offshoot of English literature but as worthy of study in its own right. The journal *American Literature* was founded in 1929 and universities began to offer multidisciplinary courses that allowed students to study American literature, history and philosophy alongside one another. By 1947 some sixty institutions were offering such an option. The success of this movement was based on a method-ological consensus Wise called 'the intellectual history synthesis'. Governed by a set of basic assumptions, this paradigm 'guided scholarship in the field and helped set boundaries within which students of American Studies were trained for well over a generation'. These assumptions were based around the principle of American Exceptionalism: that there was a more or less standardised 'American Mind' common across classes and history; that the American Mind was distinguishable because it was located in the 'New World' that made Americans individualistic, hopeful and pragmatic.[48]

The national emphasis of this project can be seen quite explicitly in Tremaine McDowell's 1948 book entitled *American Studies*. For McDowell, the purpose of American Studies was for students to reduce the diversity of the United States 'to some degree of unity'[49] in order to escape the political and economic nationalism that marked Germany and Japan in the 1930s and instead to create 'an acceptance of cultural nationality'.[50] For McDowell, American Studies was clearly as much a political as an intellectual project, but not just a domestic one. In terms echoing some of the campaigners I mentioned earlier, who at the end of the nineteenth century opposed United States territorial expansion but were keen to see business and investment expansion overseas as a way of diffusing 'American' values, McDowell suggested that 'loyalty to the nation ... may in turn expand into the brotherhood of man' and that American Studies could 'contribute to the creation of world order ... through the education of America for critical self-knowledge'.[51]

McDowell paints a very benevolent picture of American cultural nationality, and clearly, in a post-war environment when the United States had assumed the status as the world's most powerful nation, he needed to distinguish it from the dangerous economic and political nationalism of Germany and Japan. Yet what becomes clear in Wise's account of the growth of American Studies after the Second World

War is how intertwined it was with just the kinds of economic and political forces McDowell tries to resist.

Wise describes the 1950s and early 1960s as an era of 'corporate organization' in the field of American Studies. In 1949 and 1954, the University of Pennsylvania's American Civilization programme received grants from the Rockefeller foundation, while in 1954 it also received a five-year, $150,000 grant from the Carnegie Corporation, which also donated funds to American Studies programmes at the University of Minnesota in the late 1940s, to Bennington University, and to Barnard University. In 1950, Yale announced a $4.75 million expansion of its American Studies provision.[52] The American Studies Association and *American Quarterly* were founded in 1951 and 1949 respectively. In the fourth issue of this new journal, C. E. Ayres can be found trying to come to terms with the industrial wealth that lay behind this corporate reorganisation of American Studies and the responsibility he believed it placed on the United States, now that 'the civilization of the Old World has been swept away by the holocaust of war' and people were looking to the United States 'not only for material aid but even more for a renewal of spiritual strength'.[53] Arguing against the belief – which, tellingly, he attributes to 'representatives of an older civilization', that is Europeans – Ayres suggests that 'civilization comes only when the pursuit of riches is no longer necessary, when free enterprise has been abandoned in favor of free spirit'.[54] The wider context of the article would suggest that free enterprise was funding the rhetoric of free spirit; that the ideological construction of a national cultural identity, and the 'world order' that could be secured by that identity, was the project of an American Studies movement driven by not only business funds but by business ideals of domestic and international expansion and product penetration.

The international dimension to this project has been mapped by Richard Pells who focuses more closely on government-backed initiatives to spread the gospel of American Civilization overseas from as early as the 1930s when fear of German and Italian influence in Latin America sparked the development of United States cultural diplomacy. The Division of Cultural Relations in the State Department was set up in 1938 and in 1942, four months after the Japanese attack on Pearl Harbor, the radio station Voice of America was established.[55] Walt Disney was hired by Nelson Rockefeller, at the time head of the foreign department of Chase Manhattan Bank and concurrently director of the Office of the Coordinator of Inter-American Affairs, to produce a series of animated features that would circulate the benefits of United States democracy to Latin America.[56] In the academic environment, the Fulbright Program was set up and, according to Pells 'was entangled from the beginning in the tentacles of the State Department'. The Smith-Mundt Act of 1948 stimulated cultural efforts to contest Soviet propaganda and alter the distorted picture of the United States present in Europe. The genuine interest that British and European scholars were showing in United States history and literature was also fostered. Even before the war the Carnegie Foundation provided funds for British historians to go to American Historical Association conferences. During the Second World War, Cambridge University established the Pitt Professorship in American History and Institutions while British libraries received Rockefeller grants to expand their collections of United States material.[57] Henry Steele Commager, who lectured at Cambridge and whose friend Allan Nevins helped to set up American Studies courses in British secondary schools, readily admitted, according to his biographer Neil Jumonville, that he performed a propagandist role during the war. He even stayed on in Britain as public affairs officer at the United States embassy in order to help prevent the Labour Party sympathising with the Soviet Union.[58] The CIA and HUAC were also hard at work during this period, supporting conferences and placing embargoes on the books available in United States embassy libraries overseas.

Wherever one looks during this post-war period the business of business and the business of government was the support of projects aimed at promoting an American Studies dominated by the consensus model of 'American' national identity. Even projects that began as independent exercises, like the Salzburg Seminar, soon became the object of corporate and government funding. The credibility of these kinds of academic enterprises, Pells argues, whilst 'honored in the abstract, usually yielded in practice to high-pressure salesmanship', while European scholars were both 'iconoclastic and entrepreneurial', seeing in American Studies both an exciting new field and a chance for professional advancement.[59]

What is striking about the consensus model of 'American' national identity as it was developed in the academic environment was its similarity to the vision of 'America' depicted by white male literary culture in its treatment of business and nationhood. Ostensibly antagonistic to the corporate environment of the period because of its authoritarian tendencies, and more concerned with the transcendental and philosophical continuities that were believed to span history and difference and shape the exceptional 'American' individual, American Studies was happy to implicitly endorse a liberal ideology which had been, and continued to be, the foundation of business enterprise. No wonder corporate benefactors were queuing up with their money.

During the last thirty years, this consensus model in the field of American Studies has gradually split apart, and with it has gone the corporate and government backing. Cultural consensus has been replaced by the Culture Wars. Just as white male literary culture tried to retreat to a more comforting vision of 'America' as the effects of globalisation and cross-cultural circulation during and after the Second World War became ever more pressing, so American Studies did the same. But this kind of consolidation in the face of business-driven change was untenable. Ironically, all the corporate and government efforts to have people in the United States and elsewhere study the history of United States literature, culture and society resulted in a cacophony of arguments about the viability of the consensus model of national identity. A particular line of white male literary culture continues to sulk over this dilemma, as does a particular line of American Studies criticism. It is articulated in the culture of the jeremiad. And yet, from somewhere else that is still within the United States, authors and critics continue to write the differences of identity as it is manifested within the increasingly notional borders of 'America'.

Part I
White Male Literary Culture

1
Errands in the
Post-War/Cold War Jungle

In the preface to *Errand in the Wilderness*, a collection of essays published in 1956, Perry Miller famously described an epiphany he experienced as a young man while standing on the banks of the River Congo in the 1920s. Feeling deprived at missing out on the 'adventures' of the First World War that his slightly older contemporaries enjoyed, Miller instead feels himself drawn towards the adventures that his homeland offer. Sensing a burden commensurate with that described by Edward Gibbon after he was given the task of writing the history of the Roman Empire, Miller writes:

> It was given to me, equally disconsolate on the edge of the jungle of central Africa, to have thrust upon me the mission of expounding what I took to be the innermost propulsion of the United States, while supervising, in that barbaric tropic, the unloading of drums of case oil flowing out of the inexhaustible wilderness of America.[1]

Even though it seems far from his thoughts, the comparison with Gibbon immediately raises the spectre of the United States as empire in this epiphany, and when Miller writes of his 'mission' he is mirroring his role in the founding of American Studies to the Puritan migration and the white settlement of the continent that the rest of the essays in his book will discuss. What is additionally important in the context of this book, however, is the way that Miller's epiphany is fashioned in the very midst of a business transaction. The oil drums here synecdochically stand in for the United States. Miller goes on to declare that 'What I believe caught my imagination, among the fuel drums, was a realization of the uniqueness of the American experience.'[2] It is difficult to understand quite how the fuel drums could signify such a 'uniqueness' unless one acknowledges the binding together – and the exceptionality of this binding together – of 'America' and business in the cultural imagination of someone like Miller. Perhaps, looking back from the vantage point of the 1950s, he had in mind his home town of Chicago whose university was founded and funded by money from John D. Rockefeller's Standard Oil and which would go on to award him his doctorate in 1931. Whatever prompted his epiphany, it was the experience of witnessing United States business overseas that sent Miller back to Chicago with the 'mission' of forging the Puritan origins of the cultural identity of the nation.

In this chapter I want to discuss four works which combine ingredients similar to those put together by Miller: a foreign, and, in three cases, a jungle location; the shadow of business; and a meditation on the nature of national identity. In all four cases, territorial relocation seems only to offer a better chance to reflect upon 'America', as it did for Miller. Amy Kaplan has argued that Miller's project completely erases the connection between the African setting of his epiphany and the American origins in which he was so interested. In doing so, one could argue that Miller replicates Carnegie before him by standing in opposition to one another Americanism and imperialism; the American experience that in Miller's frame is so unique is not an imperial experience since for him America existed as a wilderness. But by using this foreign location, Kaplan suggests, Miller 'turns Africa into the repository – and thus uneasy reminder – of those repressed alternatives, and it comes to embody an inventory of counter-evidence, from which one can plot shadow narratives of imperial histories underlying and contesting his story of Puritan origins'.[3]

Miller's epiphany, then, seems to exemplify the argument I made about 'empire anxiety' in the Introduction. For Michel Foucault 'Choosing not to recognize is another vagary of the will to truth',[4] and it is precisely by looking right past the African jungle that Miller wills into being a discourse of 'American' origins that defensively reconstitutes the unity of the nation at an intellectual level in full consciousness of the way that the United States was breaching its national borders – in this instance by way of its commercial and business transactions. Instead of recognizing the connection between the Puritan settlers and the indigenous inhabitants of the so-called wilderness that was America, and between the Puritan migration and the passage to America of African slaves, the project in which Miller was involved isolated American culture from the kinds of imperialism and transnational phenomena that were precisely formative of national experience.

The four texts I look at here engage in a similarly complex project. While the foreign location is at times represented as remote and disconnected from the United States and the rest of the world, at other times it becomes a crucible in which an 'American' identity is forged beyond the territorial borders of the nation, either through business, or the business of warfare. As such, these texts bear witness to the anxiety of national identity formation in white male culture immediately after the Second World War. This anxiety erupts at a faultline where the nation must, at one and the same time, fulfil the role it assumed as economic and military global superpower whilst justifying such a position by manufacturing a consensus of national, bordered identity. The conflicting strains of these centrifugal and centripetal forces produced in the imaginary field of literature a domain replete with examples of what Kaplan calls 'the multiple ways in which empire becomes a way of life' and which are too often ignored as long as imperialism is conceived as a matter of diplomatic relations, foreign policy or the economic result of market forces.[5]

ARTHUR MILLER, *DEATH OF A SALESMAN* (1949)

In many ways, the most famous of post-war texts about business seems to be not imperial in its range at all but steadfastly domestic and provincial. The kitchen that appears 'at centre' in Arthur Miller's stage directions, and the bedrooms which are placed above it, provide the setting for much of the play's dramatic action.[6] When Miller wants to take his characters and their lives beyond the borders of this domestic scene he uses the forestage in front of the apartment. So, when Willy Loman visits his boss Howard Wagner about the possibility of a desk job in New York, the scene is initiated by Howard walking onto the forestage with table and typewriter (*DOAS* 59). Crucially, however, Miller still manages to domesticate the subsequent non-apartment encounters. New York looms large in the domestic environment by appearing physically and, I would want to add, metaphorically in the Lomans' apartment. Howard, for example, enters the forestage while Willy's wife Linda is midway through a telephone conversation in the kitchen with her son Biff rather than when she has finished. In terms reminiscent of the walls that Melville used to enclose the lawyer and his employees in 'Bartleby, the Scrivener', Miller lets us see 'towering, angular shapes' behind the Lomans' apartment, 'surrounding it on all sides'; we are allowed to look at this imposing urban commercial landscape *through* the 'wholly, or in some cases, partially transparent' nature of this 'fragile-seeming home'. It is by looking through the apartment, then, that 'under and over it we see the apartment buildings' (*DOAS* 7) and also the business environment of New York come hurtling into the domestic scene.

These stage directions are a careful exercise in the demarcation of space that serve in many ways only to undermine the separateness of domestic and urban – or business – environments. In *Death of a Salesmen* the two blend into one another. The presence of Linda, Biff, Happy and Uncle Ben make the play seem as much a familial and domestic drama as it is a play about the nature of salesmanship and business. In this regard it is completely different to David Mamet's *Glengarry Glen Ross*, a play that I deal with in Chapter 3 and which utilises the sales office for its staging. Families are nowhere to be found in this most work-centred of plays. Yet what I want to emphasise here is how misleading is this omnipresent domestic scene in *Death of a Salesman*; that the geographical reach of Miller's play actually stretches much further afield than the confines of domestic New York or the United States. If it is important to understand the way in which the machinations of business and commerce, and Willy's place in this system, rush into the domestic scene to undermine and devastate not only Willy himself but his family too, then it is also important to ask to what extent these wider realms come rushing in to play a part in this process.

So far these areas have been little considered. In academic circles, despite the efforts of feminist and materialist critics,[7] the tragic qualities of Willy Loman have come to dominate discussions of the play, particularly in the twenty years after its first Broadway production. Even in the early 1990s Harold Bloom could introduce a collection of essays with a discussion of whether or not Willy could be classified as a tragic character in the classical tradition or whether he was merely pathetic.[8] Brenda Murphy has also shown how, outside of the academy in the world of business itself, Willy Loman has become the emblem for a whole professional discourse about salesmanship, the demands of work and the responsibilities of employers.[9] Yet there is an African jungle in *Death of a Salesman*, and it is a jungle that is a source of enormous wealth. This is the jungle that Willy's brother Ben walks into at the age of seventeen and emerges from four years later. 'And by God I was rich' he tells Willy, twice (*DOAS* 37, 41).

Many critics have read the jungle in purely symbolic fashion. Arthur Ganz suggests that it 'is clearly the brutal, competitive modern world in which the strong and ruthless like Ben will triumph and the weak like Willy will go under',[10] while for Jeremy Hawthorn it 'represents precisely those ... qualities of unprincipled self-seeking and ambition'.[11] The problem with treating the jungle as a moral testing ground, however, is that any references to real jungles and the development of United States capitalist enterprise in such locations can then be completely erased. In turn this means focus can be redirected to the scathing attack upon the values of the industrial-commercial nature of the United States so evident in the play, and Willy Loman as self-deluding victim. As such, the play then takes on a characteristically 'American' quality that isolates it from the worldwide economic system that was so strikingly emerging after the Second World War. I believe that the character of Ben and his business success in the jungles of Africa actually opens the way for under-standing the plight of Willy Loman in terms that situate the play quite firmly in an international domain that in turn throws light upon the complex process of imagining the relationship between business and 'America'.

As an entrepreneur, Ben stands in contrast to Willy, the salaried employee responsible to bosses above him. But just what kind of businessman Ben is becomes evident when one considers that he also stands in contrast to their father who Willy equally admires, even though he cannot remember him. For Granger Babcock, while Willy's father represents the 'unfettered and unalienated labour of mercantile capital', Ben represents 'the accumulative process of monopoly capital'.[12] What I would want to emphasise in this distinction is the geographical associations that go along with these phases of capitalist endeavour. Ben tells Willy that when they were kids their father 'would start in Boston, and he'd toss the whole family into the wagon, and then he'd drive the team right across the country; through Ohio, and Indiana, Michigan, Illinois, and all the Western states. And we'd stop in the towns and sell the flutes that he's made along the way' (*DOAS* 38).

The familiarity of these national locations are juxtaposed awkwardly with Ben who, on the other hand, according to Miller's stage directions, has only 'an aura of far places about him' (*DOAS* 34). This distinction is vital to what follows in the play and to my argument because Willy clearly fails to distinguish between the two. In the first of Willy's encounters with Ben he proceeds to tell his brother that he is trying to bring his sons up to be just like their grandfather: 'rugged, well-liked, all-around' (*DOAS* 38). And yet moments later he tells Ben that he is bringing them up to be just like their uncle: 'That's just the spirit I want to imbue them with! To walk into a jungle!'

(*DOAS* 41). What Willy does not recognise is that these are not the same qualities. Ben is not 'rugged'. He enters this scene with an umbrella and proceeds to speak in a formal manner. While Willy refers to his 'Dad', Ben refers to his 'Father' and 'Mother' and calls Willy 'William'. If Willy's and Ben's father has something of the pioneersman about him, Ben is altogether different as he rushes off for his trains and business meetings. It is not the national economy that Ben is forging but the extra-continental one that has little to do with 'America'. He offers his brother the chance to work with him in Alaska where, he tells Willy, 'you've a whole new continent at your doorstep' (*DOAS* 66). But in a wonderful piece of geographical and generational dislocation this new continent turns out to be Africa: going to find his father in Alaska, Ben reveals that 'At that age I had a very faulty view of geography, William. I discovered after a few days that I was heading due south, so instead of Alaska, I ended up in Africa' (*DOAS* 37). Which is where he exploits that continent's resources and makes his fortune from diamond mines.

Ben's seamless passage between the United States and Africa makes Willy's father's business activities look decidedly parochial. Willy himself, without even the satisfaction of running his own business, still has dreams of doing so with his sons, but all their plans are nostalgic and domestic. One idea is for a sporting goods line. 'The beauty of it', Happy tells Willy and Biff, is that 'it wouldn't be like a business. We'd be out playin' ball again ...'. Happy chimes in with 'It'd be the family again. There'd be the old honour, and comradeship.' Willy tells them 'You guys together could absolutely lick the civilized world' (*DOAS* 50). The use of a word like 'civilized' here only reiterates how these nostalgic dreams are delimited by the nation's borders when Ben is busy doing business in those extra-national areas that within such nostalgic rhetoric would be classified as 'uncivilized'. There is a sense in which Miller inscribes his play with the realisation that these Loman dreams of business success represent not only a nostalgic attempt to recapture an 'American' myth, but the way in which this nostalgia is itself exhausted. The kind of stasis that Willy is reaching now that he no longer wants to travel suggests the way in which business success is increasingly beyond the local and domestic. And while Willy dreams of living in the country – 'all I'd need would be a little lumber and some peace of mind' (*DOAS* 56) – he has not been prepared to endure the deprivations of desolate Alaska, and certainly not the jungles of Africa like Ben, to achieve success. Business has moved on and, ironically, it has left the domesticated Willy increasingly at the centre of the world as the flows of capital enrich New York, and yet even further away from sharing the rewards of, or achieving success in, that business world.

This is where the use of the word 'exhaustion' to describe Willy's appearance from the beginning of the play ties him to a specific discourse of business that deals in resources. It is a description of him that his wife Linda repeats later in the play: 'The man is exhausted ... He works for a company thirty-six years this March, opens up unheard-of territories to their trademark, and now in his old age they take his salary away' (*DOAS* 44). Again, the irony of the New England territories Willy has worked being described as 'unheard-of' highlights the parochial attitudes of the Loman family; the places in Africa Ben works are unheard of, literally. I would want to interpret Willy's exhaustion not as physical, but as a kind of used-upness equivalent to the way that mines and raw materials are used up in the course of their exploitation by business. New England no longer requires Willy to work it; the 'unheard-of territories' have been opened up. And in turn the domestic labour resource that once worked this territory and which is made up of men like Loman is less important; post-war United States business increasingly requires the resources of Africa, Asia and Latin America and African, Asian and Latin American labour.

I want to suggest, then, that Willy's exhaustion arises at that point where the American pioneer spirit and the requirements of business in the jungle become incompatible and pull in two different directions. I mentioned earlier that Willy misrecognises them as having the same qualities and it is this confusion that creates his anxiety. The jungle that is so linked with entrepreneurial wealth in *Death of a Salesman* (for all that it may represent a Social Darwinist perspective on capitalism, or the streets of New York as Miller writes about them in his autobiography)[13] embodies the imperial and global expansion that on the one hand provides economic wealth, but on the other undermines the consolidation of the 'American' nation in its mythic and nostalgic form. Willy's 'empire anxiety' arises from his deep attachment to the nostalgia of his hustling, businessman father but also his devotion to his brother Ben who he believes has the answers to his desire for success. So faithful is he to both narratives that he cannot resolve the fundamental dilemma: that to achieve success like his brother Ben would mean sacrificing the myths of a rugged, masculine, frontier lifestyle that so construct his very sense of 'American' identity. In this regard, Willy sets the tone for much brow-beating in white male literary culture in the post-war years.

NORMAN MAILER, *THE NAKED AND THE DEAD* (1949)

After being rejected for military service twice, and before achieving success on Broadway, Arthur Miller found himself during the Second World War justifying his existence by writing patriotic war plays for the radio, 'mostly sponsored by Du Pont and U.S. Steel'. Working for Batten, Barton, Durstine and Osborn, 'the largest ad agency of the time and a voice box of corporate America', Miller considered that he was 'helping to refashion the necessary profit motive into themes of high-minded service'.[14] Whilst having his scripts monitored and changed by Du Pont executives, however, Miller was hiding from them the copies of left-wing magazines like *Nation, New Masses*, or *Partisan Review* that were his staple reading. These divided loyalties are indicative of the way that an affinity with the nation is tested under wartime conditions. Miller's socialist political sympathies and his objection during the late 1930s to the decadence of European imperialism are well documented in his autobiography, but in Miller's case the war appears to have tempered his admiration for Soviet socialism at least. With a brother fighting somewhere in Europe and the prospect of 'losing half a million Americans in the onslaught against Japan' whilst New York 'seemed weirdly unaffected' by it all, Miller turned his attention instead to the national purpose of 'America':

> What meaning had all this bloodletting? If my brother dies, would it make a difference? As a non-combatant I had time for such questions. And I thought that in secret people did worry about the meaning of things but were too unsure to admit it, going along instead with the official pretensions to an overwhelming national purpose that would someday justify everything. I wished I could speak for those people, say what they lacked the art to say.[15]

In wishing to speak for these American citizens and offer a non-official narrative, Miller was writing at that point where the tectonic plate of the Republic enshrined in the Declaration of Independence rubbed abrasively against its neighbour which was moved by the governmental, bureaucratic and corporate demands of a wartime economy. But those engaged as combatants in the war would soon also have time to ask themselves the same questions on their return from the European and Pacific campaigns. The jungle warfare that would so dominate Norman Mailer's first novel, *The Naked and the*

Dead, provides the backdrop for precisely assessing the means by which the United States had achieved world military and economic pre-eminence and what had happened to 'America' as a result of the United States' ascension to this position.

In general terms, the war effort depended upon massive state intervention, both to raise money and to organise the economy.[16] According to David Ryan, 'US corporations, which received government contracts in a growing militarised economy, gained disproportionate power and influence in an increasingly centralised system.'[17] Paradoxically, this tightening of the relationship between government and business took place in order to secure victory in a war against imperialist aggressors – Germany and Japan – so that United States economic expansion worldwide via an Open Door policy could secure the values of liberty, individualism, freedom and progress. *The Naked and the Dead* asks to what extent these values are compatible with the corporate and state machinery driving expansion.

Set on the fictional Pacific island of Anopopei, Mailer's novel tells the story of a United States platoon's invasion of the island and the ultimately successful capture of it from Japanese control. The novel is dominated by two characters: Sergeant Croft, head of the reconnaissance unit whose activities and members are followed by Mailer, and General Cummings, commander of the troops on the island. Despite this setting, Mailer makes little attempt to directly address the international domain. Instead, as Nigel Leigh points out, he 'invests the material with the crises of the post-war United States'.[18] While writing the novel Mailer was a campaign worker for Henry Wallace's Progressive Party. Wallace had defected from President Truman's government fearful of the emerging domination of business and particularly the military in the immediate post-war years. Responding to the rapid rise in the proportion of government expenditure devoted to the military, Wallace argued that 'Butter and guns are followed by guns and butter and finally by guns and dry bread.'[19] In one way, then, Mailer's war novel, whilst it draws on his own combat experiences in the Pacific for its material, uses the military environment less for autobiographical purposes than as a way of imagining just how the United States was being changed during and immediately after the war. And it was being changed into a perpetual war economy. This meant not just militarisation, but the coordination of this militarisation with government and business. As Richard Godden has put it more succinctly, 'Guns mean "democracy" means Pepsi.'[20]

The similarities between military and business organisation are clearly demonstrated by Mailer in his novel. At one level, large-scale businesses as they developed along Fordist lines traditionally drew on bureaucratic techniques developed initially in the military domain: the setting-up of corporate divisions for example, and the decentralisation of operational management to these divisions, while strategic planning and control are centralised in the head office of an enterprise. The military and business are directly equivalent in this regard.[21] Even the language is carried from one area to the other: company, division, campaign. The issue of management in this kind of structure is paramount. At one point Mailer describes Sergeant Croft as being 'like an entrepreneur considering improvements, he had been calculating what kinds of patrols he could manage with seventeen men'.[22] When Croft complains to Captain Mantelli, the company commander, that he does not have enough men, he is told to 'wake up, you ain't important, the only thing that counts is to have enough clerks to keep headquarters going' (*TNATD* 57). Cummings's role is strategic. While Croft leads his men in combat missions, Cummings remains isolated in officers' quarters far back from the lines studying maps. His assistant, Hearn, says that Cummings's 'expression when he smiled was very close to the ruddy, complacent and hard appearance of any number of American senators and businessmen .... There was a certain vacancy in his face' (*TNATD* 89). This suggestion that Cummings is a member of a governing political-corporate elite is emphasised in his distance from his men and the unsparing and ruthless logic that drives his thoughts on the national war effort. He argues to Hearn that a nation fights depending on two elements: first of all in proportion to the amount of men and resources it has at its disposal; secondly, 'the individual soldier in that army is a more effective soldier the poorer his standard of living has been in the past' (*TNATD* 180).

What is noticeable in *The Naked and the Dead* is the way that the hierarchical elements of army life are constantly connected back to the hierarchical social and business ranks of non-combat life in the United States. Cummings and his fellow officers 'slept in cots a few feet away from men who slept on the ground; they were served meals ... on plates while others ate on their haunches after standing in line in the sun' (*TNATD* 83). But Cummings comes from a family for whom these luxuries are standard fare. While his grandfather owned a general store, his father Cyrus became a bank owner and the richest man in town and advised his son to go to military school. In contrast, the men who sleep on the ground have had somewhat different connections to the business world. What is important is the way that Mailer makes these connections the source of character development for his portrayal of the reconnaissance unit. In the 'Time Machine' sections of the novel Mailer pencils in the relationship to business of each member of the unit. Red Valsen, for example, grows up in a mining town where everything is owned by the mining company. Starting work at the age of thirteen he spends his 'Puberty in the coal dust' (*TNATD* 227) and ends up a vagrant during the Depression talking with other vagrants about the conspiracies of big business. Gallagher remembers a night in Cambridge, Massachusetts in the 1930s when, after being stood up by a girl, he ends up walking past Harvard Business School. Looking across the river he 'feels the earth under him germinating in the spring night, the sweet assuasive air ... I'm gonna be something', he decides (*TNATD* 277). In a similar spirit Martinez, the Mexican who has joined the United States Army, dreams of setting up his own business after the war (*TNATD* 450), while Goldstein has dreams of starting up a welding shop using the money he manages to save during the war (*TNATD* 210).

The army in Mailer's novel, then, dramatises both the increasingly bureaucratic and organisation-led nature of United States capitalist society and the ideological means by which the possibility of progression through the ranks of that society is instilled in subordinate ranks without, however, the possibility that such progression can occur. 'You can consider the Army', Cummings tells Hearn, 'as a preview of the future' (*TNATD* 329). It is a future that is decidedly apocalyptic for Mailer. Cummings preaches to Hearn in a similarly apocalyptic tone:

> There are countries which have latent powers ... And there are great concepts which can unlock that, express it. As kinetic energy, a country is organization, co-ordinated effort, your epithet, fascism ... America is going to absorb that dream [of fascism], it's in the business of doing it now. ... Our vacuum as a nation is filled with released power. (*TNATD* 326–7)

The point I want to emphasise is the way that Mailer positions the jungle as the vital stage for this portrayal of United States government-business power. In one of the early descriptions of the jungle, Mailer writes about the way that 'Everything was damp and rife and hot as though the jungle were an immense collection of oily rags growing hotter and hotter under the dark stifling vaults of a huge warehouse' (*TNATD* 53). The connections with business and commerce are explicit here and the similarities to Perry Miller's oil and jungle experience particularly compelling. But if the jungle is a huge commercial warehouse wherein the hierarchical struggles of United States class groupings take place, so too is the jungle a piece of territory that is being fought over – the same way that commercial territory is fought over – by United States and Japanese troops in a larger battle to decide who gains hegemonic control in the Pacific region. The Pacific campaign in the Second World War was an extension of those interests in Hawaii, Cuba and the Philippines that the United States developed earlier in the century and which would lead to further wars in Korea and Vietnam. For Mailer, this territorial ambition is interlinked with the desires of business as it is instituted in its corporate-military form. War is business by other means. If the army is sibling to the corporate organisation, utilising similar techniques and structures, the territory that the army fights for is sibling to the markets that commercial organisations seek to control.

The quest for territory is brought to the fore by Mailer in his use of the reconnaissance unit. They come into contact with territory first and map the possibilities for later assaults. Yet the culmination of the book provides a supplementary version of how the jungle signifies in the book. Sent on a mission to scout the far side of the island and assess the possibility of an assault on Japanese lines from the rear, the men in the reconnaissance unit, and especially Croft, engage with the jungle not as businessmen or workers might, but as colonists. The jungle is the barrier beyond which lies the promised land symbolised by Mount Anaka. While for Martinez it 'seemed sacrilegious ... to move through this empty land disturbing the long untrampled earth', for Croft it was different: 'The land was foreign to him, and spawned a deep instinctive excitement at the thought that noone had trod this earth for many years' (*TNATD* 496). It is this hunger to control and conquer the island that drives Croft to try and climb Mount Anaka, despite the opposition from his subordinates. Croft's single-mindedness and his violent treatment of the men under his control situates him as an equivalent of Cummings. Together they represent the reactionary forces that are coming to hold power in the United States. They both, however, also witness that anti-rational element that Mailer opposes in *The Naked and the Dead*, and elsewhere in his fiction, to the bureaucratic machinery of what he variously called 'the Great Society' or 'technology land'. It is by representing the success of men like Croft and Cummings, and the powerlessness of a liberal intellectual like Hearn to stop them, that Mailer is directly asking questions about the fate of 'America'. Cummings humiliates Hearn and Croft is eventually responsible for his death. But instead of a defence of liberal values, as Sean McCann has argued in one of the most powerful recent appraisals of Mailer's work, *The Naked and the Dead* sets the tone for Mailer's writing career by fulminating against post-war liberalism. Mailer believed this liberalism threatened what he called in *Advertisements for Myself* 'our American republic'.[23] It is important to understand that for Mailer this liberalism incorporated the rationalism of post-war life that drove business and governmental organisation and what McCann calls an 'atomistic notion of individual rights'; that is a belief in rights that do not contribute towards a wider national cause.

Mailer's objection to the reactionary nature of United States society, and his suspicion of the liberal consensus that developed after the war and sanctioned the growth of a prosperous war economy, might initially seem to position him as a powerful critic of such developments. But the ending of *The Naked and the Dead* also opens the novel up to a less positive reading, one that places Mailer as a writer deeply regretful at the threat to the nostalgic vision of 'America' he holds dear.

Two important incidents bring the novel to a climax. First, Croft's mission to climb Mount Anaka fails when the unit disturbs a hornet's nest and his men scatter across the slopes of the mountain. Secondly, Cummings's master plan to surprise the Japanese from behind never comes to fruition and instead the Japanese are defeated by a sequence of accidental troop movements initiated by Cummings's weakest officer while Cummings is away from the island. McCann reads this ending in a way which coincides with my notion of 'empire anxiety'. What these events foreshadow, he argues, is the defeat of the reactionary – Croft, Cummings – and the reformist – Hearn – by 'the bureaucratic and the contingent, and we see not the victory of power but its diffusion'.[24] And it is this diffusion which most disturbs Mailer. The empire that would be created as the United States rolled its commercial carpet across the globe, and the values of internationalism and common values that would be its philosophical support, Mailer considered to be too rootless. His objection to this kind of United States imperialism follows in the tradition of those nineteenth-century writers who opposed military excursions abroad because of the potential dilution of 'America'. For Mailer, according to McCann, 'international hegemony proceeded less from the interests of American power than from the lack of cohesion in American society ... imperialism for Mailer ... is inevitably cosmopolitan and proportionately less republican.'[25] The vision of 'America' that Mailer is thus defending is one that is coercive and exclusionary; it is based on a sense of a common and bounded history and certain civic goals that may be achieved through strong and combative political will; finally, it is one that holds to the fore the idea of the exceptional American nation. In *The Naked and the Dead*, Mailer constructs this vision primarily by way of a critique of the interleaving of business, government and military, while his exasperation and polemical fury at the prospects for 'America' signal an acute anxiety about the way that the ever-expanding United States empire is threatening this vision.

SLOAN WILSON, *THE MAN IN THE GRAY FLANNEL SUIT* (1955)

Although Sloan Wilson's novel has been little considered in any critical detail in the course of debates about the 1950s, it was fifth on the 1955 bestseller list and the following year was made into a film starring Gregory Peck. Much of the novel's popularity was due to its culturally resonant depiction of Tom Rath, an ex-soldier struggling to come to terms with life in the stultifying post-war corporate world of United Broadcasting and his job for company president Ralph Hopkins. Horrific wartime memories are still fresh in Tom's imagination; the lovechild from a European wartime relationship threatens to dissolve his suburban family, and the need for money to support this family cannot be reconciled with his dissatisfaction at work. Above all, *The Man in the Gray Flannel Suit* is a novel about a man under pressure and as such represents an important continuation of the kinds of anxiety being expressed in *Death of a Salesman* and *The Naked and the Dead*.

When Miller and Mailer were writing in the 1940s, however, the immediate aftershocks of the Second World War were still being felt. By the mid-1950s on the other hand, as the stand-off with the Soviet Union turned into Cold War, as the House Un-American Committee activities gathered pace, and as the economy reverted to producing goods to satisfy booming consumer demand as well as the demands of the 'garrison state', it became clear that post-war United States business culture was in the process of completing a transformation that had begun in the final years of the nineteenth century, namely the consolidation of the large corporation as the principal generator of wealth in the economy. Compared with other capitalist economies the shift in scale of business enterprises in the United States had been dramatic. Almost from their very beginnings companies embraced new managerial techniques and organisational structures to facilitate their own and the market's expansion.[26] This phenomenon was particularly marked in the railway and communications industries which were themselves the means by which a vast capitalist system spread across the continent, and the means by which many small towns lost independence and autonomy and came to rely on those distant cities that not only bought what they produced but supplied what they needed to participate in the consumer market.[27]

Ironically, however, as the distance between citizens and consumers in the market economy of mass culture began to shrink in terms of time and distance, the distance between many workers like Tom Rath and the process of production (if there was one at all) steadily grew. The new kinds of business organisations were staffed by new workers who spent their days engaged in vicarious production, merely facilitating or oiling the production or service delivery process that took place out of their sight. Such was the growth in clerical and ancillary employment that two years after *The Man in the Gray Flannel Suit* was published, for the first time in America the number of non-manual workers surpassed the number of manual workers.[28]

The causes of the rapid transition of business in the United States are one of the ways in which the link between business and being 'American' has been consolidated in the discourses of business, whereas in Britain or France or Germany, for example, this national dimension remains, at the very most, unarticulated. For George Babbitt it was the way the American man did business that differentiated him from 'the decayed nations of Europe':

> One thing that distinguishes us from our good brothers, the hustlers over there, is that they're willing to take a lot off the snobs and journalists and politicians, while the modern American business man knows how to talk right up for himself, knows how to make it good and plenty clear that he intends to run the works ... He's not dumb, like the old-fashioned merchant. He'd got a vocabulary and a punch.[29]

This classic piece of Babbittry equates a certain way of doing business with an American spirit, as well as equating it with a certain kind of modernity – not 'old-fashioned' – a certain kind of masculinity – a 'punch' – and with a certain kind of honesty, mastery and straight way of talking. But even though Babbitt's speech, and his whole personality will pass into the businessman folklore of United States capitalism, this speech will become by the mid-1950s an impossible template for most men since fewer and fewer of them will be in a position to exhibit these kinds of business attributes. Even executives in some position of power within these new corporations would lose personal experiential contact with the kind of 'sane and efficient' business life Babbitt promotes as 'American'. In 1900, it was estimated that two-thirds of executives had run their own enterprise. In 1950, the figure had dropped to one in ten.[30] More and more men were working not as businessmen but, like Tom Rath, as employees in offices. The world of business, dominated by Scientific Management techniques, thus became loaded with a freight of contradictions: it was the place where one was supposed to prove oneself to be an 'American' and a man, yet the place which was mechanised and feminised and where one did what one was told by a hierarchy that for many men was literally out of sight. In *The Man in the Gray Flannel Suit*, after Tom Rath starts working for United Broadcasting, one of his new colleagues tells him he's been working there four years and has 'never laid eyes on Hopkins ... I have no idea in the world what kind of man he is'; and for all his power inside the company, he says, outside of it 'he's nothing'.[31]

In many ways what took place in the 1950s was a renewed backlash against the business organisation. And so tight was the relationship between business and male national identity in the United States at an ideological level that the changes that took place in the first half of the twentieth century produced a rich and valuable testimony to the process, culminating in a whole raft of books in the 1950s. These included not only Wilson's novel, but a series of sociological works of which the most famous are William H. Whyte's *The Organization Man*, David Riesman's *The Lonely Crowd* and C. Wright Mills' *White Collar*. Products of the same mass market which had created the changes to which they address themselves, these books are testimony to the extent to which this backlash gripped the popular imagination in the post-war period. Echoing the potential threat to 'American' manhood, William H. Whyte, in the final chapter of his analysis of post-war corporate change, urged men that they 'must *fight* the Organization ... the peace of mind offered by organization remains a surrender'.[32]

This rhetoric of fighting is utilised by Tom Rath, who draws on his experience of combat not only to differentiate himself from those executives he despises, but also to negotiate his daily working routine. Going to visit Hopkins for the first time, and conscious of the company president's reputation for toughness, Tom thinks how he 'would like to have seen how tough he was when the sergeant opened the door of the airplane two thousand feet up' just before a parachute mission. Tom's resentment turns into what he calls 'crazy anger'. This is the feeling he developed during the war 'when he'd been scared and seen some poor inoffensive colonel who never had to jump sitting behind a desk ... wisecracking with a sergeant about when they were going to get their next leave' (*TMITGFS* 39). To help 'soothe him' in this business culture, and as 'one of many men holding newspapers on their laps' on the commuter train, Tom remembers and repeats the catchphrases he used during the war when he tried to disguise his fear: 'It doesn't really matter', 'Here goes nothing', and 'It will be interesting to see what happens' (*TMITGFS* 69).

The implicit argument here is twofold. First of all, it is clear that toughness in business for Tom is not comparable to the authentic toughness demanded in combat. Secondly, and as a consequence of this fact, post-war business culture is not the inheritor of the kind of 'American' way of doing business as outlined by George Babbitt. Indeed, this is a point emphasised by Whyte in *The Organization Man*: 'No matter what name the process is called – permissive management, multiple management, the art of administration – the committee way simply can't be equated with the "rugged" individualism that is supposed to be the business of business.'[33] What Tom is fighting against, then, is a business culture threatening a national tradition. What this leads to in Wilson's Cold War novel is the depiction of corporate business as un-'American'. The gray flannel that has become 'the uniform of the day' (*TMITGFS* 8) is the marker of a military-style standardisation and bureaucratisation of non-combat life more in keeping with communism than individualist capitalism.

At one level, *The Man in the Gray Flannel Suit* is a novel that seeks to expose this vision of corporate business to a public audience, hence the importance of Tom Rath's job which gives him access to the upper echelons of the organisation. As with *Death of a Salesman*, the impact is also seen to undermine the domestic environment, although in this instance the urban is replaced with the suburban.[34] Tom's wife Betsy is constantly ratifying her husband's masculinity and determination. 'I never saw a man I thought could get away with making you really angry', she tells him (*TMITGFS* 64). However, also like *Death of a Salesman*, it is not just United States business that threatens the Rath household. While Tom's reliance upon his combat experience brings Europe and the Pacific into his post-war life indirectly – even though he argues the war is 'incomprehensible and had to be forgotten' (*TMITGFS* 96) – his time abroad threatens the stability of his life more directly when the experiences he wants to forget are brought back to him by the elevator attendant he finds working at United Broadcasting, Caesar Gardella.

What I am suggesting here is that the business organisation is the conduit through which the extra-national feeds back into national and domestic life and that it is the perfect literary device for this process because of its material role in a globalising economy. Rath's recognition of Gardella in the elevator instigates much of the anxiety we witness in the novel. Until then, Tom has been trying to convince himself that 'it's a disconnected world' (*TMITGFS* 98). But Gardella has shared the three most important moments in Tom's wartime career: his violent murder of a young German soldier whose leather jacket he takes to keep himself warm and then passes on to Gardella; his affair with an Italian woman, Maria, and his accidental killing of his best friend, Hank Mahoney, which results in him avenging his guilt by murdering a cave full of Japanese soldiers in the Pacific part of his duties. The world is clearly not disconnected now, since Tom has to face these foreign experiences at work on Rockefeller Plaza and at home on Greentree Avenue, Westport, Connecticut. Tom's anxiety thus proceeds from the same war that established United States hegemony – politically, economically and militarily – in western Europe and the Pacific. It is no coincidence either, it appears to me, that Tom works in an industry – media and broadcasting – well-placed to exploit and drive these new global interests. Again, it is this extra-national expansion that Tom finds alienating and that in the novel requires resolution if he and his family are to survive.

Here we come back to the issue of territory and its mapping and control, for it is in the realms of real estate that the Raths plan to escape the drudgery of business and suburban life and in the process sever themselves from the conduit of that business culture which contaminates the national and the domestic with the foreign. During the war Tom is a paratrooper. Being dropped before or behind enemy lines, Tom's job is to make initial inroads into enemy defences thus paving the way for territory to be taken by supporting units. Back in the United States, his mother's death allows him to inherit her house and the surrounding land. The family plan, since much of the impetus here comes from Betsy while Tom is bemoaning his job and life in the organisation, is to use the property for a housing development. This corresponding mapping and control of land stands in stark contrast to the sort of territorial procurement of war, however. Not only is it utilising family land, it is an entrepreneurial venture that is steadfastly connected to domestic territory and the spirit of family enterprise that represents a previous era of capitalist development. Nostalgic for this mode of enterprise in the same way as the Lomans, the Raths take advantage of the opportunity bequeathed to them to make it succeed. They lobby for the building of a new school in the locality, hoping that it will encourage potential house-buyers, and against the charge of self-interest Tom, somewhat ironically, defends himself with a rhetoric of change: 'What I'm trying to say is, the town *is* changing, and we can't take a vote to stop change' (*TMITGFS* 244).

The success of this housing development coincides with Tom telling Betsy that while in Italy he fathered a son with Maria. Caesar Gardella is the source of this information. Having returned to Italy after the war, he married a friend of Maria's and on Maria's behalf he tries to get Tom to send her money. While the financial aid of the Marshall Plan after the Second World War was backed up by a range of cultural and philosophical support structures as I pointed out in the Introduction, Tom is anxious to keep his obligations entirely monetary, although this also means he receives the tax benefits for having another child. But this is where he wishes his responsibility to end. If anything the payments he organises are a way of severing his ties with Maria and the child. He certainly does not want anyone to know about them (*TMITGFS* 275).

To sum up then, Tom Rath's anxiety is one that is born overseas and which meets him again in the business organisation. It is born on the Pacific jungle island where he kills his best friend in order to secure victory for the United States; a victory that ten years later seems only to have benefited corporations like United Broadcasting whose national allegiances in this novel are severely questioned, while at the same time turning out gray flannel men in their masses to service the demands of such organisations. It is born in war-torn Europe where he fathers a child during a furlough between campaigns, a furlough that subsequently becomes a threat to his 'American' family and which he contains by setting up a trust fund. This fund will depend for its money, like Tom depends for his peace of mind and the Rath family for their future, on the success of the housing development project; on the consolidation, that is, of familial and domestic property as a way of ringfencing the domestic and national from the international empire that Tom played his part in securing.

JOSEPH HELLER, *CATCH-22* (1961)

During one of the more fanciful of his excursions in *Catch-22*, Milo Minderbinder is accompanied on a trip through the Middle East by Yossarian and Orr, where they witness the full extent of Milo's international standing. As well as seeing him as the Vice-Shah of Oran, the Caliph of Baghdad, the Imam of Damascus and the Sheik of Araby, they also listen as Milo boasts that 'deep inside the jungles of Africa ... large graven images of his mustached face could be found overlooking primitive stone altars red with human blood'.[35] Whilst this hyperbole is part and parcel of a novel that revels in the possibilities of linguistic and narrative excess, Milo's transnational status in *Catch-22* serves the purpose of emphasising the scope and penetration of business that is encapsulated by the syndicate he runs. And, just as it did for Perry Miller, the sight of United States business taking place in the least 'American' of settings serves to raise questions about the very nature of what it means to belong to a nation. For Heller the United States is now a nation intent on supervising this business expansion, and, as he himself noted, *Catch-22* is not a novel about 'the causes or the results of World War II or the manner in which it was fought ... *Catch-22* is about the contemporary, regimented business society depicted against the backdrop of universal sorrow and inevitable death that is the lot of all of us.'[36]

In effect, Heller is following Mailer by using the war to dramatise his attitudes towards post-war United States. Although not published in full until 1961, *Catch-22* is very much a novel that echoes with 1950s discourses. Mention of a 'regimented business society' positions Heller closely beside Sloan Wilson whose description of gray flannel as 'the uniform of the day' witnesses a similar fear about the links between business and the military. David Seed has written about the influence of *The Naked and the Dead* on *Catch-22* and the way that *Catch-22* parodies Mailer's novel, particularly in the form of the bandaged Texan patriot with whom the novel opens and who, Seed argues, is a version of Sergeant Croft. But as well as these affinities with other works, and as well as the similarly directed attacks upon the corresponding hierarchical structures of military and business life that one finds in *The Naked and the Dead* and *The Man in the Gray Flannel Suit*, Heller's novel is different in two important ways: first of all it is a satire where the other texts I have dealt with in this chapter are naturalistic; and secondly it approaches the relationship between the individual and the nation in logical terms, the logic of Catch-22. The fusion of these literary effects help Heller to further redefine the white male response to business in the post-war period.

Like many satirical novels, *Catch-22* uses a scattergun approach whereby little escapes attack. Heller is relentless in his treatment of the discourses of business. Colonel Cargill, troubleshooter for General Peckham had, we are told, 'been an alert, hard-hitting, aggressive marketing executive' who 'could be relied on to run the most prosperous enterprise into the ground. He was a self-made man who owed his lack of success to nobody' (*C22* 40). Major Major's father is a farmer and a 'proud and independent man' but one who 'never hesitated to whine, whimper, wheedle and extort for as much as he could get from whomever he could' (*C22* 110). His speciality is alfalfa and he makes money out of not growing any:

> The government paid him well for every bushel of alfalfa he did not grow. The more alfalfa he did not grow, the more money the government gave him, and he spent every penny he didn't earn on new land to increase the amount of alfalfa he did not produce. Major Major's father worked without rest at not growing alfalfa. (*C22* 110)

The idiocy of bureaucratic organisation is epitomised by General Peckham who suggests that nothing they do in his department is very important; what is important is that they make people think they do a great deal (*C22* 406). But it is with Milo's Syndicate that business logic reaches its pinnacle of absurdity for Heller. Milo argues that all he wants to do is put the war on a more 'businesslike basis' (*C22* 325). To this effect he organises a fleet of planes and quickly has flamboyant squadron emblems 'illustrating such laudable ideals as Courage, Might, Justice, Truth, Liberty, Love, Honor and Patriotism' painted over with 'M & M ENTERPRISES, FINE FRUITS AND PRODUCE' (*C22* 321). The only country with whom he will not trade is Russia. German planes land at the airfield loaded with produce with their Swastikas similarly covered by Milo's lettering. 'Right before their eyes', Milo 'had transformed his syndicate into an international cartel' (*C22* 321) and 'Business boomed on every battlefront' (*C22*

324). This means, of course, that Milo has international obligations. He manages to balance these obligations, and return a profit, when he agrees a contract with the American military to bomb a bridge at Orvieto at the same time as agreeing a contract with the German military to defend the same bridge. But such international obligations can lead to a conflict of interests. In order to rescue a deal for Egyptian cotton that is sending M & M Enterprises under, Milo signs a contract with the Germans that results in him bombing his own air force base and killing his fellow countrymen. The furore that results is dissipated when 'he opened his books to the public and disclosed the tremendous profit he had made'. But the logic of business does not stop there. Milo is exempt from reimbursing the government for damage to the base since in a democracy, Milo explains, 'the government is the people ... We're the people, aren't we? So we might just as well keep the money and eliminate the middleman' (*C22* 329–30). By the same logic, every citizen is a shareholder in the syndicate even though they receive none of the profits. Milo is such a shrewd businessman that he can even buy eggs in Malta for seven cents each and sell them in Pianosa for five cents each and still make a profit (*C22* 293–5). The confusing logic which makes this possible rests upon the basic principle that the syndicate both sells and buys. In a circular economy of exchange it manages to make profits through the duplication of selling and buying the same products, thus allowing it to sell at what appears to be a loss unless one sees the wider picture.

Clearly, Heller's motive is to expose the wider picture of the circular world economic system that so benefits from war. That the profits generated by business rely upon circular exchange rather than any intrinsic value only seems to add to the more disturbing argument that drives the satirical logic of *Catch-22*: that the business and military power of the United States, and the institutions upon which this is built, are sustained by a value system that is corrupt, inefficient and absurd. The logic of Catch-22 works to dissolve rather than to unify or sustain; it empties the hands of United States citizens and leaves them with nothing with which to resist this inefficiency, corruption and absurdity. At educational sessions for the squadron, Colonel Korn decides that 'the only people permitted to ask questions were those who never did'. And as the people who wanted to ask questions stop attending as a result of this edict, the sessions are discontinued altogether since, Korn and Clevinger agree, 'it was neither possible nor necessary to educate people who never questioned anything' (*C22* 49). Similarly, to ask for release from combat duty because it is sending you crazy can only be taken as a sign of sanity and thus ample proof that one is able to fight more missions. Any argument is automatically diffused by the logic of Catch-22.

There is a problem with Heller's logic of Catch-22, however. Just how is it possible for a value system that is so patently absurd to be at the same time also so oppressive, dangerous and omnipresent? This is not to say that business and military institutions are not all of these things; rather, it is to question the mode of critique with which Heller attempts to expose them. Catch-22 actually relies on being applicable universally and indeed Heller's novel is wonderfully versatile in the way that it seeks out and represents the minutiae of how Catch-22 operates. Yet this universality surely imitates the logic that it seeks to criticise. By pre-determining the outcome of each and every instance of confrontation, it is Heller's conceptual logic and not that of United States business or the military that is intent on building hermetically sealed systems of circular exchange.

To illustrate this point, take the example of Chief White Halfcoat, 'a half-blooded Creek from Enid ... who hated foreigners ... and wished they'd all go back to where their lousy ancestors came from' (C22 59). Assigned to Captain Black as an assistant intelligence officer, Chief White Halfcoat can neither read nor write since when he was younger every time his family pitched their tent oilmen would come along, drill a well and find oil, thus requiring them to be moved on and for schooling to be curtailed. At each place they tried this pattern would be repeated. Heller is clearly filling in that wilderness Perry Miller imagined as he stood watching oil drums being offloaded on the Congo and drawing attention to the history of oppression that the development of the continent witnessed. Yet such are the demands of his satire, and so persistent is he in ensuring that the logic of Catch-22 be fulfilled, that Chief White Halfcoat's story is propelled forward only, it seems, by the demand to demonstrate the absurd logic of business: soon every oil company in the world is chasing his family around thinking they are 'human divining rods'; every time another member of the family is born the stock market goes up; and soon the oil companies 'began to follow us around from in front', Chief White Halfcoat explains, guessing 'where we were going to stop next ... drilling before we even got there' (C22 60). As Chief White Halfcoat drifts into the background, the spectre of business emerges to dominate the scene.

My concern with this kind of approach is that Heller treats what may be *his* relationship with business as not only symptomatic of everybody else's relationship with business, but also axiomatic and therefore short-sighted in the way that it elides other experiences. The constant demand is for business to assume this overbearing monolithic and systemic role. It may well be the case, as Brian Way has pointed out, that writers after the Second World War were seeking new literary modes to confront the new modes of multinational capitalism, and that *Catch-22* succeeds in undermining the supposedly rational logic of business and bureaucracy.[37] But it seems that this potentially radical reimagining of United States business very quickly hits two stumbling blocks: its adherence to a discourse of 'emptying out' or exhaustion that signals how new modes of business represent some kind of loss, and a corresponding desire to resurrect a discourse of individuality that might sustain one against this loss.

This is where I would want to position Yossarian, the novel's hero, who is constantly situated by Heller as an outsider. For a start 'There was much about business matters that always puzzled him' (*C22* 88). Milo is incredulous when Yossarian gives away the fruit provided to cure his non-existent liver complaint instead of selling it (*C22* 82–3). Despite this fundamental difference between them, Yossarian and Milo do spend time together in the novel and this is one way that the reader learns about the operating logic of the syndicate. But whereas Milo does everything he is told to do (*C22* 113), Yossarian constantly tries to evade the institutionalisation of the military. In his resistance to the absurdity of the military, Yossarian – like Tom Rath – is fulfilling William Whyte's instruction that men should fight the organisation. For Yossarian, there is little to choose between the people he is supposed to be fighting for and the people he is fighting against: 'The enemy ... is anybody who's going to get you killed, no matter *which* side he's on' (*C22* 161). This belief that it is anyone and everyone who is trying to get him killed leads to a paranoia that is completely justified, since for General Cathcart the name Yossarian 'was like the word *subversive* itself. It was like *seditious* and *insidious* too, and like *socialist*, *fascist* and *Communist* ... It was not at all like such clean, crisp, honest, American names as Cathcart, Peckham and Dreedle' (*C22* 268).

The injection of an 'American' dimension here raises questions about Yossarian's allegiance to the nation, and indeed for Yossarian it is the nation that is trying to get him killed, albeit supposedly in the aid of a larger cause. Part of Yossarian's resistance is that he does not equate himself or his own self-sacrifice with these national war aims: 'History did not demand Yossarian's premature demise, justice could be satisfied without it, progress did not hinge upon it, victory did not depend on it' (*C22* 90). When Milo accuses him of a whole list of unpatriotic behaviour, including 'jeopardizing his traditional right of freedom and independence by daring to exercise them', all Yossarian can do is nod in agreement (*C22* 511–12). These national ideals are difficult for Yossarian to locate, since he argues that between himself and every ideal he always finds men like Cathcart and Peckham, 'And that sort of changes the ideal' (*C22* 560).

What Heller's novel articulates, then, is Yossarian's complete alienation from the structures of post-war United States organisation culture, including both corporate business and the military. Such a situation would suggest that this is what ultimately alienates him from the nation. It should be remembered, however, that for Yossarian his experience of war has revealed how fragile the nation has now become in an era when business, in the guise of the syndicate, is constantly overriding national boundaries in its global operations, changing the relationship between individual and nation. Instead of Yossarian abandoning the nation, I would suggest that Heller's novel actually depicts the nation abandoning the individual because of its extra-national aspirations. Under these circumstances, Yossarian experiences a sense of loss for which he compensates by reverting to individualism. Timothy Melley has argued that Yossarian's paranoia is itself actually 'a method of protecting an integral self against social pressures, including those of the nation', and that as such is 'a form of individualism that is especially uncompromising'.[38] It should be noted that whilst 'regimented business society' may attempt to inhibit Yossarian exercising 'his traditional right of freedom and independence', this only makes him more determined to exercise them. Thus Yossarian does not recognise the ideological status of these values but again treats them as axiomatic to his sense of self. At the end of the novel, instead of returning to the United States and becoming incorporated in the global system, Yossarian decides to desert to Sweden. And yet this decision to sever himself irrevocably from the system that so oppresses him, stands as the ultimate act of self-preservation; an act that, as Melley points out, means rejecting social commitment 'in a familiar flight to the displaced American frontier'.[39]

Ultimately *Catch-22* shares with Mailer's *The Naked and the Dead* a fear about the diffusion of power as centrifugal business spreads the interests of the nation beyond its traditional borders. Yossarian comes to believe that Catch-22 does not exist, but that this is no longer what matters: 'What did matter was that everyone thought it existed, and that was much worse, for there was no object or text to ridicule or refute, to accuse, criticize, attack, amend, hate, revile, spit at, rip to shreds, trample upon or burn' (*C22* 516). As an antidote to this emptying-out of traditional structures and traditional modes of political engagement, Heller offers us Yossarian who tries to gather and pull towards himself the reassuring remnants of the traditions that are passing. Rather than refiguring the tenets of individualism or engaging with the altered dimensions of selfhood in an emerging transnational business system, Yossarian remains inhibited by the very discourses he accuses 'regimented business society' of abandoning. Rather than being an outsider, Yossarian is inside a system that is passing away.

2

Entropy, Postmodernism and Global Systems

In many ways, Joseph Heller's *Catch-22* ushered in a new era of post-war white male literature about business that would remain dominant until the late 1970s. While on the one hand Heller's novel retrospectively reconstructs the end of the Second World War through the lens of those 1950s fears about the business organisation and bureaucracy, on the other hand one can see in the central motif of Milo Minderbender's syndicate an obsession with international 'systems' that goes beyond the naturalism of Miller, Mailer and Wilson. *Catch-22* pre-empts, then, an emergent mode of postmodernism associated with writers with whom Heller also shared a satirical and comic style: Thomas Pynchon, John Barth, Robert Coover, William Gaddis and Donald Barthelme. What concerns me in this chapter is the coincidence of this shift in what might be called, after Donald Pease, the 'field imaginary'[1] of white male literary culture – from naturalism to postmodernism – and three other trends: the demise of the consensus model of American Studies that had been fostered after the Second World War, the increasing visibility and politicisation of marginalised social groups in the United States, and a corresponding sociological concern with global systems.

In his periodisation of the discipline, Gene Wise has suggested Alan Trachtenberg's *Brooklyn Bridge* (1965) as the high-water mark of the corporate phase of American Studies whose rhetorical dominant was the myth and symbol approach perfected in the immediate postwar years by Leo Marx, Henry Nash Smith and R. W. B. Lewis, amongst others. By 1972, with the publication, for instance, of articles like Bruce Kuklick's revisionist 'Myth and Symbol in American Studies',[2] this period was over. The subject had entered what Wise, following the lead of William O'Neill's treatment of the 1960s, called 'the "coming apart" stage' which would lead to its 'disintegration'.[3] The viability of studying United States history and culture within a framework that stressed the commonality of the 'American' mind and 'American' identity was unable to withstand the kind of social change taking place in the 1960s. Frederick Buell, for example, in writing about the series of events that marked the history of United States ethnicity in the 1960s – civil rights and immigration legislation, the rise of the Black Power movement – has argued that these events caused the seams of 'American' identity to split apart.[4] Add to this the challenges of a revivified feminist movement, the politicisation of an urban sexual politics movement that erupted in the Stonewall riots and the undertow of the disastrous war in Vietnam nightly shattering the domestic scene, and one can see why such disillusionment with a consensus model would take hold.

What Buell is keen to stress, however, is how the transgressing of such a model was not simply a local or national issue; that as much as the history of United States immigration, nation building and social conflict both before and after the Second World War might be explained by a discourse of American Exceptionalism, these events are 'intricately embedded in global relationships' and are 'part of a series of reshapings of the globe that has accelerated as the century has progressed'.[5] It was the accelerating pressures of these global trends that not only created social change in the 1960s, but that also undermined the viability of an area studies model rooted in the discourse of national ideals. The inadequacy of this area studies model was made explicit by Immanuel Wallerstein's contention in the early 1970s that the social system was not equivalent to the national state, and that the territorialisation of culture which had helped define the national state in the past was being undermined by the deterritorialisation of culture that partnered globalisation. Wallerstein instead posited the overwhelming importance of a world-system and a world-economy that he divided into core, periphery and semi-periphery, thus replacing the old three-world system with a model that suggested the interactivity of these locations. Driving this system was the business of capitalism.[6]

This sense of business-inspired interactivity is crucial to my argument here. Buell argues that 'Conceiving the world as a single social system ... represents a dramatic alteration ... in a core startled by profound changes to itself', changes that 'emanate both from the center and the margins'.[7] It is a sense of alarm and anxiety that I think is negotiated in the fictions produced by startled postmodern writers when they approach the discourses of business. Distrustful of the world-system of capitalism and international finance threatening to deterritorialise the cultural and national boundaries of 'America' on the one hand, and also the inheritors of an identity increasingly unmoored by the upheavals of the 1960s on the other, white male literary culture in the United States was left struggling to justify itself. John Barth's 'The Literature of Exhaustion' signalled as much in 1967,[8] and it is interesting that Barth, in writing about the 'used-up'-ness of naturalistic literary techniques, echoes Willy Loman's condition in *Death of a Salesman*. Just as multinational capital no longer prioritises Willy's labour, so multinational capital could no longer be adequately represented by naturalistic literary techniques, Barth seemed to be suggesting.

There are, of course, different ways to read the literature that postmodern writers produced in response to this situation. My approach to three of these writers starts from a singular position: that being threatened on all sides by the pressures mentioned above, the business fictions of Pynchon, Gaddis and Heller mark a distinctly defensive response. While they each created literary worlds that ostensibly seemed to critique and short-circuit the oppressiveness of the 'system' by assembling information too copious and/or too conflicting for any system to handle, these worlds can also be seen as attempts to fend off the centrifugal effects of the 'coming apart' and 'disintegration' described by Wise and the splitting apart at the seams suggested by Buell. First, their literary worlds are meticulously structured and organised; secondly they rely on an underlying scientific system – the Second Law of Thermodynamics popularised in the concept of entropy – that seems strangely to detach these novels from the material world that was changing around them; and finally, they all retain at their 'core' a narrative about the relationship between business and 'America' that tries to negotiate the changing status of this relationship.

THOMAS PYNCHON, *THE CRYING OF LOT 49* (1966)

Much has been made of the textual and philosophical uncertainties in Thomas Pynchon's second novel. Embarking on her role as executrix of the will of her former lover Pierce Inverarity, Oedipa Maas – and likewise the reader – is confronted by a whole catalogue of information whose status is at best unreliable and which may or may not be connected. The symbol of the muted post horn and the letters W A S T E that Oedipa first sees on the toilet wall of a bar lead to 'the languid, sinister blooming of The Tristero', or the 'Tristero System',[9] the secret organisation through which an underground communicate and whose history and existence Oedipa will try to determine. Ostensibly a reader of signs, Oedipa is drawn towards the resolution of this Tristero dilemma by way of events and characters that exemplify Malcolm Bradbury's characterisation of United States postmodernist fiction: 'data in excess of system'.[10] And, as Brian McHale has pointed out, so reliant is the reader upon Oedipa's solipsistic narrative that resolution is permanently deferred.[11] Oedipa supplies four possibilities for the status of her experience: 'Either you have stumbled ... onto a network by which X number of Americans are truly communicating ... Or you are hallucinating it. Or a plot has been mounted against you ... Or you are fantasying some such plot, in which case you are a nut, Oedipa, out of your skull' (*COL49* 127–8).

For McHale, then, Pynchon's novel is a story of poetics that begins where it ends, with an epistemological dilemma: the 'sunrise over the library slope at Cornell University that nobody out on it had seen because the slope faces west' (*COL49* 5) is likened by McHale to Bishop Berkeley's conundrum of the tree that falls in the forest with no one to hear it.[12] And yet, as Pierre-Yves Petillon has argued, the novel 'not only focuses on Oedipa's epistemological bewilderment, but also charts the gradual "opening out" of her field of awareness. Her foray into the land of the Tristero ... is a venture into a dark foreign territory.'[13] Indeed, Pynchon's introductory paragraph just as surely begins by suddenly immersing a suburban Californian housewife into the 'dark foreign territory' of the dramas and histories of national and multinational business which are to be played out around her during the course of the novel. Cornell University, Pynchon's alma mater, was founded by Ezra Cornell, inventor and entrepreneur who built the telegraph line between Washington and Baltimore on which, in May 1844, the first message was sent: 'What hath God wrought?' When Oedipa thinks of the hotel room door slamming in Mazatlán she is thinking of a city which was the most important commercial centre on the west coast of Mexico during the eighteenth and nineteenth centuries and which had close trading links not only with California but with Hawaii too. When she thinks of the 'whitewashed bust of Jay Gould' slipping from the shelf above Pierce's bed and killing him she is thinking of the railroad magnate responsible for the commercial opening-up of vast tracts of the continent. It is into this lineage that Pierce fits, 'a founding father' (*COL49* 17) who 'put down the plinth course of capital' (*COL49* 15) in California upon which everything else was built. Oedipa is forced to confront this world of business by becoming executrix. And while, in the course of the novel, she is 'to have all manner of revelations', few will be about herself or Pierce. Instead they will be about 'what remained yet had somehow, before this, stayed away. There had hung the sense of buffering, insulation, she had noticed the absence of intensity' (*COL49* 13). What I want to suggest Oedipa has remained insulated from up until now, what has 'stayed away', is precisely this world of business and its connection to 'America'. From cosy Tupperware parties and Kinneret-Among-the-Pines markets, Oedipa has revealed to her the extent and consequences of Pierce's global dealings.

The horror of these global business transactions and their connection to the betrayal of national citizenship is witnessed most clearly in Oedipa's trip to Fangoso Lagoons, a housing development around a lake and one of Pierce's last big projects before he died. Oedipa's co-executor, the lawyer Metzger, has already told her about Pierce's involvement with Beaconsfield Cigarettes and his 51 per cent share in the filter process which uses bone charcoal (*COL49* 23). Oedipa wonders 'Bones of what?', and finds out on her trip to Fangoso Lagoons that they are human bones. As well as bones sold on by the highway contractors Pierce had bought into – obtained by ploughing up cemeteries in the course of their projects – some of the bones used by Beaconsfield come from conventional sales, albeit with the Mafia. Part of one batch decorate the bottom of Lake Inverarity, the centrepiece of Fangoso Lagoons. The rest have been sold on to Beaconsfield where they 'were used in the R&D phase of the filter programme' (*COL49* 44). The bones themselves belonged to GIs killed in Italy during the Second World War. Along with Milo's bombing of his own squadron in *Catch-22* it is difficult to imagine a harsher indictment of the idiocies and misplaced priorities of United States business and its role in the global circulation of products than this: the recycling of United States soldiers killed defending the nation during a war into products that will themselves kill United States citizens during peacetime.

Not that the revelation of this incident seems to affect Oedipa at this stage of the novel. She is too preoccupied with the observation made by one of the women accompanying the Paranoids on the trip to the lake. The bones-in-the-lake story, she notices, resembles the plot of *The Courier's Tragedy* she has recently seen. Metzger mistakes Oedipa's interest in the similarity for social concern. 'I don't care what Beaconsfield uses in its filter', she corrects him. 'I don't care what Pierce bought from the Cosa Nostra. I don't want to think about them. Or about what happened at Lago di Pietà ... I want to see if there's a connection. I'm curious.' It is this curiosity that initiates Oedipa's entry into the mystery of the Tristero system. What I want to emphasise is how the system of connectedness Oedipa potentially reveals is the way in which she ultimately manages to perceive the relationship between business and the idea of 'America' and to demonstrate her social concern. The Tristero system is the layer which she must understand and pass through in order to explore the 'dark foreign territory' in which business resides and from which, up until now, she has remained protected.

Oedipa's curiosity for the connectivity of a system is established through a fascination with hieroglyphics that she confronts, again, in the world of business upon becoming executrix. Driving into San Narciso to meet up with Metzger, Oedipa looks down at the 'ordered swirl of houses and streets' that assume the 'astonishing clarity' of a circuit board in a transistor radio: 'Though she knew even less about the radios than about Southern Californians, there were to both outward patterns a hieroglyphic sense of concealed meaning, of an intent to communicate' (*COL49* 16). When she watches the TV commercial for Fangoso Lagoons, Oedipa gasps only at the point when a 'map of the place flashed onto the screen', reminding her of the printed circuit she has seen earlier and suggesting 'some promise of hierophany' (*COL49* 21). Then it is in the toilets of Scope – a bar frequented almost exclusively by the employees of Yoyodyne, the aerospace arm of Galatronics – that Oedipa is first confronted with the muted post horn which she copies down: 'God, hieroglyphics', she thinks to herself (*COL49* 37).

There is good deal of 'looking past' going on in these sections. Confronted by the world of business, Pynchon has Oedipa look through the printed circuit board, the television advertising commercial, and the Yoyodyne aerospace plant in order to try and decipher the guiding patterns and systems that lie behind or beneath them. It is during the course of this process that Oedipa is introduced to the concept of entropy. Whilst she complains that the word 'was too technical for her' as she listens to John Nefastis' explanation (*COL49* 78), we know that Pynchon's fascination with the subject goes back to his 1960 short story of the same name. According to the Second Law of Thermodynamics, the entropy of a closed system shall never decrease, and shall increase whenever possible, where entropy is a measure of molecular disorder. Wrapped up in a moment of comedy, Pynchon provides a simple example of this principle: the aerosol can that ricochets around Oedipa and Metzger's motel room (*COL49* 25–6). The energy needed to launch the aerosol can is provided by the difference between the concentration and orderliness of the molecules in the can and the existing molecules in the room. This is a situation of low entropy. As the molecules from the can disperse through the room – the closed system – and lose concentration, entropy increases, energy is lost, and the can comes to rest.

While entropy, however, is an explanation of the world that originated in physics, it was adopted elsewhere, most famously in Norbert Wiener's *The Human Use of Human Beings* (1950). Social entropy emphasised the disappearance of distinctions within a social system. Just as energy is lost as the molecules in the aerosol can and the molecules of the motel room lose distinction from one another, so social energy is drained from a society when the values of orderly difference and distinction are replaced by the qualities of sameness. Furthermore, in this vision of social entropy it is those institutions – the corporate organisations, bureaucracies, and the social 'system' – that make up society which create this situation, since these institutions work as normalising and de-individuating forces. Social entropy, then, as Timothy Melley has suggested,[14] can be seen as part of those same discourses of fear and paranoia about the fate of the individual that dominated the critical treatments of post-war United States culture by writers like William H. Whyte and David Riesman.

At this stage I think it is worth thinking about social entropy and its points of equivalence with the kind of 'coming apart', 'disintegration' and 'splitting at the seams' that I mentioned above. Initially, there would seem to be a discrepancy between, on the one hand, the idea that the consensus model of 'American' identity was being fractured by multiculturalism and the politicisation of marginalised groups and, on the other, the idea that United States society was becoming increasingly homogenised and de-individuated. It should be remembered, however, that the discourse of entropy was taken up primarily in the works of white male writers. The emphasis on entropy in these works suggests a presumption that the battle between institutionalised society and the individual is of greater importance than the differences and confrontations between social groups. White male literature was more concerned with explaining the unmooring of its own identity as a consequence of the systemic and entropic nature of society rather than having to confront the way that this group identity had in the past been privileged and how that privilege was now being questioned. White male culture, then, was experiencing the relativisation of identity as a loss of identity completely. This is a defensive manoeuvre in two ways: not only does it attempt to universalise, and therefore disguise the source of, white male anxiety, but the appeal to social entropy also leads inevitably back to a discourse about 'America' since the 'system' responsible for de-individuation is an 'Americanism' that increasingly wants to drive a global system through business. While globalisation may in fact lead to the increasing contrast and proximity of differences, in terms of the Second Law of Thermodynamics taken up so readily by white male literary culture, it means only increasing entropy and further homogenisation and leads to an appeal for a nostalgic and unified vision of 'America'.

In *The Crying of Lot 49* this appeal is complexly arranged in relation to business. On one level, and in addition to the indictment of Pierce's business dealings and their connection with the death of United States citizens, there is a quite straightforward discourse about what has happened to the individual in the corporation. Stanley Koteks complains to Oedipa that Yoyodyne makes all its engineers sign away patent rights to any of their inventions, thus stifling their creativity (*COL49* 63). Later in the novel Oedipa is told a story about a Yoyodyne executive who, on being 'automated out of a job ... by an IBM 7094', is deserted by his wife and, after some prevarication, decides to commit suicide. He stops when his wife's new lover scoffs that the three weeks he took to decide on this course of action could have been completed in twelve micro-seconds by the IBM 7094. And this is the point in Pynchon's novel: these moments when the individual is on the point of collapse in the face of corporate pressure lead Oedipa to signs that there is a possible world that escapes institutional control. Thus the gasoline the Yoyodyne executive was going to use to burn himself dissolves the printing ink of stamps on the letters in his jacket pocket, leaving a watermark of the muted post horn. The underground Tristero system in the United States possibly survives despite the fact that from the 1840s onwards the federal government has sought to monopolise the delivery of mail and outlaw private mail firms.

The importance of mail systems and stamps in the novel suggests that it is in the form of communication that Pynchon attempts to establish the possibility of an alternative realm that, just like Maxwell's demon in the Nefastis machine, might violate the Second Law of Thermodynamics. The demon, instead of letting molecules arrange themselves, deliberately organises them so that they continually release energy. What remains problematic in Pynchon's novel, however, is the way that, as Thomas Schaub has suggested, 'What Maxwell's Demon is to the Nefastis Machine, Oedipa is to *America*'[15] (my emphasis). The closer Oedipa gets to realising what is happening around her, the more tightly she starts to cling to and revalue the signifier 'America'. The clearest example of this is towards the end of the book when Oedipa walks along a stretch of railroad track whose spurs link up to factory properties that 'Pierce may have owned'. Oedipa now reads San Narciso as a synecdoche of 'America':

> San Narciso at that moment lost ... its residue of uniqueness for her; became a name again, was assumed back into the American continuity of crust and mantle ... San Narciso had no boundaries. No one knew yet how to draw them. She had dedicated herself, weeks ago, to making sense of what Inverarity had left behind, never suspecting that the legacy was America. (*COL49* 135)

Oedipa then goes on to speculate that every other town and city is like San Narciso and that 'she might have found The Tristero anywhere in her Republic' (*COL49* 136). She imagines the kinds of squatters, outcasts and drifters who might utilise this railroad location and the empty Pullman cars and who might also communicate through the Tristero. 'What would the probate judge have to say about spreading' Pierce's legacy – 'America' – amongst them all, she wonders. Here the reader is brought back to the inescapable subtext of this novel: that business as personified by Pierce, whilst it overflows into its corporate and global incarnations, has betrayed or neglected the 'American' sections of the population and has created an 'America' in which the only way Oedipa can continue to live 'and manage to be at all relevant to it, was as an alien, unfurrowed, assumed full circle into some paranoia' (*COL49* 138).

Petillon gives this aspect of the novel a personal dimension for Pynchon by suggesting how the lapse into obscurity of Pynchon's famous Puritan family in the nineteenth century 'can be viewed as an emblem of the way America has betrayed its original "errand" into the wilderness', especially in the 'thrust toward headlong conquest, land grabbing, exploitation and destruction'.[16] The wilderness that Oedipa ventures into is the railroad track mentioned above and night-time San Francisco – 'the infected city' (*COL49* 88) – where she spends the hours finding images of the post horn '[d]ecorating each alienation, each species of withdrawal': in Chinatown, chalked on the sidewalk, in a laundromat in a 'Negro neighbourhood', at the airport, and during her encounters with 'a facially-deformed welder ... a child roaming the night ... a Negro woman with an intricately marbled scar ... an ageing night-watchman, nibbling a bar of Ivory soap' (*COL49* 92). Unlike in Norman Mailer's *The Naked and the Dead*, however, there is no sense with Pynchon that the cosmopolitanism hinted at during the course of this evening's journey – Oedipa also bumps into Jesús Arabal, a Mexican café-owner she first met while with Pierce in Mazatlán – is a danger to the Republic. Instead it is a Republic founded on the plinth of Pierce's capital that has not accepted cosmopolitanism, except where it serves business, and pushes out of sight the uncomfortable reminders of that quest for wealth.

One could argue that Pynchon's willingness to imagine this other side of the Republic and to reveal it in his fiction marks a much needed counter-hegemonic intervention. Indeed, shortly after *The Crying of Lot 49* was published Pynchon wrote a now-famous piece for the *New York Times* entitled 'A Journey into the Mind of Watts'. Detailing attitudes in this Los Angeles district a year on from devastating riots, Pynchon writes about a place that lies 'uncounted miles further than most whites seem at present willing to travel'.[17] He emphasises the isolation of Watts and its isolation from much of the white culture that surrounds it. Sympathetic, pessimistic and indignant by turn, the article is written in a hard-nosed style that communicates much of the despair, violence and resignation Pynchon finds there. It stands in stark contrast, however, to the mode of representation Pynchon deploys when writing Oedipa's experience of the multiracial, multicultural city. 'America' is not mentioned once in Pynchon's *New York Times* piece. Oedipa's experience, however, seems to me to be represented in almost-epiphanic terms that can be read as a corollary to the kind of experience that Perry Miller underwent during his trip to the African jungle. While Oedipa does not look past the non-white faces and neighbourhoods during her time in the wilderness, she sees exactly what Miller saw in his epiphany. Petillon is surely right to suggest that 'The kingdom that Oedipa feels is about to come in the auction room of the novel's final scene is "another" kingdom, and yet, at the same time, it is nothing but "America" itself ... waiting to be redeemed from its captivity.'[18]

WILLIAM GADDIS, *JR* (1975)

Despite only being a short novel, *The Crying of Lot 49* manages to pack within its covers a panoply of characters, references and clues that lead to a proliferation of meanings and possibilities. Indeed, part of the success of the novel – and certainly its accessibility to the reader

– is the way that the amount of information it contains seems inversely proportionate to the size and difficulty of the narrative. William Gaddis's *JR* is an altogether different proposition. Formidable not only in terms of size, Gaddis dispenses with the cues and deceits that help the reader negotiate more traditional narratives by writing his novel almost entirely in dialogue. Other than the diction, language and tenor of the dialogue itself, there is little indication to the reader which character is talking. Devices to organise, recap and condense a plot are also absent.

Yet there is no mistaking that this novel is about business and 'America'. The novel begins with the word 'Money' and draws its title from the character JR Vansant, a schoolboy entrepreneur who early on visits the New York stock exchange with his classmates in order, as their social studies teacher Amy Joubert puts it, 'to buy a share in America' with the 24 dollars they have saved: 'The boys and girls will follow its ups and downs and learn how our system works, that's why we call it our share.'[19] Twenty-four dollars was, of course, exactly the amount Dutch settlers paid the Manhattan tribe to buy the piece of land that becomes the setting for much of the novel. Amy Joubert herself has connections that fit her into a context of business as well as education. She is daughter of Monty Moncrieff, head of Typhon International and great niece of Governor John Cates, a director of Typhon. The school principal, Whiteback, is not just in the business of education either. He is president of a local bank. Edward Bast, composer in residence at JR's school, is a member of the Bast Angel family, whose 'name was changed from Engels, somewhere along the way' (*JR* 4), and who own the General Roll company. The inheritance and ownership of this family-run company is one of the narrative threads that runs through the novel. The company is acquired by the business empire JR builds from improbable beginnings. His deal to buy nine thousand gross of surplus army picnic forks leads to a paper empire that collapses as quickly as it grows. When General Roll has to be floated on the stock exchange in order to pay the death duties of James Bast, whose death has occurred shortly before the novel begins, JR incorporates it within his portfolio. It is then thrown to the mercy of the stock exchange and is eventually dismantled.

This cursory overview cannot do justice to the extensive and continuous machinations of business that Gaddis depicts in his novel. It is a vast web of characters whose interests connect the world of business with the world of education and – through the composer

Edward Bast, the teacher and writer Jack Gibbs, the painter Schepperman, and the writers Schramm and Eigen – the world of the arts. But in many ways the entirely confusing detail of the novel, that confounds the reader at every point, is incorporated by Gaddis into a much clearer vision than that which initially appears to be illustrated by the novel. Thomas LeClair has argued that 'Gaddis's vision of America is of a land of excess, of quantitive values and uncontrollable bigness, a place where time, people, and language are atomized', and *JR* works because it 'imitates what it hates'.[20] This vision of excess is one that LeClair suggests is so out of control, and truly systemic, because it escapes human management. In this situation, those areas that one might think are beyond the reaches of business – education, the arts – are completely overrun by it too, leaving the individual no place of escape. Gaddis's motive for creating such an excessive novel, LeClair contends, 'is a radically felt need to communicate new, large, even planetary and possibly saving visions of contemporary existence'.[21]

Given the global or 'planetary' vision of the system Gaddis imagines, *JR* becomes a novel that according to Joel Dana Black is 'preoccupied ... with the overwhelming spectre of Empire',[22] where an institution-driven entropy plays the role of villain. Here the subject of entropy is on the school curriculum of physics teacher Jack Gibbs. Although his class cannot spell it, Gibbs – named after Josiah Willard Gibbs, the American physicist who heavily influenced Norbert Wiener – is determined they should know that organisation is not an inherent property of knowledge itself and that 'Order is simply a thin, perilous condition we try to impose on the basic reality of chaos.' His attempts to impress this on his students are preceded by a plea for order in the classroom: ' – All right let's have order here, order' (*JR* 20). The lawyer Coen has already told Julia and Anne Bast that 'The law seeks order ... Order!' (*JR* 8). But the students ignore Gibbs and hurry out of the classroom while Julia and Anne Bast ignore Coen's pleas. Excess and entropy lead only to disorder. And once education and the arts are brought within the realm of commercial and government institutions there is little opportunity for the kinds of feedback that might regenerate the system. 'To Gaddis', Stephen Weisenburger argues, 'when money talks, things fall apart.'[23] Individuals themselves are reduced to a state of entropy. The most explicit demonstration of this is the 96th Street apartment that Gibbs shares with Eigen and that JR uses to collect his mail and store products. The apartment, supposedly a place of artistic retreat, becomes that which confounds creativity as Gibbs has to clamber over '24–7 Oz Pkgs Flavored Loops … 24-One Pint Mazola New Improved … 36 Boxes 200 2-Ply' (*JR* 286). As Weisenburger concludes, while all 'of Jack's artist friends try to isolate themselves' in order to produce creative work, their efforts end 'in failure, despair, or suicide',[24] as in the case of Schramm (*JR* 273). Edward Bast's musical ambitions are also permanently on hold. He tries to tell JR that 'music's not a business like shoes' and that he's 'not trying to write tunes for money' (*JR* 134), but he becomes embroiled in JR's business when he agrees to act on JR's behalf and, during a meeting with a stock adviser, agrees to compromise himself and write some 'Zebra music' for a film the adviser has produced (*JR* 197–206).

The pervasiveness of these business practices combined with the ideas of an increasing disorder and entropic world indicate the way that Gaddis, like Heller in *Catch-22*, is constructing his satire at an all-encompassing level. Christopher Knight has suggested that in *JR* Gaddis imagines a world in which there 'are no vacuums, and into the space vacated by the more traditional orders, business has marched like an ur-reality'.[25] The 'planetary' business system becomes a closed system where the flows of capital are not a signal of positive interaction and rejuvenation, but of enervation. Not only this, but the overseas dealings of United States business are yet further indications of the way the business of the nation is undermined by the business of business. As in *The Crying of Lot 49*, business has on its hands the blood of its own citizens. Monty Moncrieff leaves his job as head of Typhon to take up a high-level government post in Washington explicitly to negotiate a deal that will allow Typhon to set up a smaltite processing plant in the fictional African state of Gandia. Backing Typhon to the tune of $39.7 million, and ignoring the civil war that is breaking out in the country, the government enables Typhon to take advantage of the cheap labour and mineral deposits it sees ready for exploitation (*JR* 96–7). But the cobalt recovered is then used by brewers in the United States to put a head on their beer, causing all kinds of body tissue damage according to a government report (*JR* 435). The civil war becomes an opportunity for business too, however, and JR is responsible for selling to one side in the conflict a whole shipment of weapons. They are, however, toy weapons made from plastic and result in a massacre (*JR* 709).

The intertwining of business and government in overseas projects like this and the way that the end results are detrimental both to United States and foreign citizens are part of *JR*'s discourse about the divorce between business and morality. The runaway project of business and its demand for the constant circulation of products has resulted, *JR* suggests, in the 'material-money-junk world' that Gaddis himself described.[26] It is a world in which a teenage entrepreneur can achieve success, primarily because – as a child – he accepts the ethics of business unquestioningly. There is a corresponding discourse, then, in Gaddis's novel about maturity. For Stephen Moore, the association of money in *JR* with excrement – most notably in JR's perpetual use of the phrase 'Holy shit' when he's talking business – can be considered in the light of Freud's contention that the child's anal-erotic satisfaction of producing faeces is sublimated into the production of odourless and socially acceptable products like money. In his previous novel, *The Recognitions*, Gaddis names a businessman Recktall Brown but in *JR* the association reaches its climax with Isadore Duncan's enema:

> – No such thing as free enterprise in this country since the Haymarket riots, the minute something threatens this expanding capital forma ow ...
> – That's it lie still now, just try to keep it in as long as you can that's it ...
> – Threaten this expanding capital formation and they're at the head of the line whining for loan guarantees against the, the taxes on those tips she's sitting out there counting at night on her four dollar davenport to, to ...
> – That's it now just keep it in ...
> [...]
> – See the debt burden rising twice as fast ... good time to sell out try to slow down inflation the wholse security market's co, collapsing credit shrinkage forcing a, can't ...
> – Just a minute longer ...
> – forcing a, a mass, massive outflow ...
> – Wait here's the pan! here's the pan! my ...

This fusing together of talk about business and excrement reinforces Gaddis's point that 'what America's all about' is 'waste disposal and all', a phrase repeated three times during the novel (*JR* 25, 27, 179). What one sees now is that the business Gaddis so berates is the subject of his satire because it has become – much to his regret – 'America'. It is a sign that 'America' has failed to mature in the way that was once imagined possible because the childlike nation remains fascinated with the production of waste. This linking of the nation with business and anality carries with it demonising overtones. Reminiscent of Leslie Fiedler's argument about the largely narcissistic and immature nature of homoerotic male United States literature,[27] it is homophobic in the way it uses business to constitute anality and homosexuality as threats to the nation.

What emerges in *JR*, then, is a very clear picture about the nation. Indeed, Stephen Moore has suggested that 'America has always been Gaddis's great subject' and that he has harboured 'a feeling of bitter disappointment at America's failure to fulfil its potential, to live up to the magnificent expectations held for the New World'.[28] But as well as trying to give form to, and apportion blame for, this disappointment, Gaddis has also injected *JR* with ideas about how the nation might be improved. He gives what appears to be a chaotic text that 'imitates what it hates' an underlying sense of order to try and hold together the nation that falls apart when money gets involved. William Gass has noted how Gaddis's interest in Russian writers like Dostoyevsky suggests that 'he was attempting to save his version of an acceptable country as they were endeavoring to redeem theirs'.[29] The most powerful literary allusions in the novel, however, are 'to works of cultural crises, concerned with the salvation of a society'.[30] Primary amongst these is Wagner's *Ring of the Nibelung*.

In his role as school music fellow, Edward Bast is putting on a production of the opera, with JR playing the role of Alberich so that he can get out of gym lessons (*JR* 31-7). Stephen Moore has detailed how characters in the novel are images of characters from the *Ring* – Cates as Wotan, Amy Joubert as Brünnhilde – and the way in which the rambling structure of *JR* imitates the 'uninterrupted formal design' of the *Ring*. The opening E flat pedal tone of the *Ring*, for example, which carries on for over a hundred bars is matched in *JR* by its opening word: money. In addition, throughout the course of the novel there are numerous references to Wagner's life, career and family.[31] The choice of Wagner's operatic tetralogy as a model for *JR* makes sense when one considers how it has been read as a critique of exploitative capitalism. Wagner, like Karl Marx – whose dictum 'From each according to his abilities' is hewn in stone above the school entrance – was exiled from mid-nineteenth century Germany.

What interests me about Gaddis's decision to organise his novel in relation to Wagner's *Ring* is the way that it inevitably invites parallels with the other major features of Wagner's work: his nationalism and his ideas about the role of art as a redemptive national force. Gaddis anticipates the charge of Wagner's anti-Semitism by having the school rehearsals of the *Ring* take place in a Jewish temple, but like Wagner he is drawn to some of the myths of an earlier national culture – in Gaddis's case 'late-nineteenth century social and educational reform movements, robber barons and unregulated capitalism, and the Protestant work ethic of Benjamin Franklin and Horatio Alger'.[32] By fashioning his fiction in this way Gaddis is drawn to those myths and discourses that have in the past underpinned the ideological discourses of nation building. And whilst he does so in order to attack the development of United States business and capitalism, his commitment is to an art that will be good enough to overcome the brutalities of business and value the human rather than the economic qualities of human beings. Gregory Comnes has explored the way that *JR* constructs a model of artistic value, and he concludes that the failure of the artists in the novel that I have already mentioned occurs because 'they do not recognize that there can be no art until someone makes it, whatever may be the obstacle. The artists intellectualise and complain about the depreciation evident in society yet keep themselves paralysed by waiting for something worth doing to motivate them.'[33]

In *JR*, Gaddis does something that according to Thomas LeClair amounts to 'transforming waste into art'.[34] This is the ultimate act of sublimation but also the ultimate act of productivity. And it is worth remembering at this point too how Calvin Coolidge praised the American journalist for forming out of current events not 'a drab and sordid story, but rather an informing and enlightened epic. His work becomes no longer imative, but rises to an original art.' By setting his sights to the system of business that underpinned 'America', Gaddis set himself the task of producing an art that was capable of encompassing the vastness of his subject. This artistic project ultimately is meant to redeem the nation from corruption. If, during the twenty years that it took Gaddis to write the novel, 'American' identity was splitting apart at the seams then his response can be seen almost an act of national consolidation. Fighting off the centrifugal impact of economic globalisation and the unmooring of white male identity, Gaddis deals with the business with which he was so familiar by raising above it the idealism that Coolidge argued was the chief ideal of the American people.

JOSEPH HELLER, *SOMETHING HAPPENED* (1974)

Compared to the territory of wartime Europe he depicted in *Catch-22* and the journeys over and across it made by United States servicemen, in *Something Happened* Joseph Heller turned to an altogether more domestic scene. One of the more interesting aspects of Heller's change of mode is the way that he replaced a comic third-person narration incorporating a large cast of eccentrics and villains with a sombre first-person narration that, for almost as many pages as *Catch-22*, remains confined to the mind of Bob Slocum as he engages with the kind of life during which nothing does happen except the grinding repetition of working and family responsibilities. It is a life of bland routine far removed from the missions of life and death flown by 256th Squadron or their furloughs in Rome. And whereas Yossarian perpetually refused to conform to the disciplinary and bureaucratic structures of military life, Bob Slocum is obedient to the corporate machine in which he prospers and succeeds.

Compared to *Catch-22*, then, it is as if in *Something Happened* the world has come to a standstill. Whilst the circulation of global capital continues unchecked, men like Slocum who work in the businesses driving and benefiting from this circulation are – like the aerosol can in Oedipa's motel bathroom – falling to rest and atrophying. Their careers may be taking off, but 'Look at me', Slocum says, 'I ascend like a condor, while falling to pieces.'[35] Heller's narrative represents this coming to rest that is also a coming apart by dealing not in revelation but repetition. Ordinarily, the confessional technique might lead Slocum to redemption. But Heller's prose, as Lindsey Tucker points out, is often contradictory and while it revisits incidents and characters – particularly Slocum's youthful relationship with Virginia – there is little sense that Slocum is energised or re-formed as a result.[36] Slocum's life has become a closed system with no points of reference or feedback from outside of work or family. Ultimately, it is business in its corporate mode that is responsible for this kind of effect in *Something Happened*. The nature of the company for which Slocum works is never named and its products never identified. For Lois Tyson, this suggests that the novel focuses 'on the psychology of hierarchical corporate structures rather than on the psychology of industrial production'.[37] The discrepancy between Slocum's career success and his sense of an identity falling to pieces mirrors the world of business. The calm surface that is its public face disguises a culture where 'fear is the oil that lubricates operations'.[38]

As with Arthur Miller's *Death of a Salesman*, however, and in the light of Buell's contention that the forces shaping the United States were connected with the reshaping of the globe as much as particularly 'American' developments, the domestic nature of *Something Happened* needs to be read in this global context. While *The Crying of Lot 49* and *JR* quite explicitly reference the kind of global business connections that are absent in *Something Happened*, I would connect the three novels by suggesting that *Something Happened* represents the process of economic globalisation as it is internalised psychologically by white male culture. Slocum's fear of the corporation in which he works, and fear of corporate institutions in general, witnesses a fear of the processes in which corporations are involved.

It is possible to start thinking about the link between Slocum's fear and globalising business culture by noticing the way that this relationship is condensed figuratively in Heller's opening introduction to Slocum: 'I get the willies when I see closed doors. Even at work, where I am doing so well now, the sight of a closed door is sometimes enough to make me dread that something horrible is happening behind it, something that is going to affect me adversely' (*SH* 3).

This fear of closed doors is identical to the Türschluss syndrome about which William Gaddis writes in *JR*. This syndrome is derived from the term 'Torschluss-Panik' – the fear of closed doors or gates that mean arriving too late for something, and itself the title of a play Gaddis wrote for German radio in 1998[39] – and in *JR* the Türschluss syndrome is discussed twice. First of all, Jack Gibbs uses it while in the 96th Street apartment after the suicide of the writer Schramm: 'just having a touch of the Türschluss syndrome beginning to see the doors closing, all sad words of tongue or pen the same God damned doors Schramm saw closing' (*JR* 383). Later, Gibbs refers to a 'Whole Türschluss generation, kind of paralysis sets in' (*JR* 492). In *JR*, it is the invasion of multinational business corporations into every domain of life that frustrates artists like Schramm and Gibbs and leads to an entropic 'paralysis' that is experienced at the level of the individual. In *Something Happened* this paralysis does not affect artistic production, but has become a way of life for the office worker Slocum.

I understand this 'paralysis' as the postmodern equivalent of the sense of 'exhaustion' Willy Loman experiences in the face of business. The very phrasing Heller uses – 'I get the willies' – suggests a reference to Loman. It is a paralysis, also, that is determined by the scale of the business in which Slocum works which is much bigger than the company itself. The twelve elderly men 'who helped found and build the company and now own and direct it' no longer work very hard. 'Nobody is sure anymore', Slocum says, 'who really runs the company (not even the people who are credited with running it), but the company does run' (*SH* 14). More disturbingly, though, Slocum suggests that his life is not affected by just this one company. His fear of doors extends much further and he suggests how his sense of 'falling to pieces' and failure are subject to much wider influences: 'I find it impossible to know exactly what is going on behind the closed doors of all the offices on all the floors occupied by all the people in this and all the other companies in the whole world who might say or do something, intentionally or circumstantially, that could bring me to ruin' (*SH* 15).

It is at moments like this that Heller's novel defies its domestic setting and reaches out to explore the ways in which the life of Bob Slocum is not just dependent upon local or national influences but on a network of connected businesses that stretch across the globe. The reader learns that the company for which Slocum works has offices in Canada, Latin America and eleven more that are just 'overseas'. Slocum's 'paralysis', just like that artistic 'paralysis' in *JR*, now has causes that are beyond, but tied into, a changing 'America'. Slocum feels cut off from the world around him and no longer feels able to rebel. Anything he does at work, he suggests, will be 'absorbed like rain on an ocean and leave no trace'. More tellingly, however, Slocum suggests 'it is just about impossible for someone like me to rebel anymore and produce any kind of lasting effect. I have lost the power to upset things ... I can no longer change my environment or even disturb it seriously' (*SH* 19).

The words 'someone like me' indicate how Slocum considers his condition to be a partial one. Who are the people who are not like him? They may, of course, include the African-American, feminist or gay and lesbian activists who, whilst faced with all sorts of social and political barriers, did not consider themselves incapable of changing their environment. The political changes that did occur during the 1960s were driven by a sense of identity that, however compromised by prejudice and oppression, was strong enough and committed enough to fight for change. It was the very antithesis of the kind of identity displayed by Bob Slocum. So fragile is his sense of identity that he has the 'wretched habit ... of acquiring the characteristics of other people' (*SH* 72). He finds himself talking, walking, or stuttering like the people he meets or knows. He worries about being in the presence of homosexuals because he 'might be tempted to become like them' (*SH* 73); when he talks to 'a Negro' he will, 'begin using not only his vernacular (militant hip or bucolic Uncle Tom), but his pronunciation' (*SH* 74). The identity that is splitting apart at the seams here is the 'American' identity that Bob Slocum identifies as his own falling to pieces; the identity that – by using the words 'someone like me' – he is demonstrating holds a particular relation to 'America'. He has, he complains, 'got the decline of American civilization and the guilt and ineptitude of the whole government of the United States to carry around on these poor shoulders' (*SH* 67).

This characterisation of his situation leads to a whole discourse of melancholy and self-pity in the novel. Slocum seizes on the chance offered by his besieged and disintegrating white male identity to cry, protest that 'sorrow is my skin condition' (*SH* 359), and worry over his vanity (*SH* 221). The sense of regret he feels pushes him to contemplate the office in which he first worked and the storeroom to which he would retreat, sometimes alone, but more often with Virginia. In the storeroom were kept the files for all the car insurance company's claims and it was amidst this detritus of business bureaucracy that he tried and failed to seduce Virginia, a failure that signifies for Slocum the 'absence' and loss of 'density' (*SH* 363–4) he feels so strongly as an adult office worker. And yet what distinguishes *Something Happened* is the way that at the same time as feeling himself 'falling to pieces', Slocum also takes sanctuary in this melancholy. He feels a sense of safety in 'paralysis', and at seeing his life becoming like the old records deserted in the bleak storeroom. After arguing with his wife and daughter, he says, 'I feel so sorry for myself it is almost unbearably delicious. I also feel mighty: I feel potent and articulate … I stride towards the door with tears of martyred grief' (*SH* 158–9). At work Slocum even uses the death of his son to bolster his vanity and prestige: 'Everybody is impressed with how bravely I've been able to move into Kagle's position and carry on with the work of organizing the convention' (*SH* 565).

As well as the discrepancy between Slocum's career success and his identity that is falling apart, there is another discrepancy, then, between the fear he feels at work and the comfortable melancholy he experiences there. Here, I want to suggest, *Something Happened* is different from *The Crying of Lot 49* and *JR*. While Heller's novel registers the same kinds of concern with the impact of global business on United States culture, albeit at the internalised level of Slocum's psyche, it never reaches out for 'America' in the same way as these two other novels. *Something Happened* registers the way that white-collar, white male culture in the United States is so intertwined with the culture of business that to envisage a domain beyond business would be only to clutch at ideas of 'America' that defy the very premise with which business is imagined in the first place. After all, if business in its global phase is truly as systemic and invasive as all three of these novels suggest, how can it be that one can escape it? By representing Slocum's 'falling to pieces' not as a universal condition of identity but as one determined by his status as a white-collar, white male individual, Heller begins to envisage the coping strategies that men in similar positions will need to deploy. Not always sophisticated or defensible – Slocum is unremittingly misanthropic – these strategies are as important for the options they exclude and reject as the manner in which they are played out. *Something Happened* may just be the first time white male literary culture in the United States confronted global business and did not turn around and run for 'America'.

3
Postnational Recovery Narratives and Beyond

If Gene Wise was right and the 1970s marked a disintegration of the traditional models of American Studies criticism, then it was a disintegration that prompted a reorganisation of the field on new grounds. As research in other social sciences like ethnography and anthropology, along with theoretical developments from Europe, filtered into the writing of Americanists, the field was transformed by diversification and specialisation. Wise described this general process as a shift from a 'holistic' to a 'pluralistic' approach to American culture, driven by black studies, women's studies and popular culture studies which, taken together he argued, marked 'a rediscovery of the particular in American culture'.[1]

But Wise, having written about the 'corporate phase' of post-war American Studies, carried on his business metaphors in describing a simultaneous development in the field during the 1970s that has had direct implications for the use of the word 'American' in American Studies. For Wise, this period was characterised by a *stock-taking consciousness*.[2] Had Wise lived to see the field changing in the 1980s and '90s, he would have witnessed just how much this 'stock-taking' has dominated the field of American Studies, so much so that the boundaries of what constitutes 'American' culture are regularly being questioned. One of the points of engagement for both students and academics is the knowledge that 'America' no longer has a national but a postnational culture.

The development of a postnational discourse in the field of American Studies has been driven by the kinds of extra-national events that Frederick Buell argued were changing the United States in the 1960s. But whereas the 'reshapings of the globe' that Buell discusses impacted in that decade in ways which unsteadied without entirely unseating the connection between the nation and its culture, in the last two decades globalisation has been envisaged as a threat to the very viability of the nation-state itself. Donald Pease, for example, in the introduction to a special edition of *Modern Fiction Studies* devoted to this subject, writes about how the socio-economic configuration of globalisation, and a coincidental but asymmetrical postcolonialism, 'share responsibility for the demotion of the nation-state to the status of a residual unit of economic exchange in the global economy'.[3] If in the past, as Pease suggests, national narratives were cultural forms 'wherein official national fantasies were transmitted to a "national people"', postnational narratives try to 'make visible the incoherence, contingency, and transitoriness of ... national narratives and ... reveal [a] paradoxical space'[4] between the nation and the state.

This process, however, has not been straightforward or uniform. The objective of this chapter is to look at a series of narratives written during the last 25 years, and whose main focus is business, in order to examine to what degree national narratives are revealed to be incoherent or contingent in white male literary culture. There are good grounds for scepticism. For a start, it would be optimistic to expect these narratives to be free from some of the same reservations that greeted the changing focus of American Studies and cultural studies more generally. The attention to the 'particular', about which Wise wrote so enthusiastically, has resulted in a multicultural curriculum and research culture that critics such as Dinesh D'Souza, Allan Bloom, Richard Bernstein and Arthur Schlesinger, Jr, amongst others, have castigated precisely for its failure to emphasise a national cultural narrative.[5] Secondly, just as I emphasised the sense of discomfort in the previous chapter that postmodern literature displays as it is forced to confront the impact of globalisation, so the ever-increasing rate of commercial globalisation driven by technology that has marked the last two decades will create similar ambivalent senses of dislocation. In the academic realm, Pease has written about the 'transferential anxieties' and 'investiture crises' released when one paradigm model of academic study usurps another.[6] This serves as a useful model for trying to understand just how the socio-economic shifts that are rearranging the field of American Studies are likewise altering the cognitive and conceptual experiences of non-academic life in the United States and that erupt in its cultural formations.

Finally, and perhaps most significantly, it is important to note the ways in which the postnational that is a product of globalisation may still be subordinated to the interests of a national discourse. This is a danger pointed out most convincingly by Frederick Buell when he argues that 'recent U.S. culture is characterized less by insurgent post-nationalism ... than by the invention of a new breed of cultural nationalism – a form of cultural nationalism for post-national circumstances'.[7] Taking issue with Arjun Appadurai's claim that electronically mediated globalisation helps create imagined worlds where the official and the entrepreneurial might be contested, Buell argues that globalisation is 'still substantially managed by the official mind of nations and by transnational, as well as national, entrepreneurial mentalities'.[8] What Buell contends is that after the disastrous decade of the 1970s – marked as it was by the oil crisis and by the United States becoming a debtor and importer – the idea of the global economy became 'a key term for restructuring the political discourse of national crisis and internal division into a new kind of recovery narrative'.[9] The form that this new cultural nationalism takes is, paradoxically, the globalisation and multiculturalism so affecting the study of 'America'. Buell sees the simultaneity of globalisation as an economic mode and the stylistic heterogeneity of advanced capitalist countries witnessed in multiculturalism as evidence that capitalism in the United States is recovering a nationalist discourse by commodifying and repackaging those movements which potentially threaten it. Multiculturalism and globalisation provide 'a new market for both consumer and academic diversification, as ethnicity, non-Western culture, and the study of it are all commodified'. As Buell tellingly suggests, 'phrases like "cultural diversity," "difference," and "product diversification" are strangely appropriate bedfellows'.[10] The language of business that Wise uses to describe academic 'stock-taking' is particularly apt, then, since it is the business of globalisation that is in large part rearranging the relationship between the nation and the culture produced and consumed within its territorial borders.

DAVID MAMET, *AMERICAN BUFFALO* (1975) AND *GLENGARRY GLEN ROSS* (1984)

When it comes to writing about business, no playwright has taken up the dramatic baton of Arthur Miller and Eugene O'Neill with quite so much intensity and passion as David Mamet. In both *American Buffalo* and *Glengarry Glen Ross*, two relentlessly attritional and claustrophobic plays, Mamet puts American business through the grinder of colloquial language to offer up an indictment of its myths and practices. Mamet provides no room for the characters in these plays to build a life that can shelter them from the systemic oppressiveness of the discourses of business. Indeed, one of the features of the plays is the way that they draw upon the kinds of relationship between the individual and the institutionalised system mapped out in the literary texts I have already considered. The extra ingredients that Mamet adds to his treatment of business, however, are twofold: first, a sense of empire anxiety that I want to suggest manifests itself as guilt, and secondly, a recognition of the way that the myths surrounding business are played out in practice as the brutalised relationships between, in *American Buffalo*, a group of criminals and, in *Glengarry Glen Ross*, a group of salesmen where business itself becomes a process indistinguishable from criminality.

The most evident sign that Mamet is addressing himself to the connection between business and empire is with the Buffalo nickel that acts as the catalyst for the dramatic action of *American Buffalo*. The nickel, imprinted with a buffalo's head, turns up in Don's Resale Shop. Unaware of the coin's value, Don sells it to a customer for what he thinks is an inflated price only then to learn that the customer is a collector. Don assumes the coin must be worth far more than he sold it for and determines to steal it back, along with the rest of the collection. The figure of the buffalo is the evocative reminder of what the progress of United States capital destroyed as it spread across the continent in the nineteenth century: not only the animal itself but the native Indian communities who relied on it for their survival. What Mamet does by making the buffalo nickel – which was produced in the United States between 1913 and 1938 – the pivot around which the play revolves, is to highlight not only the destructive nature of business in the past, but the way that same historically destructive dynamic is now targeting the white male culture that lies at the heart of these two plays.

Mamet does not place white male culture in structurally the same position as native American culture, however. On 4 March 1913, coins from the very first batch of buffalo nickels to enter circulation were presented to President Taft as well as to 33 Indian chiefs at the ceremonies for the National Memorial to the North American Indian at Fort Wadsworth, New York. These ceremonies, whilst they may have helped salve national guilt, were also acts of reconciliation that tried to draw – however hypocritically – what remained of the native Indian population into the nation's social and economic system. And yet the turning of the buffalo into a national coin witnessed the way that the state could not commemorate its imperial conquest of the continent without reducing native Indian culture to an object of exchange. In Mamet's play this object has now become fetishised to such an extent that it is white male culture – in the form of the coin collector, Don, Teach and Bob – that battles for control of the object. The buffalo nickel, in which is condensed the story of the theft of native Indian land in the name of the state, is itself now the object which Don and Teach plan to steal. The criminal underclass of white male culture, then, now wants to steal the buffalo nickel in the name of the free enterprise that Teach describes to Don: 'You know what is free enterprise? ... The freedom ... Of the *individual* ... To Embark on Any Fucking Course that he sees fit ... In order to secure his honest chance to make a profit ... The country's *founded* on this, Don. You know this.'[11]

This exemplifies Chris Bigsby's point that Mamet is writing in an age 'in which the self-justifying cant of the rich has filtered down through the system'.[12] The predatory phase of capitalist life about which Thorstein Veblen wrote in *Theory of the Leisure Class* has gradually diffused into everyday life. Mamet, himself a reader of Veblen's work, describes how this process links business and criminality. Talking about *Glengarry Glen Ross*, although in terms that are equally applicable to *American Buffalo*, he argues that 'The play concerns how business corrupts, how the hierarchical business system tends to corrupt. It becomes legitimate for those in power in the business world to act unethically. The effect on the little guy is that he turns to crime.'[13]

The crime that Don and Teach plan in order to recover the buffalo nickel takes on the elements of a business project. It has to be planned and it has to be managed. Questioning whether Fletch should be part of the deal, Teach makes the preparation explicitly an issue of economics: 'We're talking business, let's *talk* business: you think it's good business to call Fletch in?' (*AB* 54). He later reiterates his commitment to the theft by marking himself out as a man of business: 'I don't fuck with my business associates. I am a businessman, I am here to do business, I am here to face facts' (*AB* 86). Because of the uncomfortable relationship between business and ethics that Mamet himself emphasises, it is precisely Teach's insistence on his business credentials that should make the other characters suspicious of him.

However, what seems to get left behind in this depiction of the ways in which business and criminality are intertwined, are the racial dimensions which initially seem to motivate Mamet's play. While the buffalo nickel skilfully serves the purpose of identifying how the state is culpable in commodifying the violent acts of its own past, Mamet is himself culpable in using this token as a means of appropriating racial oppression only then to evacuate the oppression of its racial element in order to show the damage business inflicts on an all-white male group. Since business is a means of making money, either 'legitimately' or unethically, business becomes in *American Buffalo* both a system which excludes the characters by way of its class and status inequalities, but also the discourse which these same characters then use to try and justify and reintegrate themselves into the system by utilising its terminology to legitimise their money-making scheme.

Whether this attempt can succeed is, of course, open to question. But while the play, in its exaggerated and repetitious references to 'business', suggests the futility of such a course of action, what it ensures is that the fate of this particular white male group remains the primary focus. After introducing as the impetus for its dramatic action the multicultural dimension of United States history, Mamet erases this multicultural history by replicating the state's commodi-fication of the buffalo nickel, this time by condensing the damage that business has done to non-white cultures in the United States into a literary synecdoche and using it as a platform from which to address the damage that business is doing to white male culture.

In this manoeuvre Mamet almost seems to equalise oppression by suggesting that the white male criminal class with which this play deals stands in the same relation to business as native American cultures of the past. A similar desire to portray the destruction of white property salesmen in *Glengarry Glen Ross* suggests that Mamet actually has in mind a broader constituency of male culture. In fact, I would go so far as to say that the motif of the buffalo nickel is one way in which Mamet actually recuperates a particular white male vision of 'America' through a multicultural frame, since there remains in his work a centripetal discourse pulling his audience towards 'America'.

In a tradition that goes back at least as far as Emerson's complaint that the peculiar qualities of American life 'are yet unsung'[14] and Melville's demand that America 'first praise mediocrity ... in her own children, before she praises ... the best excellence in the children of any other land',[15] Mamet has set himself up as a writer who makes literature out of 'American' experience. Not wanting to be that 'honorary Englishman' who appears 'because we don't feel that our actual life is a fit subject for drama',[16] Mamet combines what Chris Bigsby has described as 'jeremiad with celebration' by attacking business in the poetry of the American vernacular and placing his male characters in *Glengarry Glen Ross* in a recognisable lineage of what Nina Baym has famously called 'beset manhood'.[17]

It is the properties being sold to unsuspecting buyers in *Glengarry Glen Ross* that fulfil the purpose of commodifying the past in this play. Named Glengarry Highland, Glen Ross Farms and Homestead, they offer up what Steven Price has described as 'a specifically Jeffersonian vision of the farm as idealized family retreat', a quality that makes them commercially valuable.[18] Selling these properties are the successors to a national fiction of frontiersmen and hard-boiled detectives: salesmen who, in temperament, are anti-intellectual, bigoted, misogynistic, xenophobic and distrustful of power.[19] Like *American Buffalo*, crime stands at the heart of the play. The salesmen rely on good leads to sell property. The importance of these leads is made evident at the very beginning of the play, where it is also clear that the lead in business submits to a Catch-22 logic. Levene wants to get on the top salesman board, but cannot until he closes deals. But he cannot close deals until he gets good leads, and to get good leads he has to get on the top salesman board. The effects of this logic on the salesman is, as in *American Buffalo*, entirely destructive of the qualities of individualism and freedom that Jeffersonian ideology promises. Business, according to Price, 'is conducted in terms that bind the salesman to the same rules from which they are attempting to escape: the desire [for freedom] can be effected only through more crime, through an act of theft from the parent company'.[20] This act of theft, which separates the two acts of the play, is the theft of the leads from Williamson's office.

Mamet sets up some familiar targets to represent the system of business. Williamson, the office manager, is despised by all the salesmen for being a 'company man' and for Roma this is also equivalent to being a '*fairy*'.[21] The bosses of the real estate company, Mitch and Murray, remain hidden during the course of the play and signify the faceless power brokers of capitalism as they manipulate the salesmen, most directly with the sales contest: the winner receives a Cadillac while the loser will be fired. It is Richard Roma in particular who rails against what he sees as this 'world of clock watchers, bureaucrats, officeholders ... what it is, it's a fucked up world ... there's no adventure *to* it' (*GGR* 62). The scams the salesmen pull, the violence of their language and the culture of competitiveness they occupy, become understandable responses to a system that so ruthlessly exploits them. But it is Roma's choice of words when condemning this system that make it imperative that *Glengarry Glen Ross* is read with the same multicultural perspective as *American Buffalo*. Concluding his attack, Roma suggests that he and his fellow salesmen are a 'Dying breed. Yes it is. *(Pause.)* We are the members of a dying breed' (*GGR* 62).

With the buffalo nickel in mind here, it is hard not to think about the discourse of the vanishing Indian that dominated early twentieth-century thinking about native Americans. Fuelled by *The North American Indian*, Edward Curtis's twenty-volume collection of photographs published between 1907 and 1930, this discourse combined the myth of Manifest Destiny with social Darwinism to explain the disappearance of native American culture in the United States. As self-fulfilling prophecy, such a discourse actually helped implement and carry out the destruction. What is interesting, and at the same time discomforting, in *Glengarry Glen Ross* is the way that Mamet appropriates this discourse. Drawing on the rhetoric and, in *American Buffalo*, on the iconography of United States multicultur-alism, Mamet uses them to display a reverence for the subcultures of white male identity.

Steven Price has suggested that in his screenplays for *The Untouchables* and *Things Change*, Mamet displays a 'measured admiration for the Mafia hierarchy precisely because it embodies the values of American capitalism, without the hypocrisy of official business'.[22] In *Glengarry Glen Ross*, this admiration is reserved for the 'dying breed' of white males fighting official business and is articulated in Mamet's glitteringly visceral colloquial dialogue. What Mamet brings into view, then, is the anxiety and the suffering of white male culture faced with the system of business. What 'vanishes' in this scenario are the histories of racial oppression that provide Roma with his rhetoric of protest.

At this point it is possible to see how Mamet's plays – and this would apply to the works of the other male writers I have so far considered – actually fit into a clear tradition of what has been considered to be the best and the most appropriate subject of 'American' literature. According to Nina Baym, the quality that drove the 'nationalist orientation' of literary criticism was not just a belief that 'America as a nation must be the ultimate subject of the work', but that the 'cultural essence' of the nation was the tension embodied by white males who were part of the dominant social group but also alienated from it.[23] The literary form that this tension produced was the 'melodrama of beset manhood'. Baym's argument that it was precisely the valuing of this kind of literature that produced the neglect of writing by women, makes the glaring absence of female characters in Mamet's two plays all the more telling. And while Mamet may write about men who are not part of the dominant social group, they certainly use that dominant group's ideological discourse of business to imagine themselves and their place in the nation. The sheer desperation of a character like Levene in *Glengarry Glen Ross* as he begs for Williamson to give him decent leads, or the ruthlessness of Roma as he lies to customers he has duped, are testament to the way in which Mamet imagines the centrality of white male experience to national experience.

My main point, then, about Mamet's plays is that whilst they draw subtly on the multicultural dimensions of United States history and culture, they do so in a way that ultimately leads back to a familiar discourse about the white male who stands as the essence of what constitutes 'America'. While the buffalo nickel and Roma's description of himself as part of a 'dying breed' gesture towards a racially violent past driven by business and empire building, there is little sense in the plays of how that past has consequences for, and creates, a multicultural 'America'. The use of such a multicultural element may mark a new departure in the texts I have looked at so far, but what Mamet's plays testify to is the process whereby a nationalist culture – in the realms of often dazzling dramatic language – recognises its guilt, before appropriating the rhetoric of victimhood from this multicultural discourse the better to reimagine again the plight of white manhood and so shore up the traditions of a national literature.

BRET EASTON ELLIS, *AMERICAN PSYCHO* (1991)

The reaction that greeted the publication of Bret Easton Ellis's third novel certainly proved that literature in the United States could still generate national debate, although the debate in this case was often concerned more with the 'psycho' in *American Psycho* than with the 'American'. Attacked by the National Organization for Women for being a 'how-to' manual, and elsewhere by women for its graphic depiction of sadistic sexual violence, defenders of the novel cited its value as social satire and its attention to the detail of contemporary culture.

The critical response to *American Psycho*, on the other hand, has been organised more by the discourses of global postmodernism and Fredric Jameson's analysis of the 'cultural logic of late capitalism'. It is exactly business in its late capitalist phase that Ellis represents in *American Psycho*. From the hub of his Wall Street office, Patrick Bateman does his job of trading bonds in the global exchange market by relying on micro-electronics and information systems. Incredibly wealthy, he has succeeded in the free-market, post-industrial landscape that defined 1980s Reaganomics. What concerned Jameson was the cultural response to the emerging global economic system of multinational capitalism from the 1960s onwards and which, by the time of the 1980s, had become so pervasive in people's everyday lives. Not only was multinational capitalism employing them, it was increasingly determining the information, the images, and the commodities with which they interacted. For Jameson, this situation marked nothing less than a new form of historical engagement. In a world where all times and styles were available but new ones remained unavailable to the individual, in a world where we 'live in a perpetual present and in a perpetual change that obliterates traditions of the kind which all earlier social formations have had in one way or another to preserve', the proliferation and availability of information and objects within late capitalist culture lead, for Jameson, to 'the disappearance of a sense of history'.[24] Jameson identifies two key features of this condition that impact on cultural production: 'the transformation of reality into images' and 'the fragmentation of time into a series of perpetual presents'.[25] These manifest themselves as cultural modes of representation in the form of pastiche and schizophrenia respectively.

It is understandable that *American Psycho* be considered in these critical terms. Not only does it root itself firmly in what, during the 1980s, was the most visible cultural spectacle of global capitalism – Wall Street yuppiedom – but it quite consciously uses the formal techniques Jameson identified. Written for all but the briefest of sections in the first person,[26] the narrator Patrick Bateman often relies upon the pastiche that Jameson called 'the wearing of a stylistic mask' or 'speech in a dead language'.[27] It is the 'dead language' of selling, advertising and consumption in which Bateman narrates. The descriptions of clothes and technology are reproduced as if from catalogues, brochures, voice-overs and sales pitches while brand names litter the narrative as they do the rest of contemporary culture. Characters are introduced in similar terms: 'Courtney opens the door and she's wearing a Krizia cream silk blouse, a Krizia rust tweed skirt and silk-satin d'Orsay pumps from Manolo Blahnik' (*AP* 8). In Bateman's apartment stands a Toshiba TV set: 'it's a high-contrast highly-defined model plus it has a four-corner video stand with a high-tech tube combination from NEW with a picture-in-picture digital effects system (plus freeze-frame)' (*AP* 25). The description continues in copious detail, along with a description of the rest of the room in a similar style. There are interludes during the narrative when Bateman stops to discuss some of his favourite pop stars – Genesis, Whitney Houston, Huey Lewis and the News – and these sections read like music press biographies. Huey Lewis and the News, for instance, 'burst out of San Francisco onto the national music scene at the beginning of the decade, with their self-titled rock-pop album released by Chrysalis, though they really didn't come into their own, commercially or artistically, until their 1983 smash, *Sports*' (*AP* 352–3).

While one might argue that these sections do in fact create the laughter and parodic effect Jameson considers absent from pastiche, it should be remembered that what they actually draw attention to is not any object of parody – a person, a piece of technology, a band – but the styles of expression available to describe and explain these objects. As such these sections evidence that process whereby individuals are increasingly dependent upon the styles circulated to them by the world of multinational business. The schizophrenic temporal effects of this process are also evident in *American Psycho*. A 400-page novel whose aleatory narrative is given some semblance of continuity by its diary-like chapter headings, it actually refuses connections, linearity and resolution. The repetition of hypertrophied descriptions of all manner of consumer items stall the narrative on a vertical axis; the lack of any apparent motivation for Bateman's murders means the narrative resists a psychological explanation of cause and effect, and the concentration on image, style and physical appearance are all narrative effects that exemplify Jameson's notion of a perpetual present. They also seem to refuse the notion of epistemological depth and conform to that situation whereby, according to Philip Simmons, 'gestures toward "depth" of historical understanding are continually returned to the "surface" of postmodern image culture.'[28] The importance of surface and image means that 'the distinctions between inside and outside, self and society no longer hold and the self merges with its image environment'.[29] Bateman's continual references to *The Patty Winters Show* serve to reiterate this point in the novel. A show that anticipates the Jerry Springer phenomenon, it is that most postmodern of cultural products: real-life television.

The scenario I have mapped out for *American Psycho* here fits the novel snugly into Jameson's 'logic of late capitalism'. And yet there are problems with treating the novel in this way, problems that arise at that point where the business of multinational global capitalism meets the subject of this book: the business of 'America'. While it is necessary to recognise the extent to which globalisation is driven by United States capital, it would be a mistake to equate the two. As I explained earlier with reference to Immanuel Wallerstein, the spread of United States business interests overseas produced multidirectional flows, however unequal. The problem with Jameson's attempts to explain the cultural response to global capitalism is that by positing a totalising phenomenon he automatically deduces totalising effects. It may be an obvious point, but Ellis chose to call his novel not *Global Psycho* or *Capitalist Psycho*, but *American Psycho*. Rather than inferring generalised cultural conditions it is worth thinking about how this novel might be interpreted as both a response to that 'rediscovery of the particular in American culture' of which Gene Wise wrote, and how Patrick Bateman is brought into existence at that point where 'America' meets the multilateral forces of globalisation.

Although there is little meditation in the novel itself about the connection between Bateman's murderous violence and the rise of global business systems, Ellis uses other devices to frame his novel quite carefully and give it a historical perspective that belies the idea that the rest of the novel is halted in a perpetual present. The epigraphs, for instance, introduce a clear sense of societal development and change. The extract from Dostoyevsky's *Notes from Underground*, while reiterating the fictionality of both character and events and giving *American Psycho* a comparative twist, states that such a character 'must exist, considering the circumstances under which our society has generally been formed'. Furthermore he – and it is, I think, safe to assume that Ellis wants the reader to equate Bateman with the author of *Notes from Underground* – 'represents a generation that is still living out its days among us'. The use of words like 'formed' and 'generation' here emphasise some sense of historical change. In the next epigraph, Ellis locates the novel much more specifically by quoting *Washington Post* columnist Judith Martin's criticism of the 1960s for loosening the restraints on what people could or could not say: 'In civilization there have to be some restraints.' The implication, then, is that what has happened after the 1960s represents some degradation of American civilisation. The final quote, from a track on the Talking Heads' 1988 album *Naked*, takes us right back to the issues I dealt with in the previous chapter: 'And as things fell apart/Nobody paid much attention'.

Ellis appears to be situating his novel within a conservative discourse that reassesses changes in 1960s United States culture in negative terms. The multi-ethnic landscape of New York is depicted in apocalyptic terms. 'Abandon all hope ye who enter here' (*AP* 3) are the first lines of the novel and a warning about the text as much as the city. Bateman's frustration at not being able to make his Chinese dry cleaners understand what he wants, indicates how Ellis sees the absence of dialogue across ethnic boundaries leading to a fragmented urban experience and the potentially violent consequences of such ethnic proximity: 'she keeps blabbering something in some spastic, foreign tongue. I have never firebombed anything and I start wondering how one goes about it' (*AP* 83). The way the novel is framed suggests little sympathy with any notion that the 'rediscovery of the particular', driven by the splitting apart of 'American' identity into categories based on ethnicity, gender or sexuality has produced positive results. But it is not primarily through the discourse of multi-culturalism that Ellis approaches the falling apart of 'American' civilisation. It is through the artefacts of consumer culture that Ellis can concentrate, like Mamet, on the fate of white male culture in the global business order.

The similarity – that is, the detail and stylised language – with which Bateman narrates both consumer products and murderous violence suggests a link between the two. The nature of this link is clarified when one considers that, in a world dominated by surface and image and in a narrative that refuses to acknowledge epistemological depth as an explanatory mode, causality is communicated by metonymic means. It is the contiguity of consumer culture and murder in Bateman's life that makes the latter the result of the former. Once this link is made, it is possible to see just how damning is Ellis's vision of the circulation of consumer goods in a global business system. The questing after and the worshipping of consumer goods result in an emptying-out of Bateman's 'civilised' self. There are no restraints in Bateman's world, and there are no restraints because of the *excess* of products and choices available to him. Ellis depicts Bateman's problem not as one that is psychologically rooted but that is a consequence of this excess flooding into his life. The combination of Bateman's wealth and his immorality suggests that Ellis envisions the decline of 'American' civilisation into a kind of consumer decadence. Crucially, however, Ellis depicts this decline not as being driven solely by the forces of United States capitalism, or by a globalisation that is dominated by United States capitalism. What is striking about *American Psycho* is that the products that create this excess come from a whole range of non-United States sources: Bateman's Toshiba TV and NEC video recorder are manufactured by Japanese companies, his Rolex watch comes from Britain, his A. Testoni loafers from Italy, he goes to see the Irish band U2 in concert, and so on. One gets a sense that the Americanness of the world in which Bateman lives is being diluted by the forces of global consumer culture; that there is the local in which people spend their everyday lives and then the world of global consumer capitalism which provides their lifestyles, entertainment and accessories. The national domain gets squeezed out of the equation. Early on in the novel Bateman is goaded into discussing the pressing problems faced by the United States:

> Ensure a strong national defense, prevent the spread of communism in Central America ... We have to ensure that America is a respected world power ... We also need to provide training and jobs for the unemployed as well as protect existing American jobs from unfair foreign imports. We have to make America the leader in new technology. (*AP* 15)

Not only does Bateman slip into the stylised discourse of contemporary, spin-driven, politics, but his speech is met with discomfort, 'bemused disbelief' and, most importantly, by silence. Someone quickly changes the subject to dessert. There is no conception amongst Bateman's friends and colleagues that this national dimension registers on their lives.

Ellis's novel is, ultimately, a cry in the dark. We see not an appropriation of globalisation for national ends in the terms described by Frederick Buell, but a novel whose judgement of global capitalism is that it destabilises the national project of 'America' in the most violent and murderous terms. Ellis utilises a formal postmodernism – Jameson's pastiche and schizophrenia – and puts it to work in the context of business in order to try to refocus attention on the nation. It is a conservative project and one that relies too heavily on demonising the changes of the 1960s. If that decade is a subtextual villain in the novel, then it seems only appropriate that Ellis christened his protagonist after Norman Bates, another American *Psycho*, who first appeared on film in the year which ushered in that decade.

WILLIAM GIBSON, *NEUROMANCER* (1984)

While Ellis's *American Psycho* charted the dystopic transformation of fashionable New York society in the 1980s at the hands of new business systems, William Gibson's landmark novel *Neuromancer* mapped out a dystopic future for the entire globe. In so doing, Gibson – more than any writer I have considered so far – gives the lie to John Carlos Rowe's suggestion that in the post-Second World War world, literary culture loses its place as primary arbiter of ideas about cultural imperialism. According to Rowe, 'we can no longer speak of "literary culture" as central to the formation of the dominant symbology or for those practices critical of [cultural imperialism]'. Instead, 'the new dominance of telecommunications, computer, film, television, and video in the communicative practices of different people and cultures has changed significantly our understanding of cultural imperialism'.[30] Yet it was Gibson's literary fiction that most influentially reimagined the relationship between business – or Biz – in its global and cybernetic variant and the culture of 'America'. Films such as *Blade Runner* played their role here, but Gibson's *Neuromancer* provided the terminology and the blueprint for the subsequent growth of the cyberpunk genre in the realm he named cyberspace.

The literary dimension is important here, since one aspect of the culture wars of the 1980s in the United States, according to Frederick Buell, was a lament about declining literacy standards and the devaluing of literature. Books like Sven Birkerts's *The Gutenberg Elegies: The Fate of Reading in an Electronic Age*, defended print culture on grounds that for Buell repeated theories emphasising 'print culture as a foundation of Enlightenment ideas of individual selfhood' and 'print as a key factor in the creation of national "imagined communities," and therefore the creation of citizenry, place, and national-cultural traditions'.[31] The fact that Birkerts was himself the son of Latvian immigrants, who explains his veneration of the imaginary world of print as a way of constructing identity and reality, leads Buell to declare that print culture in this discourse 'is a line of local defense against penetration at a variety of sites by suddenly, sickeningly integrating globalizing forces'.[32]

The literary effect of *Neuromancer* was to regenerate the science fiction genre in the 1980s. It did so in terms that imagined the cyborg, David Brande argues, 'as an effect of advanced capitalism's restructuring of modes and relations of production and its corresponding transformations of ideological reproduction'.[33] What the man in the grey flannel suit was to the 1950s, so the cyborg was to the 1980s. Whereas the suited white-collar worker of the 1950s engaged with business in the office, however, the cyborg is 'jacked into a custom cyberspace deck that projected his disembodied consciousness into the consensual hallucination that was the matrix'.[34] As Brande points out, the vision one finds in *Neuromancer* is not one that simply reflects the conditions of late capitalism. In literary terms, it is not a book which operates in a realistic mode. Instead, 'the cyborg is the "consciousness" of the techno-capitalist dream' and *Neuromancer* 'is a dream of late-capitalist ideology'.[35] Gibson, it could be argued, actually brings into existence with his neologism 'cyberspace' a territory which provides business with its ultimate market.

According to Marxist accounts, capitalism is beset at various points with crises of overaccumulation where markets are unable to sustain levels of production. At these moments – and the 1970s would represent such a moment in the United States – capitalism is forced to respond both by reorganising itself so that it operates more efficiently and by developing new markets. In geographical terms, this means finding new territories which will absorb the investment of capital and labour. The spectre of ongoing economic imperialism clearly raises its head at moments like these, especially as new crisis points will develop when these markets are exhausted. What remains the only solution to these intermittent crises in capitalist production is a territory that expands in unison with the constantly changing modes of production that Marx described. According to Brande, 'Gibson's construction of cyberspace responds to the tendency toward crises of overaccumulation with a fantastic – although not entirely incredible – vision of limitless virtual space for market expansion.'[36]

To imagine this world in these terms *Neuromancer* prioritises an image of corporate penetration into every aspect of life. Given the opportunity of a cyberspace market, corporations have reached new stages of sophistication and exploitation although, like much science fiction, in its composition of the future much of what appears to be prediction is drawn from the cultural context and legacy in which the book is written. So when the main protagonist, Case, tries to describe the relationship between power and the corporation, his words echo those used by Tom Rath and Bob Slocum: 'Power, in Case's world, meant corporate power. The zaibatsus, the multinationals that shaped the course of human history, had transcended old barriers. Viewed as organisms, they attained a kind of immortality. You couldn't kill a zaibatsu by assassinating a dozen key executives' (*NM* 242). And the bosses themselves, Case imagined, 'would be both more and less than people ... He'd always imagined it as a gradual and willing accommodation of the machine, the system, the parent organism' (*NM* 243).

The status of the individual within this system of corporate power likewise bears similarities with the way in which men in business fictions had previously considered themselves as victims. *Neuromancer* picks up on the literally sickening possibilities of employment. Case opens the novel in the Japanese city of Chiba trying to find a cure for his damaged nervous system. After stealing from his former employers – providers of 'exotic software required to penetrate the bright walls of corporate systems, opening windows into rich fields of data' – they release mycotoxin into his body. When he agrees to carry out a job for Armitage in return for being cured, Case is still medically dependent. Armitage implants slowly dissolving sacs of mycotoxin into Case's body. Only if Case completes the job as requested will Armitage give him the enzyme and the blood transfusion necessary to prevent him returning to the state in which Armitage first finds him. When Case's new colleague, Molly, explains to him that 'Anybody any good at what they do, that's what they *are*', she is witnessing a model of identity that Catherine Casey has described as the 'corporate colonization of the self'.[37]

Gibson also clearly conceives this new territory of cyberspace in terms of discourses of globalisation. Cyberspace in *Neuromancer* is where corporate penetration produces complete deterritorialisation. National borders have disappeared, and home for Case is not the United States, but the Sprawl, the 'Boston-Atlanta Metropolitan Axis' (*NM* 57). The virtual network of the matrix and the interconnectedness and free-flowing, unrestricted operations of Biz, eliminate the necessity for discrete borders. Again, cyberspace enacts a perfect market. Like *American Psycho*, though, it is not what might be recognised as United States capital that dominates cyberspace. The novel makes much of the importance of Asian corporate power, especially in the way that it uses terminology drawn from Japanese business culture. Case steps out of the way of a 'dark-suited sarariman' in Ninsei and sees 'the Mitsubishi-Genentech logo tattooed across the back of the man's right hand' (*NM* 18). 'Sarariman' is the Japanese version of 'salaryman', the worker who gives their all to make the 'zaibatsu' or large company successful. So successful it seems in this vision of cyberspace, that Mitsubishi – the Japanese industrial giant – has absorbed the United States genetic engineering company Genentech. Mitsubishi has also established the Mitsubishi Bank of America (*NM* 69).

So, while on the one hand cyberspace in *Neuromancer* enacts the deterritorialisation suggested by some discourses of globalisation, one can also see how Gibson stages this development in terms of national penetration by foreign capital. At the time Gibson was writing, in the early 1980s, one of the dominant visions of Japan in the United States was as an economic competitor who was overtaking the United States because of more flexible production methods and greater technological expertise. This vision also applied to other so-called 'tiger economies' in the Pacific Rim which relied on low labour costs to make their products competitive. The dystopic landscape of cyberspace in *Neuromancer* thus symbolises a fear of strengthened Asian economies and a weakened United States economy. It is at this point, then, that cyberspace also marks a reterritorialisation of space in national terms. For it is by creating a dream of the perfect market that cyberspace becomes a contemporary frontier. In the nineteenth century the frontier not only stimulated United States capital by acting as a voracious market capable of funding the imperial settlement of the continent, it also operated mythically as a fantasy of limitless space. Gibson recreates this myth of the frontier in an era of advanced capitalism under the name of cyberspace. David Brande frames his scepticism about Gibson's cyberspace in just these terms: 'Cyberspace is Gibson's fantastical geography of postnational capitalism, fulfilling the same basic functions as did the frontier and the nation-state in an earlier era.'[38]

And on this cyberspace frontier works Case, a figure repeatedly imagined as cowboy: 'Case was twenty-four. At twenty-two, he'd been a cowboy, a rustler, one of the best in the Sprawl' (*NM* 11). Case is not just constantly called a cowboy, he also embodies those attributes that mark the cowboy out as the repository of all that is valued by white male culture: independence, anti-authoritarianism, risk taking, virility. In *Gunfighter Nation: The Myth of the Frontier in Twentieth-Century America*,[39] Richard Slotkin has argued that with the closing of the frontier the cowboy was reborn in the figure of the hard-boiled detective, and the essential elements of the frontier myth re-enacted in the urban crime fiction of writers like Raymond Chandler and Dashiell Hammett. Case's very name puts him into this lineage and Gibson's prose style – if not his language – clearly owes a lot to the hard-boiled style:

> Case picked at a shred of bacon that lodged between his front teeth. He'd given up asking her where they were going and why; jabs in the ribs and the sign for silence were all he'd gotten in reply. She

talked about the season's fashions, about sports, about a political scandal in California he'd never heard of. (*NM* 62)

This mixture of urban low-life and high-tech created the successor of hard-boiled detective writing: cyberpunk.

In Gibson's depiction of advanced capitalism as cyberspace, then, one can see the construction of a three-tiered approach to globalisation. First of all, *Neuromancer* imagines the possibility of new and limitless opportunities for the penetration of multinational businesses in a world stripped of its current borders. Second, in an anxious manoeuvre that recognises the threat to 'American' hegemony in such an unregulated geography, it imagines cyberspace in dystopic and chaotic terms. Finally, in order to save the original vision, the novel resurrects the figure of the pulp hero as 'the privileged insider'[40] of cyberspace. This reconfiguring of globalisation in explicitly national literary terms helped, Buell observes, to recuperate many of the old attitudes associated with the frontier, but also to counter a basic fear that 'the national space – its culture, social relations, and even geography – is being undone by contemporary capitalism'.[41] In Case we find another American male who, according to Molly, 'is coming apart at the seams' (*NM* 40). In order to reconstitute himself, the narrative has him turn to 'America' in its mythic mode at the same time as it creates the technological world of cyberspace which will itself become the location for the regeneration of United States business and 'a crucial place for the corporate restructuring of American identity'.[42]

DOUGLAS COUPLAND, *MICROSERFS* (1995)

In *Microserfs*, Douglas Coupland offers us a vision of just how this restructuring in the field of technology impacts on one particular demographic group in the United States: the sons and daughters of the white professional managerial classes who were born during the turbulent decade of the 1960s and who entered the labour market during the 1980s and '90s. Coupland had already provided a label for this group in his earlier novel, *Generation X*. In that book, and in the method – if not the spirit – of the consumer culture that so dominates the lives of Dag, Claire and narrator Andy, Coupland provided a marketing label whose brand associations defined the constituent elements of this group's cultural, emotional and socio-political make-up. Some of the chapter titles in the early part of the book are telling: 'OUR PARENTS HAD MORE', 'QUIT RECYCLING THE PAST', 'I AM NOT A TARGET MARKET', 'QUIT YOUR JOB'. In addition, Coupland turns to a whole series of neologisms to help him in his process of definition and these are collected as footnotes. Almost a handbook for a generation, then, it is possible to explain the formation of this group in a way which is directly related to business in the United States.

If their parents did have more, then it was because they belonged to what Fred Pfeil has called the 'baby-boom professional managerial classes', people who benefited from the buoyant economy of the post-war years. Driven by expansion in the areas of mass media, corporate bureaucracies and consumption, opportunities in this economy grew commensurately and with them so did the middle classes. This group also, Pfeil suggests, had a particular cultural-aesthetic sensibility. Exposed to high culture by university education, the middle classes also lived an everyday life in which they consumed mass culture and where they did not recognise any incompatibility between the two.[43] Clearly this environment was not, as I hope I have demonstrated, devoid of anxiety. The same businesses that were so rapidly expanding and providing material opportunity were also the locus for much antagonistic sentiment. Yet, looking back from the 1980s and '90s, this period represents for Coupland's characters a much more benevolent and secure era. The shift into a post-Fordist business regime during and after the crises of the 1970s – a decade when economic growth and middle-class expansion slowed dramatically and when real wages actually fell – produced a business culture in which, as Nick Heffernan says, people 'faced far greater difficulties and pressures in converting their cultural capital into secure and materially rewarding professional positions within the fluid and volatile occupational structure of post-Fordist capitalism'.[44]

Heffernan goes on to provide a compelling analysis of Coupland's work, and Microserfs in particular, that explains much of the texture of the Generation X world as a threefold response to these declining middle-class fortunes and to the fear of downward social mobility. First of all there is 'boomer envy', one of Coupland's neologistic handbook entries.[45] Coupland describes this in material terms, but the envy of the baby boomer generation is cultural too. Their parents' lives were animated by changing attitudes towards sex and drugs, by new music, by the civil rights movement, feminism and anti-war protest. In contrast, the culture of post-Fordist employment and consumerism seems bland and apathetic. 'Our systems had stopped working', Andy explains about his, Dag's and Claire's lives before they escape to the desert. They were 'jammed with the odor of copy machine, Wite-Out, the smell of bond paper, and the endless stress of pointless jobs done grudgingly to little applause' (*GX* 14). Second, there is a tendency to ironise the cultural capital that no longer converts to material wealth. This 'wilful erasure of the boundaries between knowledge, education and the detritus of commodity culture'[46] may owe something to the cultural-aesthetic sensibility of the boomer generation, but irony issues at that point where there is no political purpose to which cultural capital can be put. Both of these coping mechanisms contribute towards the third response: a 'slacker' ethic, or an ideological anti-capitalism for the professional middle classes that works as a 'strategy for managing middle-class anxiety ... by willingly embracing, even seeking out, downward mobility as a form of personal expression, thus pre-empting failure'.[47] For Heffernan, what characterises these responses is a sense of 'play', the medium for which in *Microserfs* is information technology.

I want to go on and discuss Coupland's treatment of information technology shortly, but it is worth pausing here for a moment to register just how different a narrative about the past emerges in Heffernan's depiction of Generation X culture. Here, the 1960s exists not as a period when 'America' took a turn for the worse but as a decade that is imagined nostalgically. Things started to go wrong from this perspective not with identity politics and multicultural-ism, but with the stagnation of the economy in the 1970s and its violent restructuring during the 1980s. This may well be a partial perspective borne out of waning class authority, but what I want to suggest it offers is a response that is grounded in a particular experience of business change in the United States that does not, as a result of this experience, reach for a recovery narrative of 'America'. This is in stark contrast to the other texts I have looked at in this chapter.

As far as *Microserfs* is concerned, Heffernan remains sceptical about the discourses Coupland relies upon to think through the quandaries of this class. He complains that the narrator Daniel Underwood's 'critiques of power inequalities and hierarchy' within the Microsoft corporation 'are expressed in terms of personal style rather than politics or ideology',[48] and that politics is deflected and absorbed into a discourse of community that 'at its centre is tightly homogenous in terms of class (and, of course, race)'.[49] There is something to be said for both of these arguments, but I want to approach *Microserfs* from a vantage point that, while recognising the limits within which it operates, still sees it – in comparative terms at least – as a bold attempt to negotiate the discourses of United States business and of 'America' in original ways in the electronic age. It is a novel that does not draw on theories of globalisation to depict this age in either of the two extreme and contradictory ways described by Frederick Buell. The world of *Microserfs* is neither the 'futuristic world wholly penetrated by capital and catastrophically commodified' like *American Psycho* and *Neuromancer*, but nor is it a world of 'democratic global interactiveness' where the global economy is domesticated and Americanised.[50]

To refine both Buell's and Heffernan's arguments about information technology and the electronic age, it is worth pointing out that *Microserfs* is about the cultural impact of living in a software age. The early development of the computing industry in America was certainly marked by a preoccupation with hardware, as companies like UNIVAC, DEC and IBM filled the nation's corporate and government offices with mainframes, but according to Paul Ceruzzi, by the 1990s the development and marketing of software had started to overshadow the hardware that 'was becoming in some cases a cheap mass-produced commodity'.[51] It is Abe, work colleague and housemate of Daniel Underwood, who pinpoints the particular spatial consequences of this change. He complains to Dan about the architecture of the 1990s: 'He said that because everyone's so poor these days, the '90s will be a decade with no architectural legacy or style – everyone's too poor to put up new buildings. He said that code is the architecture of the '90s.'[52] Computer code is what the occupants of the group house in which Abe and Dan live deal with all day in their jobs at Microsoft, the writing of it and the testing of it; the software that is produced from it has made Bill Gates the richest man in the world. And although Abe may not be poor – he is the 'in-house multimillionaire' (*MS* 5) thanks to his work as a coder – he has no desire to own, let alone build, his own property. He rents his room instead, just like the others, and in this regard is well-placed to draw attention to one striking fact: for people working in the software industry, the most important forms of architecture are migrating from the spaces that surround us – homes, workplaces, public buildings – to the code that is invisible and mostly incomprehensible to us inside our computers.

Microserfs, then, like *Neuromancer*, treats late capitalist technology in terms of its spatial consequences. But whereas *Neuromancer* imagines new vistas of space into which business can infinitely expand, *Microserfs* turns our attention instead to the space where labour and capital increasingly now meet: in code. Thinking about the migration of architecture from a visible space surrounding us to the invisible space of code, offers the opportunity to refine another more national narrative of migration that often gets told about the development of the computing industry in the last 25 years: this is the *Neuromancer* version of technology as the new frontier. The metaphors of the road, the journey and the Gold Rush that Bill Gates uses in his book *The Road Ahead* rely on just this narrative;[53] the same narrative compelled Gates and Paul Allen to migrate to New Mexico in the 1970s, and compelled a similar migration to California in the 1990s of people who wanted to get their computer code onto the most important road in the world, the information superhighway.

Dan and his housemates embark on this journey once they decide to leave the stifling corporate atmosphere of Microsoft and head for Silicon Valley to help work on *Oop!*, a computer game developed by their co-worker and housemate Michael. Although they are joining Arthur Kroker's 'Virtual Class', a new economic grouping that, he argues, is 'compulsively fixated on digital technology as a source of salvation from the reality of a lonely culture',[54] Kroker's assessment of this class – the managers of 'the endgame of postcapitalism'[55] – hardly helps us understand Dan and his colleagues. This is especially true for someone like Abe who, despite the millions of dollars he has made from computing by the age of 30, has 'nothing to his name but a variety of neat-o consumer electronics and boxes of Costco products purchased in rash moments of Costco-scale madness' (*MS* 10–11). More helpfully, Peter Stoneley has noted that while the most keenly-sought transformation of Gold Rush hopefuls in the nineteenth century was the change from being poor to being rich, the literature of those who experienced such attempts often points 'toward a much more general sense of change and disorientation'.[56] It is just such a sense of change and disorientation in *Microserfs* that interests me. It is a novel that takes on and intersects with the national narrative of pioneering entrepreneurism only to render that narrative unfocused and imprecise. Dan, in fact, touches on the transitional nature of this experience when he is persuaded to keep his diary more regularly by his girlfriend: 'Karla got me to thinking that we really *do* inhabit an odd little nook of time and space here, and that odd or strange as this little nook may be, it's where *I* live – it's where *I am*' (*MS* 63). It is the consequences of changes like this, I would argue, that contribute toward 'the general sense of change and disorientation' that is experienced by the characters in Coupland's novel as their lives cross the path of this particular historical moment.

The importance of Silicon Valley in *Microserfs* is not, then, its importance as a new frontier town, but the fact that it exists as a visual phenomenon on the same level as the computer code on which its importance as a place is built: it is invisible. Po Bronson has described it as 'an endless suburb, hushed and nonchalant, in terrain too flat to deserve the term "valley"'.[57] But, as Dan himself says, 'invisibility is invariably where one locates the ACTION' (*MS* 137). The principle on which software products and Silicon Valley are founded – code as architecture – has literally altered the epistemological organisation of capitalist working space and social relations.

An engagement with code and encoding beats away at the heart of Dan's narrative in *Microserfs*. The first hint we get that Coupland is drawing attention to it is early on when Todd invents a program called 'Prince Emulator' that converts 'whatever you write into a title of a song by Minnesotan Funkmeister, Prince' (*MS* 18). Dan rewrites part of his diary with it and then begins to keep a file on his computer called 'Subconscious' that consists of random words that come into his head, and which then begin to appear at the end of his diary entries, creating almost a second level of narrative which might be read as a condensed – although alternative – account of that day or week's diary entry (see *MS* 46, 49, 52 for examples). Ethan, the businessman Michael teams up with to help raise venture capital for the *Oop!* project, first meets Michael 'inking out all of the vowels on his menu' in a diner; Michael explains that he was '"*Testing the legibility of the text in the absence of information*"' (*MS* 109). Dan copies this attempt and converts another of his diary entries (*MS* 308); and then converts it so that it has no consonants.

These entries allow a glimpse at the workings of Dan's techie, '90s-acculturated mind, and it is clear that this is sometimes not a contented place. The word 'Windows' translates into 'Prozac' within the space of a few lines (*MS* 182). The cult of Bill outlined by the novel also clearly suggests the way that computing technology is implicated in the consolidation of economic power and capital. And yet it would be hard to draw such causative associations from these messages, especially since *Microserfs*, I would suggest, is a novel that demands attention not as an arbitrator between two competing schools of thought about computing technology – that is, technology is good/technology is bad – but as a novel that represents the territory that is left unexamined by such a polarised debate: the way in which technology is experienced.

My point here is that in this strange transitional landscape that Dan and his friends are negotiating, code has become not only the engine driving capitalist accumulation and economic expansion, but the very means by which communication proceeds and the way, therefore, by which we – following Dan – might understand how meanings and institutions might sometimes be at odds with one another. Code is important in Coupland's narrative because, by being in such close relation both to the businesses and the economy that rely upon it *and* to the non-visual form of communication that people are increasingly using, it stands as the mediating object through which the people in that economy try to come to terms with the 'general sense of change and disorientation' that accompanies the experience of important economic change. This disorientation may manifest itself as 'little fears' as it does for Dan: 'fear of not producing enough; fear of not finding a little white-with-red-printing stock option envelope in the pigeonhole' (*MS* 38). It may manifest itself in the 'Perfectville' train set landscape that Dan's father builds, or in gay Bug's desperation to 'find a niche' (*MS* 306), or in Dan's anxiety about the diminishing distance between man and machine (*MS* 228). Code, because of its encrypted nature, signals in an ambiguous way and this is why *Microserfs* is a novel where things do not line up. Work and leisure have stopped being discrete domains of one's life; the workplace and the home can now be the same place, or different places that look the same; architecture is now not only visible but invisible as well, a virtual space formed by code and not just the space that one is surrounded by. Ultimately the different significations of code may not line up behind one another either. But as a form of response to the changes that they are living through, code can be about something other than work for the *Microserfs*: 'It's about all of us staying together' (*MS* 199).

For Heffernan this sentimental note clearly seems to grate. This is where he accuses *Microserfs* of producing a community that is 'tightly homogenous'. But Heffernan underestimates – in fact ignores – the dimensions of both gender and sexuality that Coupland adds to his novel. The 'all of us' includes not just Dan and his girlfriend Karla, but gay Bug, bodybuilding coder Todd, Michael, mother and coder Dusty, Susan and Barcode too: a mixed gender and a mixed sexuality group of friends. This kind of 'all of us' has – literally – been unimaginable in any of the texts I have looked at in the first part of this book. And in a culture that has in the past so denigrated the closeness of the relationship between sons and their mothers, how loving it is that, virtually paralysed after a stroke, Dan's mother is surrounded at her bedside by Dan and his friends. She can find only one way to communicate: 'part woman/part machine, emanating blue Macintosh light' she moves her fingers across a computer keyboard. Dan, anxious to confirm that it is his mother typing and not the machine, asks her a question that only she will be able to answer. 'Tell me something I never liked in my lunch bag at school.' She types 'PNUT BUTR'. 'Here it is', Dan says, 'Mom speaking like a license plate ... like the lyrics to a Prince song ... like encryption. All of my messing around with words last year and now, well ... it's real life' (*MS* 369). This sentimentality seems to me to be of a different order to that sentimentality that has so often been identified as a weakness, one subsequently used to denigrate and oppress women and homosexual men. It is instead one that, arising from a childish anxiety about transition, focuses on Dan and his friends' place within post-Fordist culture, how they cope with a culture that is often hostile to their nurture, and upon the reparative impulses that can help them to cope.

This is just one of the ways in which *Microserfs* resists the temptation to fall back on mythic national discourses in its representation of United States business. The development of the *Oop!* project completely obliterates the link between masculinity, business and entrepreneurism that has preoccupied so many of the white male writers I have looked at in the first half of this book. The kinds of anxieties Dan and his friends feel seem not to be connected to globalisation either. The falling apart at the seams that male protagonists undergo as they come into contact with the business and culture of globalisation – from *Death of a Salesman* all the way through to *American Psycho* – is replaced in *Microserfs* by a much more localised sense of confusion and dislocation that is the product of a destabilised class rather than national position. Coupland's Canadian background and his peripatetic education and residency suggest that this de-stabilisation might be local to the issue of class, but strikingly transnational in the sense that comparable class groups across national borders live through similar experiences.

Part II

The Difference of Gender, Race and Sexuality

4
Objectivist Fantasies and the Industry of Writing and Piracy

The first part of this book looked at how white male writers have engaged with the discourses of United States business after the Second World War and the various forms of 'empire anxiety' manifested when the literature they have produced tries to manage the expansionary nature of United States capital overseas and the often discomforting ensuing cross-cultural flows. One point I have emphasised is the frequency with which these writers have relied upon a recovery narrative of 'America'. At those points where the 'powerful imperial desire' of United States business collides with the 'profound anti-colonial temper'[1] of many white male writers and intellectuals, the faultline of national identity has been covered over – with minor exception – by recourse to a narrative of 'America' that is by turns mythic, nostalgic and exclusionary.

In the Introduction I suggested various reasons why it might be possible to identify an alternative tradition in writing about business during this same period. In this and the remaining chapters, I want to ask whether such a tradition emerges if one considers how gender, race and ethnicity and sexuality modulate the way in which United States writers have responded to the discourses of business. As far as gender is concerned, my thinking in this chapter is driven by two major ideas that are well-rooted in United States cultural history: first, Veblen's distinction between 'exploit' and 'industry', and second, the framing of imperial contact between the United States and other territories in terms which emphasise a male/female relationship.

As Michael Spindler shows, Veblen developed the guiding principles and vocabulary of his work very early in his career and with close reference to the status of women in United States society, especially in essays such as 'The Economic Theory of Women's Dress' (1894) and 'The Barbarian Status of Women' (1899).[2] While these essays dealt with marriage, status, fashion, and property rights, issues that Spindler argues were central to 'the world-view of respectable people in turn-of-the-century America', Veblen wrote about them in such a way that he was 'systematically undermining them, and in so doing undercutting any complacent sense [respectable people] might enjoy of being part of an advanced civilisation'.[3] For Veblen, married women in the United States were little more than captured slaves. They were proof of male 'exploit', and their 'capture', together with the patriarchal household of which they became a part and which signified the new importance of property-ownership, belonged to a predatory, warlike phase of historical development. A woman's dress was an economic issue for Veblen because of the place of women within the patriarchal household. Dress was an indication of the wealth of its owner, and since in Veblen's terms 'wearer' was not equivalent to 'owner', and women were owned by men, women's dress indicated male wealth.

The place of women in Veblen's thought can be seen to be more closely linked to business and work when one considers the way that he saw male 'exploit' to be an indicator of what he described as the increasing 'irksomeness of labour'. Where once social honour and esteem – the key motivations in life for Veblen – had been based on an 'instinct for workmanship', by the end of the nineteenth century the United States had reached a point where labour had fallen into low esteem and social respect was gained through ownership, by conspicuous consumption, and by non-participation in productive work. So while labouring-class men and women were left to carry on the productive labour, or 'industry', property-owning, wealthy men were engaged in status-enhancing 'exploits'. And even though not all men could leave behind the world of work, what is important is the way that this division operates ideologically. 'Work was no longer regarded as a "vocation"', Spindler argues, and 'the commonest dream of all was to escape from it, by means of unexpected inheritance, say, or a "lucky break".'[4] Rather than seeking freedom *in* work, the dream was freedom *from* work.

Although Veblen's deterministic and social Darwinist explanations for his ideas are open to question, his writing marks an intervention in the gendered nature of work and business and offers a chance to think about why gender may affect the way that business and work are represented differently across gender lines. Veblen's ideas certainly offer one way of explaining the antagonism towards business in white male culture. Because of the systemic nature of business in the United States since the Second World War, the dream of entrepreneurial success has become increasingly distant. Instead, business represents that which keeps men *in* work and *from* which there is no escape. Thus working in this business world no longer enables them to cast off the 'irksomeness of labour' and cross into the leisure class. Business is that which blocks the fulfilment of an 'American' freedom. The difference between men and women is that in Veblen's terms, women do not stand in the same relation to 'exploit' as men do. Therefore the dream of freedom from work may not be as important as freedom in or at work. Consequently, women might be drawn to discourses that emphasise not the 'irksome' nature of work and its stifling effect on social honour, but the productive potential of work once it can be disentangled from its position in the predatory phase of modern industrial life and recast as the 'instinct of workmanship' which Veblen argued organised social honour in earlier, more peaceable and collectively minded times.

If the acquisition of women by men through marriage was an example of what Veblen considered to be property ownership in the predatory phase, then it could be argued that the acquisition of territory was similarly an example of the warlike nature of this phase, albeit at the level of the nation and state. This connection seems to be even more explicit if one considers the gendered language used to describe territorial conflict. Shelley Streeby makes the point that in the 1840s and '50s, around the time of the United States–Mexican war, 'relations between the United States and Mexico were often imagined as relations between male and female', where 'U.S. national strength was metaphorically aligned with manhood, and Mexico was figured as a woman'.[5]

In a more broad-ranging intervention, but with a similar goal of connecting the language of gender and nation, Amy Kaplan has reconceptualised the notion of the 'domestic' in United States culture by emphasising the word's double meaning. The domestic is not only the site of the familial household but also the national as opposed to the foreign. If the domestic sphere has traditionally been used to separate the realms of female and male activity, by emphasising the national dimension of domesticity Kaplan brings men and women together as 'national allies against the alien'.[6] She is, however, equally alert to the ways in which imperial expansion also disrupts the domestic by incorporating 'foreign subjects in a way perceived to undermine the nation as a domestic space'.[7] As a result, for Kaplan the domestic is 'an ambiguous third realm between the national and the foreign, as it places the foreign inside the geographic boundaries of the nation'.[8]

Both Veblen's gendered distinction between 'exploit' and 'industry' and the gendered language of imperial territorial expansion suggest ways in which women have historically been placed in different relation to 'America' compared to men. This chapter will look at the way that women in the United States since the Second World War have negotiated the legacy of these discourses in literature about business and work.

AYN RAND, *THE FOUNTAINHEAD* (1947) AND *ATLAS SHRUGGED* (1957)

In a recent essay, Paul Giles has argued that Russian émigré Vladimir Nabokov produced in *Lolita* 'a metafiction of area studies: a text which holds up a mirror to the implicit assumptions of American Studies and renders them translucent'.[9] Giles is concerned with the way that during the 1950s Nabokov engaged with the key themes of youth and virginity so integral to the nationalist ideas of United States American Studies (think of book titles like Leslie Feidler's *An End to Innocence* [1955], R. W. B. Lewis's *American Adam* [1955] and Henry Nash Smith's *Virgin Land* [1950]), but engaged with them in a such a way as to question the viability of such themes. 'While Nabokov's narrative teases us with the idea of a metaphorical relationship between Lolita and America',[10] Giles suggests, Humbert Humbert's status as a 'duplicitous European' means that '*Lolita* fails signally to accommodate itself to any form of the national imaginary'.[11]

Ayn Rand, another Russian émigré writing in the United States during the 1940s and '50s, poses questions about allegiance to myths of the nation altogether different to the ones Nabokov addressed in his complex and subtle aesthetic. Born in 1905 as Alissa Rosenbaum, Rand moved to the United States in 1926 before becoming a naturalised citizen in 1931. One apocryphal story suggests Rand took her new surname from the Remington Rand typewriter she used to type her first screenplay, although Rand herself suggested that her new name was an abbreviation of the Cyrillic spelling of Rosenbaum. Renaming herself after a piece of machinery so integral to female employment from the end of the nineteenth century onwards would certainly provide a meaningful coincidence for this chapter, but, rather than any association with the world of women's work, Rand is best known now for the Objectivist philosophy she dramatised in her fiction and which, in later years, she explicated in numerous books and articles.

Although Rand chose to argue the reverse, claiming that 'I came to America because this was the country based on my moral premises',[12] Objectivism was a philosophy whose principles were based upon pre-existing nationalist ideas of 'American' individualism and self-interest that were already understood to be fostered best in a *laissez-faire* capitalist system. So where Nabokov was exposing the myths of national identity formation, Objectivism for Rand acted as an *a posteriori* philosophy for pledging her allegiance to 'America'. The extent to which Rand had established this allegiance is witnessed by her willingness to appear before the House Un-American Activities Committee (HUAC) on 20 October 1947 as part of the 'Hearings Regarding Communist Infiltration of the Motion Picture Industry'. As a Hollywood scriptwriter with local knowledge – albeit twenty years out of date – Rand was asked to comment on Gregory Ratoff's 1943 movie *Song of Russia*, the story of a visiting American conductor who falls in love with and marries a lovely Soviet peasant woman during the Nazi invasion of Russia. Rand offered a critique that ignored the wartime propaganda value of a film depicting a harmonious Soviet–United States alliance in the battle against Nazism, seeing it instead as a film that benevolently – and falsely – represented life under a totalitarian, collective regime. Rand's philosophical obsession with individualism meant that Objectivism treated any kind of collective activity based upon principles of altruism not only as something to be despised but also as that which was capable of destroying free market civilisation.

At one level, Rand's treatment of business in both *The Fountainhead* and *Atlas Shrugged* is similar to other fictional and sociological accounts of business that became popular in the 1940s and '50s. Like many white male writers Rand was concerned with the stifling conditions of large businesses and the way they inhibited individualism. To counteract this perceived condition, Rand's Objectivism held at its core the idea of the heroic male individual who could overcome such restrictions. Howard Roark in *The Fountainhead* epitomises just such a man. The novel follows the careers of Roark and his college acquaintance Peter Keating. They both attend architecture school together, but while Keating comes top in the year and ends up with a position at Francon and Heyer, a large and prestigious New York company, Roark is expelled for his maverick and iconoclastic approach to design and can only find work with the disregarded, although himself once also maverick, Henry Cameron. Keating embarks on a swift rise through the company and the institutions of architectural conformity, while Roark lives and works in isolation, struggling for commissions and spending time working in a quarry when he cannot make money from designing buildings.

Rand's choice of architecture as the business field through which to approach the ideal of the heroic 'American' male, means that *The Fountainhead* is literally a novel about construction. Just as Tom Rath in *The Man in the Gray Flannel Suit* seeks to escape the drudgery of business by way of his real estate development, so Rand makes the development of land central to her conception of 'America'. But Rand takes this idea of nation building a stage further by way of two strategies. First, the heroic individual is given a special connection with the land. The reader first finds Roark standing

> ... naked at the edge of a cliff ... He did not laugh as his eyes stopped in awareness of the earth around him. His face was like a law of nature – a thing one could not question, alter or implore ... These rocks, he thought, are here for me; waiting for the drill, the dynamite and my voice; waiting to be split, ripped, pounded, reborn; waiting for the shape my hands will give them.[13]

Later Roark tells Cameron that he wanted to be an architect 'because I've never believed in God ... I don't like the shape of things on this earth. I want to change them' (*TF* 40). Second, it is not only the development of real estate that is important, but how one develops it and the types of building constructed on it. One of the reasons Roark is expelled from architecture school is his unwillingness to repeat historical – mostly classical and European – designs. Wanting to be 'an architect, not an archaeologist' (*TF* 14), his buildings 'were not Classical, they were not Gothic, they were not Renaissance. They were only Howard Roark' (*TF* 11). While Keating and other members of the architectural profession are only too willing to replicate these old designs, Roark is a modernist who turns down commissions that will mean compromising his principles. When one customer asks him to build a house in Tudor style, Roark sums up the customer like this: 'There was no such person as Mrs Wayne Wilmot; there was only a shell containing the opinions of her friends, the picture-postcards she had seen, the novels of country squires she had read' (*TF* 152). This customer represents the kind of selfless character Roark despises. Selflessness for Roark is not an admirable quality, but indicates precisely a lack of self, a kind of self similar to the 'other-directed self' about which David Riesman wrote in *The Lonely Crowd*.

More than this, selflessness is also associated with collectivism, most evidently in *The Fountainhead* in the character of Ellsworth Toohey.

Toohey is a respected architectural journalist and liberal thinker. He considers marriage, much like Veblen, to be 'an economic device to perpetuate the institution of private property' (*TF* 77) and architecture to be a group project, calling on architects 'to abandon their selfish quest for individual glory and dedicate themselves to the embodiment of the mood of the people' (*TF* 68). Toohey and Roark, then, are ideological rivals and Toohey repeatedly tries to ruin Roark's career. In terms of Rand's Objectivism, Toohey and Roark represent the opposite forces who are battling for control of the nation. Toohey helps set up a new architectural organisation to be run by Keating, and when Keating is made a partner at what was formerly Francon and Heyer, Rand writes about 'a grave feeling of brotherhood in the room' who are saluted as 'the future of American Architecture!' (*TF* 189). Roark, on the other hand is almost entirely isolated in his battle: 'You, against the whole country!' Keating tells him. Rand joins with her male counterparts – people like William H. Whyte, who declared later that 'collectivization ... has affected almost every field of work'[14] – in seeing something suspicious and destructive in this brotherhood of business. *The Fountainhead* culminates in the trial of Howard Roark after he blows up a building in New York that he designed but whose original principles have been compromised. Toohey wants Roark in prison, 'In a cell. Behind bars. Locked, stopped, strapped – and alive. He'll get up when they tell him to. He'll eat what they give him ... And he'll obey. He'll take orders' (*TF* 619). In his own defence, Roark rehearses precisely an argument about the dangers of collectivism as a form of mass imprisonment, and its betrayal of 'American' virtues:

> Now observe the results of a society built on the principle of individualism. This, our country. The noblest country in the history of men ... Now, in our age, collectivism, the rule of the second-hander and second-rater, the ancient monster, has broken loose and is running amuck. It has swallowed most of Europe. It is engulfing our country. (*TF* 669)

The reference to Europe here suggests that the corruption by collectivism comes from outside the nation and that any resistance must come from an endogenous cultural heritage based on individualism. In the New York skyline Roark sees the embodiment of this nationalistic enterprise. He describes it as 'the will of man made visible' and then goes on to compare it with foreign offerings: 'What other religion do we need? And then people tell me about pilgrimages to some pesthole in a jungle where they go to do homage to a crumbling temple ... Let them come to New York, stand on the shore of the Hudson, look and kneel' (*TF* 433).

The building of the nation in Rand's terms requires that Roark escapes conviction and Keating's career and life collapse. Rand imagines architecture in *The Fountainhead* as that place where the spirit and the practice of 'American' business achieve their most visible symbolic manifestation. By the end of the novel, as Roark's buildings start to take their place in the New York skyline, the national recovery from collectivism seems to be on course. Yet in her 1957 novel, *Atlas Shrugged*, Rand is still dealing with similar problems. In many ways, Objectivism is a philosophical project bound up in what Sacvan Bercovitch described as the American Jeremiad.[15] It relies upon an idea that those values laid down by the founding fathers, and which should properly constitute the nation, are being undermined. Only some form of spiritual renewal can put things right. If it is Howard Roark who offers the blueprint for the shape of this renewal in *The Fountainhead*, in *Atlas Shrugged* it is John Galt and Hank Rearden.

Rand sets this later novel initially in the business environment of the railroad industry, and more particularly in the firm of Taggart Transcontinental. A less realistic novel than its predecessor, *Atlas Shrugged* represents business and capitalism in organic terms. A map on the wall in the offices of Taggart Transcontinental, shows the company's routes as a 'network of red lines slashing the faded body of the country from New York to San Francisco' that 'looked like a system of blood vessels' (*AS* 15). When Dagny Taggart, Vice President in charge of Operation and sister of Transcontinental president James Taggart, arrives at the offices she thinks 'of the Taggart Building standing above her head ... growing straight to the sky ... These are the roots of the building, hollow roots twisting underground, feeding the city' (*AS* 25). But if business serves as the organic lifeblood of the nation, then the nation is fast becoming a corpse. The problem as Rand represents it in *Atlas Shrugged* is twofold: the undertaking of commercial ventures by businesses on other than economic grounds, and the interference of government in business. Both indicate that wealth creation has lost its place as the engine of national unity.

Taggart Transcontinental's misguided corporate strategy means it is buying steel for its railroad from Associated Steel who cannot supply them with the necessary quality or efficiency. Dagny manages to solve this problem by turning instead to Henry Rearden who has patented a new metal alloy both stronger and longer-lasting than traditional steel. Like Roark, Rearden is a maverick, 'incapable of half-way concerns' (*AS* 151). Dagny cannot, however, stop Taggart building a railroad to San Sebastian, a venture that while supposed to enhance trade with Mexico and transport an 'inexhaustible supply of copper' is not based on 'any mineralogical fact about the San Sebastian Mines' (*AS* 57). Instead the reasons given are, in terms of Rand's Objectivism, anathema:

They've never had a chance. It is our duty to help an underprivileged nation to develop ... When considering an investment, we should in my opinion, take a chance on human beings, rather than on purely material factors ... Since a man must think of the good of his brothers before he thinks of his own, it seems to me that a nation must think of its neighbours before it thinks of itself. (*AS* 57)

When the Mexican government nationalises the copper mines at San Sebastian along with the railroad that serves it, Taggart has to write off 30 million dollars of investment.

This malaise in the decision-making capacities of United States business organisations is exacerbated in the world of *Atlas Shrugged* by collectivism and the involvement of government at every turn. The National Alliance of Railroads passes regulatory rules that force strong individual companies out of business (*AS* 75), while the government-sponsored State Science Institute tries to buy the rights to Rearden's new alloy. When Rearden's production of metal exceeds the government's Fair Share Law he is put on trial after a visit from a government official who tells him that 'The day of the barons of industry is done! You've got the goods, but we've got the goods on *you*, and you're going to play it our way.' Rearden's response is to tell his secretary 'I think I'm discovering a new continent ... A continent that should have been discovered along with America, but wasn't' (*AS* 407).

Faced with these kinds of restraints, *Atlas Shrugged* represents a United States in which business can no longer be conducted in *laissez-faire* conditions. The novel, in a bizarre and romantic twist, then imagines the withdrawal from the system of innovators and individualists like Reardon, and men like Dr Hendricks who 'quit when medicine was placed under State control' (*AS* 687), into a secret, pastoral oasis organised by John Galt. This withdrawal is a means of speeding the destruction of corruption. The United States gradually collapses and the novel culminates with mass panic and the city of New York disappearing from the face of the earth as the lights go out. Once this stage of total destruction has been reached, recovery can begin. John Galt announces that 'The road is cleared ... We are going back to the world. He raised his hand and over the desolate earth he traced in space the sign of the dollar' (*AS* 1074).

This gesture epitomises the way in which *Atlas Shrugged* conceives of 'America' as a monetary phenomenon. Earlier Francisco d'Anconia, head of a huge copper corporation and one of the first men to join Galt in exile, has outlined just this position. America, he says, is '*a country of money*', but a country, he tells his audience, in which people now 'look upon money as the savages did before you, and you wonder why the jungle is creeping back to the edge of your cities'. 'Americans', he argues, have an exceptional historical relationship to money because 'they were the people who created the phrase "to *make* money" ... Americans were the first to understand that wealth had to be created.' In contrast, d'Anconia refers to 'the rotted cultures of the looters' continents', nations who created wealth by force and exploitation (*AS* 386). Although he may be Mexican by birth, d'Anconia clearly believes in 'Americanism'.

While the rhetoric of Rand's novels is that of the jeremiad and suitably apocalyptic and hyperbolic, her treatment of the condition of business and nation does include an element that many of her white male counterparts pass over. More than any other writer during this post-war era, Rand builds into her novels a discourse about work. As I mentioned in the Introduction, white male writers have often been drawn towards narratives of personal alienation, and 'lives of quiet desperation'. With the exception of Douglas Coupland's *Microserfs*, they have not had their characters respond to the oppressive conditions of corporate culture by turning to other forms of work. Alienation from a particular mode of business manifests itself as alienation from all modes of business. For Rand, however, it is precisely a commitment to work that will help alter the mode of business. Henry Cameron tells Howard Roark 'You love your work. God help you, you love it! And that's the curse. That's the brand on your forehead for all of them to see ... Do you ever look at the people in the street? … The substance of them is hatred for any man who loves his work' (*TF* 55).

In contrast to Roark, Keating has no passion for his job and wants to be successful merely for the sake of success. More than this, Roark has an affinity with the world of work and workers. He becomes good friends with Mike, an electrician who hates architects and big business and who also 'loved his work passionately and had no tolerance for anything save for other single-track devotions' (*TF* 84). And when Roark's own business fails to prosper, he leaves New York to spend long hours working in a granite quarry, walking two miles each way to the site and living in squalid conditions. The therapeutic nature of this kind of work is partly what attracts Roark: 'He liked the work. He felt at times as if it were a match of wrestling between his muscles and the granite. He was very tired at night. He liked the emptiness of his body's exhaustion' (*TF* 190). As an antidote to the enervation of corporate culture, this passion for work – and certainly in this instance its muscular qualities – help Roark regroup and prepare himself for a renewed assault on the architectural business practices of New York. Similarly, in *Atlas Shrugged* it is the dedication to work of the heroic male individuals like Galt, d'Anconia and Rearden that will renew the nation.

Unearthing the idealisation of hard work and 'industry' from beneath the foundations of the white-collar world of corporate business, then, Rand returns it to what she considers its proper place: as part of a pioneering discourse inseparable from a discourse about nation formation. In this way, her fiction creates an odd amalgam of ideas about business. While she joins in the white male literary critique of post-war business, she is additionally committed to establishing for work a central role in the organisation of social honour, in a renewed nation, in terms strikingly reminiscent of Veblen. And yet, while emphasising work in this way, the gender discrimination that was implicit in Veblen's description of modernising 'America' is in no way confronted or overturned in Rand's fiction. If anything, her allegiance to *laissez-faire* economics and mythic, pioneering and masculine discourses of the nation sanction a penetrative logic that not only would have money colonise every aspect of nationhood so that the dollar sign can stand in for the nation at every point, but that also means Rand imagines female heroines constantly in thrall to an aggressive masculinity that is itself aligned with a potent business logic. In *The Fountainhead*, for example, Dominique Francon is attracted to Roark after she sees him working in the quarry, which her father owns. 'She knew it was the most beautiful face she would ever see', Rand writes, 'because it was the abstraction of strength made visible ... He stood looking up at her; it was not a glance, but an act of ownership' (*TF* 194). While Dominique, powerful and independent, makes Roark suffer by trying to destroy him, what attracts her to him is precisely the strength that will prevent him from being destroyed and that separates him from the other men who try to love her. This strength is both mental and physical. When Roark enters Dominique's bedroom and rapes her, Rand describes it 'as a symbol of humiliation and conquest ... the act of a soldier violating an enemy woman' (*TF* 205).

Dominique's ownership by Roark is, then, depicted as both ideological and territorial. Not only does Roark embody those 'American' virtues that Rand wants to see wrest control of the nation's future, he will fight and conquer that which stands in his way. So, for all Rand's attention to work, she still sees it as that which serves the 'exploits' of business and a martial economics that will fulfil the exercise of nation building. Indeed, this national dimension of Rand's Objectivism was resurrected in the immediate aftermath of the attacks on the World Trade Center in 2001. On 20 September 2001, Leonard Peikoff – Rand's legal heir, one-time collaborator and, like her, a naturalised United States citizen – placed a full-page advertisement in the *Washington Post* under the headline 'IT'S TIME TO DECLARE WAR'. Peikoff's argument – in ways that take us right back to Perry Miller's epiphany – links oil, individualism and Americanism in a dizzying political intervention:

> Fifty years ago, Truman and Eisenhower surrendered the West's property rights in oil, although that oil rightfully belonged to those in the West whose science, technology, and capital made its discovery and use possible ... Arab dictators were denouncing wealthy egotistical capitalism. They were crying that ... oil, like all property, is owned collectively, by virtue of birth ... Our Presidents had no answer. Implicitly, they were ashamed of the Declaration of Independence. They did not dare to answer aloud that Americans, properly, were motivated by the selfish desire to achieve personal happiness in a rich, secular, individualist society.[16]

The conflicting centrifugal and centripetal tensions of business and nation I outlined earlier are evident in Peikoff's rhetoric. While United States business – supported by the state if necessary – should be free to claim resources globally, irrespective of national borders, the borders of the United States must remain sacrosanct and protected by the martial powers of the state. Objectivism has become the philosophy of choice for many right-wing commentators in the United States and the grounds for attacking a variety of developments that are seen to threaten the sanctity of an 'American' United States: multicultural education, environmentalism, government intervention in business. It was just this connection between business and the ideals of an individualist 'Americanism' that Rand addressed in her two most famous novels.

JOYCE CAROL OATES, *EXPENSIVE PEOPLE* (1968)

During her prolific writing career Joyce Carol Oates has turned her hand to a variety of fictional and non-fictional themes, but approaches the issue of business most directly in her 1968 novel *Expensive People*. It is narrated by Richard Elwood, an 18-year-old boy who ends the novel a murderer after killing his mother as she walks into their expensive suburban home in the fictional town of Fernwood. *Expensive People* takes up the discourse of 'disintegration' that I dealt with in Chapter 2 but locates it here as a condition brought on for Richard by the domestic unrest that exists between his businessman father, Everett, and his artistic mother, Nada, the daughter of Russian immigrants. Richard begins 'to disintegrate as a child'[17] when the family move to a new home in the 'expensive, innocent town' of Fernwood and Richard enters Johns Behemoth private school; it is this moment when the financial prosperity provided by his father's business career is married with his mother's social and vocational aspirations. Richard is Nada's 'darling prodigy who was to carry the genes of genius into the future, brought all the way to America from sad, dark Russia' (*EP* 85). But, while both parents care for and have high expectations of their son, they are constantly embroiled in a domestic battle that can be interpreted in both cultural and ideological terms.

One of three brothers, all of whom have developed successful business careers, Richard's father has moved through innumerable jobs, 'from bolts manufacturers to underwear manufacturers ... to vice-presidencies in seat-belt companies, wastebasket companies, certain curtain companies, certain steel companies' (*EP* 25), and during this time 'was always being promoted and shoulder-tapped by other corporations, transferred and stolen and relocated back and forth across the country as if he were a precious jewel' (*EP* 24). The fruits of this rise through the corporate system pay for the suburban Fernwood home and take him on business trips to Ecuador (*EP* 94) and other parts of South America (*EP* 119), giving him the confidence and 'the liberal abandonment of an American businessman who does not flinch at seeing a foreign industry patronized' (*EP* 21). According to Richard, Nada is herself at times 'jauntily beautiful and suburban' (*EP* 85), but she also aspires – through her work as a professional writer of fiction – to a style and a world beyond the suburbs. Richard's father's decision that the family move to Fernwood after he receives a promotion, leaves Nada infuriated, especially when Everett belittles her in front of Hanson, the real estate agent selling the house. Lecturing Hanson about the economy, Everett ignores every attempt Nada makes to intervene in the conversation and in the decision about buying the house. 'Oh, you humiliate me!' she objects. 'You know nothing, you're ignorant, you're vulgar – you and your goddam promotion! Who the hell wanted to come here anyway? Why do we have to move?' (*EP* 17).

Nada's description here of the world of business and promotions as 'vulgar' sets up a clash between 'American' business and a non-'American' – in this instance Russian – intellectualism that ruptures the domestic scene and drives the narrative development of the novel and of Richard's experience. The point where they meet is the point where Richard begins to disintegrate. As a young boy he recognises the discrepancy in his parents' relationship. Not only do they have vastly differing backgrounds, but they also have nothing in common. Out walking together one day, they appear to be, Richard suggests, like 'a happy family even though we had the look of being three strangers who have met by accident ... and are waiting for the first chance to get away from one another' (*EP* 20). When both Nada and Everett touch him and urge him on during this walk, it is because, Richard feels, the two of them were 'perhaps using me to show that they had something in common after all' (*EP* 20).

Attempts like this to cover the gaps in their relationship prove futile, however. Nada leaves Everett and Richard for a third time and Everett's response is to try to cement his relationship with his son by introducing him to the world of business while demonising the intellectual world that Nada belongs to. Taking Richard to work with him, he shows off the company's products and the offices that fall under his control (*EP* 121) before accusing women in 'this good old America' of being like Nada: 'she has everything she wants and then doesn't want it, she doesn't know what she wants, she never does any work – good sweet Jesus, never, never!' (*EP* 124). As for intellectuals of the kind Nada mixes with – like 'Dean what's-his-name, that fairy with the English accent' (*EP* 124) – 'Those intellectual bastards ... are filthy, and it comes out disguised as a joke' (*EP* 124). From there Everett moves on to voice his fears about immigration and the 'fake Russians' he imagines Nada has mixed with in the past, the ones who haven't 'stayed over on their side of the ocean ... and I don't exclude those spics and crud coming up and landing in New York' (*EP* 126).

What Everett accomplishes in this section as he heads towards a nervous breakdown, and in full visibility of his son, is the linking together of an exclusionary and nationalist conception of the nation with a gendered idea of male work as the platform upon which the nation is built. Women's work and non-partisan intellectual work are dismissed in this equation in much the same way that they have been dismissed in much of the white male fiction I have looked at in the first half of this book. But rather than ratifying this lament like Rand and other white male writers do, Oates actually relativises it by having Richard himself see beyond it. Richard does not accept his father's version of the link between business and a white 'American' nation. And he is able to do so because at the heart of the domestic space in which he grows up is his Russian mother. If, as Amy Kaplan suggests, 'Through the process of domestication, the home contains within itself those wild or foreign elements that must be tamed',[18] then Richard observes at first hand the way that Nada refuses to be domesticated in both of Kaplan's senses of the word. She does not remain at home to concentrate on the family space but has ambitions beyond it, and – through her commitment to an intellectual culture that Everett sees as alien – she does not become 'American' either. The model of citizenship that Nada displays to Richard, therefore, is at odds with the one suggested to him by Everett.

While it is his mother Richard kills and not his father, this piece of evidence is misleading if used in isolation to try and suggest which model Richard is drawn towards. In shooting his mother, Richard is in fact acting out the role of a sniper he finds in one of her ideas for a short story. And it is this connection with his mother through her work that distances Richard from his father and his father's conception of an 'America' built upon business. Before he shoots his mother, Richard declares that he wants Nada to realise that he is 'a darker, more secret child of hers, a boy who belonged only to her and dedicated everything to her' (*EP* 283). Playing out the role of sniper with his mother as victim may seem a strange kind of dedication, especially when it is at the point that Richard pulls the trigger 'that the world cracked in pieces around' him (*EP* 297), but it is precisely the connection with his mother that is established in the act of shooting her – the playing out of a role created by her in her story – that leads Richard to such an act.

In many ways, by killing Nada, Richard prevents her from walking out on him for a fourth time. Having returned from leaving the third time, Nada's relationship with Everett is gradually pulled apart again by their differing conceptual models of citizenship. Initially Everett seems to be making an effort to realign himself with Nada. He takes Richard to see Antonioni movies and reads the *Partisan Review* at the breakfast table (*EP* 167). However, he also starts a new job in a 'Top-security business' – the making of bombs – which has a clear 'tie-in with the government', and the intimation is that Everett is showing an interest in non-United States culture and United States literary culture not because of his wife but as a form of reconnaissance now he has a place in the national defence industry that is funding his suburban home. 'I almost lost my top clearance because of your mother' (*EP* 173), he tells Richard. Frightened, Richard watches as his father 'speeds into the domestic American darkness' (*EP* 191) while his mother, moving in the opposite direction, starts an affair with the editor of *Transamerican Quarterly*. Falling to pieces in the middle, Richard tries to cling to his mother by dedicating himself to her.

Following her death, Richard embarks upon a dedication that draws him into emulating his mother's work as a writer. The narrative of *Expensive People* is Richard's narrative. Like *Lolita*, it is a confessional narrative, but one where the whole process of writing is emphasised as work. Richard tells the reader that 'Writing this is such hard work that I have to stop and wipe myself with a large handkerchief' (*EP* 4) and he describes himself 'dripping sweat over his manuscript' (*EP* 7). Locked up in prison, with no prospect of doing any other form of work, writing the manuscript is his 'life's work' (*EP* 25). He remains 'Earnest also, because who else would stay laboring over this miserable typewriter … dripping lardy sweat onto the keys, for no reward' (*EP* 32). In the context of his relationships with his mother and father, this depiction of himself as a 'laboring' writer clearly suggests where his allegiances lie.

The role of writing in Oates's novel, then, and writing as a form of work, undermines the easy connection between business and 'America' that Everett represents and which he tries to enshrine in the suburban home. Misjudging the extent to which his Russian wife can be 'domesticated', Everett's project is undermined by Nada's writing, a form of work whose purpose is not the support of business. Produced at home in the domestic space, Nada's writing is the 'wild or foreign element' that is not tamed and therefore destabilises the 'American' project that Everett sees to be underpinned by business. Richard's narrative and his work as a writer allow us access to this process, and by doing so Oates creates a novel whose power lies in the way that it picks apart the discourses of business and nation not in order to create a recovery narrative, but in order to illustrate the tensions that lie at the heart of the ideological production of the nation.

KATHY ACKER, *EMPIRE OF THE SENSELESS* (1988)

In more radical fashion, Kathy Acker develops this model for a different phase of capitalist development some twenty years later. When, in the very first sentence of *Empire of the Senseless*, Acker describes her central female protagonist Abhor as 'part robot',[19] then the reader is being led into a terrain of cybernetics similar to the one William Gibson explored in *Neuromancer*. I have already argued that Gibson's response to digitised late capitalism is innovative – in the sense that it creates a new vocabulary and discourse of the 'cyber' through which to discuss changes in capitalist organisation – but ultimately that this innovation is compromised by a conservative national discourse that attempts to recover the myths of the frontier and the cowboy in order to 'Americanise' this new 'cyber' location. The fictional comparison between Gibson and Acker is all the more apt here, since Acker engages with *Neuromancer* quite explicitly in *Empire of the Senseless*. Using a plagiarising style that she deploys elsewhere in her fiction, Acker lifts sections from *Neuromancer* and transfers them into *Empire of the Senseless*, altering the context and some of the details in the process.

Brian McHale has suggested that 'Acker's rewrite has no discernible purpose apart from that of producing the "sampling" effect itself.'[20] He sees no point in Acker's modifications, nor her substitution of Sense/Net with American Intelligence, Panther Moderns with Moderns, and Wintermute with Winter. In contrast, I see Acker's intertextuality as a much more active engagement with Gibson's novel and with the discourse of cyberspace he develops. More particularly, Acker's novel – replete with images of multinational corporate power and control just like *Neuromancer* – resists Gibson's recovery narrative of the frontier and the individualistic anti-hero of the cowboy by creating a cyborg incarnation that is, in Donna Haraway's terms, 'outside of salvation history'.[21] For Haraway, the cyborg 'is a matter of fiction and lived experience that changes what counts as women's experience in the late twentieth century'.[22] *Empire of the Senseless* charts precisely this experience as the relationship between female labour and multinational corporate capitalism shifts into its latest incarnation.

At one level, Acker's version of multinational capitalism is the familiar one where capital is paradoxically both omnipresent and unlocatable. Before this current phase of multinational capitalism, Acker suggests, it was possible to leave behind alienating places like the ghettoes of pre-Nazi Germany as Abhor's family did – where 'Wealth was the price and cost of political escape' as well as the 'price and cost of capitalism' (*EOTS* 3). Now, however, 'there're multi-nationals' (*EOTS* 3) from which no escape seems possible. 'My father's no longer important', Abhor suggests,

> ... cause interpersonal power in this world means corporate power. The multinationals along with their computers have changed and are changing reality. Viewed as organisms they've attained immortality via bio-chips ... So killing someone, anyone, like Reagan or the top IBM executive board members, whoever they are, can't accomplish anything. (*EOTS* 83)

Multinational corporate business in this vision has territorialised all domains, including – as in *Neuromancer* – the mind. However, the political dangers of this development are signalled much more explicitly in *Empire of the Senseless* than they are in *Neuromancer*. When Acker has Williams, a businessman who deals in comic books, say that 'Any revolution, right-wing left-wing nihilist, it doesn't matter a damn, is good for business ... Because the success of every business depends upon the creation of new markets' (*EOTS* 182), then she is offering a critique of the new domain of cyberspace as one more of these new markets. In the previous chapter I argued that cyberspace for Gibson marks a reterritorialisation of space in national terms, specifically in the way that by creating a dream of the perfect market cyberspace becomes a contemporary frontier, allowing Gibson to recreate the myth of the frontier in an era of advanced capitalism under the name of cyberspace. It is precisely this national recovery narrative that Acker gestures towards in her plagiarising of Gibson's novel, but, in an attempt to retain some sense of political human agency within this environment, it is also a narrative she resists by way of a twofold manoeuvre.

First, Acker tackles the political dangers of an abstract economic system by detailing the gendered nature of its operation. The first chapter of the novel is called 'Rape by the Father'. If Abhor is 'part robot', then she is also a woman who comes from a family of women for whom there has always been a connection between work, money, business and sexual exploitation. At the behest of her parents, Abhor's grandmother works as a child prostitute in Paris after leaving Germany. She endures 'bloody periods of hard labour' (*EOTS* 4), Acker writes, and from this the narrative segues into a digression on Karl Marx's 'new continent' of class struggle, ultimately pulling the two elements back together when a Parisian Vice Squad captain makes the link between hard labour and class struggle and assumes that Abhor's grandmother and her friend Alexander are political terrorists. Acker's mode of writing often works in this way, by juxtaposing non-contiguous temporal, spatial and philosophical elements. The effect achieved here immediately redirects the narrative away from the systemic nature of business and instead drills down to uncover the sex-workers who exist at that point where doing business literally means selling one's gendered body.

Social institutions such as marriage and the family help maintain this kind of sexual violence that Acker identifies as the burden of women's work in capitalism. Not only does Abhor's father keep his daughter in a room so that he can whip her while telling everyone that she is a cripple (*EOTS* 15–16), but her father and grandmother have a telling conversation where marriage and 'fuck[ing] for money' become interchangeable:

'What's this shit about you not letting my granddaughter fuck for money? I mean, get married?' Grandma always got her terms mixed up. 'Do you want your daughter to be a freak? After all she carries our name.'

'I don't have enough money to let her marry, Florrie. Marriage's too expensive a business.'

'I'll finance it,' Grandma replied.

'If you finance her fucking for money,' said my father whose IQ was 166, 'I'll let her do it.' (*EOTS* 16)

The female body is at one and the same time, then, an object of both sexual and economic exchange. Until he disappears, Abhor's father spends much of his time in a brothel which also doubles as the location of a sex-show. It is this location – where what takes place is 'the exploitation of sex for commercial and assorted equally venial reasons' (*EOTS* 16) – where the fusion of the economic and the gendered body takes place, in the minds of the performers as well as 'the "fans" ... Their buyers' (*EOTS* 17).

For Acker, then, it is impossible to write about business without writing about the sexual violence that is carried out against women. The geographical location of this early part of the book indicates that this is not a uniquely 'American' phenomenon, but a result of capitalism as an economic system and it also suggests that Acker is more concerned with the political dimensions of this situation as they affect women rather than how they affect Americans. Hence her thoroughgoing critique of the United States – of Ronald Reagan and IBM – is not matched by a recovery narrative of 'America'. Acker sees herself alienated from such narratives too. So, while she dismisses the intrusions of business and state in the global as well as the personal domain in the post-war years in summary fashion – 'Just as the USA now desperately needed new economic markets for its coke (the mild variety) and McDonalds, so the American CIA needed new drug-test victims' (*EOTS* 144) – she is equally damning of the discourses of freedom and individualism that so many white male writers have fallen back upon: 'As for Liberty. Liberty's a nail which was thrust into my head. It's also a nail they stuck in my cunt. Only I know my cunt is my diseased heart' (*EOTS* 163). Again, Acker reinserts the dimension of gender into any discussion of liberty, showing how women have been placed differently in relation to this discourse compared to men.

None of this is to suggest that Acker does not come up with her own version of a recovery narrative, however. But the second way in which she resists the hegemonic narrative of national recovery as written in Gibson's cyberspace is to create an imaginative realm that persistently undermines a bounded national identity. Pre-eminent here is the figure of the sailor or the pirate. 'Reagan's heart is empty', Acker writes, while the 'sailor is a human who has traded poverty for the riches of imaginative reality' (*EOTS* 114). It is this emphasis upon the imaginary and the dream world that, in Acker's novel, separates the official and the unofficial domains of United States and world business. The spatial dimensions of the sailing ship are important here. Michel Foucault, in his description of heterotopias, or places where 'all the other real sites that can be found within the culture, are simultaneously represented, contested, and inverted', calls the sailing ship the 'heterotopia par excellence' because

> ... the boat is a floating piece of space, a place without a place, that exists by itself, that is closed in on itself and at the same time is given over to the infinity of the sea ... the boat has not only been for our civilization, from the sixteenth century until the present, the great instrument of economic development ... but has been simultaneously the greatest reserve of the imagination ... In civilizations without boats, dreams dry up, espionage takes the place of adventure, and the police take the place of pirates.[23]

Acker seems clearly to be dealing with similar issues in *Empire of the Senseless*. Her determination to resurrect the image of the pirate is partly to imagine a world where power and the nation-state are not conjoined in the pirate's successor, the police official. Thivai dreams of being a pirate and Acker's narrative fulfils this desire. Being a pirate is, of course, both an occupation as well as an adventure, but one that Acker reminds us has an ambiguous relation to the nation.

> In 1574 there were pirate ships.
> By that time the total halt of legal, or national, European wars forced the French and German soldiers either to disappear or to become illegal – pirates. Being free of both nationalistic and religious concerns and restrictions, privateering's only limitation was economic. Piracy was the most anarchic form of private enterprise. (*EOTS* 26)

It is the anarchic and illegal nature of pirate life that attracts Acker. As such, pirate ships and piracy represent a form of existence that is outside or beyond the borders of national capitalism. As an imaginative domain they form a counter-hegemonic world of national and cultural mixing and intersection where the world of national capital may be suspended or resisted, where the empire that has been created by the senseless operations of post-war United States capitalists and politicians may not quite reach. In this context, it is important to note the determinedly internationalist nature of Acker's novel – her willingness to incorporate foreign characters, locations and languages – and this quality is a telling counterpoint to the kinds of anxiety I noted in earlier chapters when white male writers confronted the non-United States world.

By way of a conclusion, it is also worth returning to Amy Kaplan's reconceptualisation of the domestic and asking just how Acker's narrative might be incorporated in this idea. One problem with Kaplan's account is that although it makes the connection between the domestic household and the domestic nation, by writing about the domestic as 'an ambiguous third realm between the national and the foreign' because of the way that 'it places the foreign inside the geographic boundaries of the nation', Kaplan is still relying on binary oppositions of national and foreign. One might usefully ask where are the geographic boundaries of the nation in *Empire of the Senseless* and how a writer like Acker conceives of her characters in terms of national and foreign. Kaplan's terms seem to be inadequate to cope with the fluid and narratively anarchic geography and characterisation of Acker's novel. The cybernetic Abhor immediately resists categorisation as domestic or foreign since it seems unlikely that a robot could have a national identity when such identities are usually conceived in humanistic terms. In *Neuromancer*, Gibson turns to cowboy rhetoric to give his hero Case a national identity, but Acker resists effects such as this at every turn. Instead she relies on a vision of the contemporary world that is alert to the hegemonic practices of multinational business and the gendered impact of these practices, but that also seeks to cope in this world by creating an imaginative domain that does not rely on the recovery of 'American' qualities. Acker's response to the increasing importance of global cultural flows is to recognise how these flows have economic imperatives but also to note the opportunities for reconceptualising discourses of identity in a non-national way.

5
Assimilation, Citizenship and Post-Ethnicity

If the intellectual emergence of gender studies during the 1970s can be identified, in Gene Wise's terms, as one of 'the earthquake-like jolts' that destabilised the discipline of American Studies and deprived it of 'a larger cultural synthesis' with which to think about United States culture,[1] then ethnic and race studies did precisely the same thing during and after the 1960s. In many ways it has been the combination of these two intellectual approaches, together with work on the labouring classes and popular culture, that has forced American Studies towards its recent postnational self-consciousness. Race and ethnicity are key to this emerging condition for someone like John Carlos Rowe, for instance, who has argued that a postnationalist American Studies curriculum must not only 'incorporate the various intellectual traditions in a multicultural United States', but also be taught by 'faculty of color who specialize in the study of specific/ethnic groups in the United States'.[2]

Yet the amalgamation of American Studies and race and ethnic studies has not been a straightforward one. Indeed, Rowe's repeated efforts to create a 'new' American Studies signal the work that still needs to be done. One of the problems American Studies has faced as it tries to come to terms with the concept of the postnational is the tenacity of an intellectual tradition that has emphasised a demarcated geographical area delimited by the borders of the nation-state as well as the kinds of exceptional values associated with the nation that are assumed to correspond to these borders. This disciplinary model stands in uneasy juxtaposition with other critical disciplines that often predicate their critical enquiry on cross-national developments and on the basis of difference and/or conflict. Even before the institutionalisation of race and ethnic studies in the United States, this internationalist model had been a feature of the work of writers like Jose Martí and W. E. B. Du Bois. Martí's 'Neustra America', published originally in 1891, envisaged an 'America' that was hemispheric in dimension and capable of acting as a bulwark against both European and United States imperialism.[3] The impasse between these contrary critical approaches was the subject of Janice Radway's presidential address to the American Studies Association in 1998. There, she drew attention to 'the problem of how to think difference and the idea of a specifically "American" studies together' and conceded that 'It is not easy to deal with either the most generative or the most limiting effects of difference if you already assume the unity and coherence of a distinctly "American" history.'[4] Radway's suggestion that the American Studies Association consider renaming itself (Association for the Study of the United States and Inter-American Studies Association were two of her suggestions), reiterates just how deeply the national model of American Studies has been challenged.

But it is not just the security of a national model of disciplinary study that ethnic and race studies have undermined. As I wrote in the Introduction, Paul Gilroy's notion of the Black Atlantic is an exemplary instance of this kind of approach. And the way in which he envisages the importance of spaces beyond and between nation-states for fashioning racial identity, suggests that ethnic and race studies have also undermined a national model of citizenship. By being drawn to extra-national locations, the link between identity and nation has become a fragile one. As American Studies scholars have tried to cope with this postnational challenge to 'American' identity, one figure who has attracted a good deal of critical attention is Olaudah Equiano, who published *The Interesting Narrative of the Life of Olaudah Equiano, or Gustavus Vassa, the African* in 1789. As a way of leading into this chapter's discussion of race, ethnicity and business, Equiano's autobiography is a useful entry point. One of the notable aspects of the book is that it was published not just in the moment of national founding, but also, as David Kazanjian points out, that it recounts – as well as his birth in Africa, his experience of slavery and antislavery protest – Equiano's time in the transatlantic merchant marine trade at a time when the United States Congress was passing tariff bills which can be understood as 'one manifestation of an extensive system of economic nationalism known as "mercantilism"',[5] the system of centralised effort by governments to accumulate gold, avoid a balance-of-trade deficit, and be self-sufficient in agriculture and manufacturing.

In a complex argument, Kazanjian draws on two major ideas in order to ask how race, nation and identity intersect in Equiano's experience of transatlantic business. First, he takes up Etienne Balibar's contention that the nation-state does not emerge inevitably from capitalism but is created by – amongst other things – the discourses of mercantilism. Second, he uses Marx's notion that mercantilism helps establish the value form and how this in turn creates 'citizenship as an institution of formal and abstract equality supplemented by codified particularities such as "race" and "nation"'.[6] What Kazanjian suggests is that Equiano, although nominally free and equal, is never able to experience freedom and equality because the 'supplementary' codifications of race and nation that go hand in hand with mercantilist trade constantly exclude him, since he is black and not a United States citizen. Although he manages to buy his freedom from slavery, his attempts at trading are ultimately unsuccessful because of the way in which the business with which he is engaged is conducted not in a 'free' market, but in a trading environment where the imperatives of trade are to produce and consolidate a white 'American' nation. As Kazanjian puts it, Equiano's business failures 'are neither incidental nor unique, but systematic' and represent 'a *constitutive* exclusion ritually iterated and reiterated' in the form of physical violence, swindling and robbery.[7]

While Equiano's life may, historically, be fairly distant from the post-war world of writers like Ralph Ellison, Octavia Butler, Gish Gen and Chang-rae Lee who I consider in this chapter, what his experience suggests is that the interweaving discourses of business and nation have consequences that materially impact upon racial identity and in many ways help construct concepts of national racial citizenship through the kinds of exclusion about which Kazanjian writes. Equiano's retelling of such incidents at a moment of nationalist mercantilism can be seen as one of those 'narratives of acculturation' which, I suggested in the Introduction, are produced when an investment in the national project is restricted by one's subject position. It is experiences of this kind that I want to explore in this chapter.

RALPH ELLISON, *INVISIBLE MAN* (1952)

In his introduction to the thirtieth anniversary edition of *Invisible Man*, Ralph Ellison notes not only how his writing of the book was ultimately achieved by 'keeping a businessman's respectable hours',[8] but how the novel itself grew out of an altogether different, and transnational, project: a narrative about the wartime experiences of a black American pilot who is captured by Nazis and interned in a prisoner-of-war camp. As the only black American in the camp, but the most senior in rank, Ellison writes about the way in which this character has to fight both 'native and foreign racisms' (*IM* xxx), and how his determination to help his white American colleagues, even though they despise him because he is black, leads to an inner struggle of which neither they nor the German guards are aware. By emphasising the international dimension of racism, Ellison is drawing attention to the fact that 'historically most of this nation's conflicts have been – at least for Afro-Americans – wars-within-wars' (*IM* xxx). The personal war that results for Ellison's character erupts at that point where an allegiance to the nation-state is undermined by the knowledge that the nation-state regards black life 'as of lesser value than the lives of whites making the same [wartime] sacrifice' (*IM* xxx). This point is reiterated by an awareness that once the war is over, the German guards 'could immigrate to the United States and immediately take advantage of freedoms that were denied the most heroic of Negro servicemen' (*IM* xxxi).

Like Equiano, Ellison served in the merchant marine, and while he did so because he considered it a 'more democratic mode of service' during the war (*IM* xxxi), his experiences of wartime Europe and the accounts he heard from other black servicemen he met on his trips, suggest that – like Equiano – Ellison was forced to confront the contradictions and *non sequiturs* of his own racialised national identity during this time. The 'existential torture' (*IM* xxxi) that he finds, comes to shape the character who 'upstages' the narrative of the black American pilot – Invisible Man. As a novel, *Invisible Man*, then, is forged in the same transnational wartime domain that undergirds the texts I wrote about in Chapter 1: *The Naked and the Dead, The Man in the Gray Flannel Suit* and *Catch-22*. *Invisible Man* differs from these texts in important ways, however. Rather than starting from a position where the interests of nation and individual are *expected* to coincide, *Invisible Man* originates from an historical legacy – and what Ellison calls an 'archetypal American dilemma' (*IM* xxxi) – of racial exclusion and inequality. Rather than experiencing in times of transnational contact the ways in which the nation is stretched and distorted by global commitments to such an extent that 'America' is considered perpetually under threat, *Invisible Man* forges from the experience of transnational contact a representation of racial identity that is alert not only to the consequences of exclusion and inequality but also to the 'divisions of class and diversities of culture' (*IM* xxx) within a racial group produced by such conditions and that themselves generate feedback, further distorting the stability of racial identity. Rather than a nostalgic appeal to 'America', *Invisible Man* registers the extent to which 'America' remains an occluded concept to this particular black citizen because he cannot see himself reflected back in the national imaginary.

The knock-on effect of this situation is precisely the visual logic that drives Ellison's novel. Invisible to the white nation, but not part of any homogeneous racial group either, the central, unnamed character becomes invisible to himself as well. While this situation is clearly connected to a visual logic of racism that has interested critics from Frantz Fanon to bell hooks,[9] I want to emphasise the central place of the paint factory (*IM* 196–230) in Invisible Man's journey to his underground hideaway and how a logic of visibility is also linked to the discourses about business and nation as they developed in the 1940s and 1950s. While McCarthyite purges relied upon a logic of hidden un-American activities and J. Edgar Hoover saw communism as a plot and a conspiracy that was 'virtually invisible to the non-communist eye, unhampered by time, distance, and legality',[10] Vance Packard was declaring in *The Hidden Persuaders* – a book about business and advertising – that efforts to control the thought processes of US citizens were taking place 'beneath our level of awareness; so that the appeals which move us are often, in a sense, "hidden". The result is that many of us are being influenced and manipulated, far more than we realize, in the pattern of our everyday lives.'[11] This kind of rhetoric was part of the backlash against business corporations and other large bureaucratic organisations that took place in the post-war years, and it increasingly relied on the idea that those in control were anonymous, unseen and consequently beyond the limits of democratic controls.

If this suspicion is in many ways constitutive of Timothy Melley's 'agency panic', what Ellison does is to appropriate such a discourse of invisibility and use it not to question the motives of business and bureaucratic elites, but to highlight the way in which, when business and the nation come together, what is made invisible is the way that business is underpinned by racial distinction. Ellison therefore sets himself the task of reinserting this racial dimension. When Invisible Man arrives at the paint plant he immediately sees 'a huge electric sign' announcing to him: 'KEEP AMERICA PURE WITH LIBERTY PAINTS' (*IM* 196). As the 'hidden persuader' who has dreamed up this advertising slogan, Ellison is asserting the national value that accrues to business when it sells products by underlining the product's association with a racialised concept of national purity and freedom.

What is striking about the slogan is the way that the word 'KEEP' insists not only upon a past vision of nationhood – 'America' as a nation that has developed by asserting white freedom – but also upon the future effects that can be achieved by purchasing Liberty paints. Invisible Man is struck by how looking at the combination of this slogan, together with the 'maze of buildings below the sign', is 'like watching some vast patriotic ceremony from a distance' (*IM* 196). I would suggest that 'distance' here can be interpreted not as a simple form of geographical distance but as a kind of exclusionary distance where space is demarcated on racial grounds. Invisible Man quickly finds out that race is one of the factors prompting his employment, allowing the company to get away with paying him less than union wages. And all this for a firm closely connected not just to the nation, but to the nation-state too, since they 'Make a lot of paint for the government' (*IM* 197). The batch of paint that Invisible Man works with is 'heading for a national monument!' (*IM* 202).

Taking the importance of this particular business product still further, it is vital to Ellison's weaving together of business, nation and race that the colour Liberty paints is best-known for is 'Optic White'. Invisible Man's job is to make this paint as white as possible, as white, his 'slave driver' (*IM* 199) supervisor Kimbro tells him, as 'a George Washington's Sunday-go-to-meetin' wig and as sound as the all-mighty dollar! That's paint ... That's paint that'll cover just about anything!' (*IM* 201–2). If the purpose of this product is literally to paint the nation white and to make invisible the existence of a multiracial 'America', then the labour of Invisible Man reveals to the reader the process whereby the whiteness of 'Optic White' relies upon non-white elements. Invisible Man has to work on a batch of paint that does not meet the standards of whiteness required. The solution is to put ten drops of black dope into each bucket of paint and mix it together until it turns whiter. When he is finished, however, Invisible Man notices a grey coming through the white, the kind of grey that just a couple of pages before he has used to describe the unpainted buildings that surrounded his old college. While the college buildings were impressive 'because they were the only buildings to receive regular paintings', the surrounding cabins and houses 'were left untouched to become the dull grained gray of weathered wood' (*IM* 201). There are places like Trueblood's cabin and, more importantly, the Golden Day, the saloon-cum-brothel that is filled with black First World War veterans who, after fighting overseas for 'American' freedom, have returned home only to find segregation laws still in tact. The fact that Kimbro does not see the grey coming through the white paint leads Invisible Man to 'a feeling that something had gone wrong, something far more important than the paint' (*IM* 205–6).

What has gone wrong here is that what is visible to Invisible Man is not visible to Kimbro. The 'gray' that Invisible Man sees coming through the white paint is a result of his experience with, and links him quite explicitly to, Trueblood and the Golden Day and the episode where he takes Norton to the Golden Day and which ultimately leads to Invisible Man's expulsion from college: 'it was strange how life connected up ... If, I thought, one could slow down his [Norton's] heartbeats and memory to the tempo of black drops falling so slowly into the bucket yet reacting so swiftly, it would seem like a sequence in a feverish dream' (*IM* 201).

It is access to this kind of racial history that changes the colour of the paint for Invisible Man. In particular, the presence of the First World War veterans in the Golden Day returns us to the contradictions of fighting for one's nation but being denied equality by that nation on the grounds of race. For Kimbro, on the other hand, the paint remains white because what is invisible to him is the racial inequality created in the process of producing paint as white as George Washington's wig.

The reliance of business on black labour is also emphasised in the next part of Invisible Man's journey through the paint plant. Lucius Brockway takes pleasure in telling Invisible Man that there 'Ain't a continental thing that happens down here that ain't as iffen I done put my black hands into it' (*IM* 218). The use of the word 'continental' here emphasises the link between business and nation and the expansion of the nation's interest not just in terms of the United States but the whole continent of America. It also urges the reader to recognise how the nation relies upon black labour and black military participation to enable that continental expansion. In addition, Brockway tells Invisible Man how he helped come up with another of Liberty paint's marketing slogans: 'If it's Optic White, It's the Right White.' Invisible Man is reminded of a childhood jingle: 'If you're white, you're right' (*IM* 217–18), and the link between an observation on white racism and the recirculation of it in a business environment hints at the way that structures of oppression repeat themselves through the discourses of business.

All of these instances witness the way in which Ellison uses this chapter in the paint factory to incorporate the vital ingredient of business into his representation of Invisible Man's acculturation. By appropriating the discourse of invisibility that was being deployed elsewhere in post-war literary culture to critique the rise of large-scale organisations, Ellison is able to racialise the link between business and 'America' and thereby implicitly offers his own critique of white male literary culture that looked in all the wrong places for some of the most harmful and violent consequences of 'American' business development. Crucially, it is the experience of work in the paint factory that helps Ellison reveal these consequences and to add them to the sense of disorientation affecting Invisible Man; a sense that ultimately leads him to his underground basement where he can try to finally see and identify himself in a racialised 'America' after so many experiences that have forced him to confront the conditions of his acculturation. If Olaudah Equiano ultimately left the merchant marine trade because of the injuries done against him, then Invisible Man can be understood to leave United States society for the same reasons. And yet it is testament to the place of business in inflicting these injuries that Invisible Man exacts some sort of revenge by stealing electricity from Monopolated Light and Power to illuminate the blackness of his invisibility.

OCTAVIA BUTLER, *KINDRED* (1979)

While the links with historical experiences of national racial formation remain implicit in Ellison's novel, Octavia Butler places them at the heart of *Kindred* by engaging with slavery and makes the link between contemporary identity formation and historical experience explicit. The novel opens with Dana, the central female character, lying in a hospital bed having lost an arm. By the end of the book the reader realises that this loss occurs as a result of her experiences of moving between 1970s Los Angeles and early nineteenth-century Maryland. As she traverses space and time returning from her final visit, Dana cannot free her arm from Maryland; it remains trapped in the grasp of the dead Rufus, the man who Dana has been returning to Maryland to save since he was a young boy. As the walls of her Los Angeles house form around her, Dana is 'still caught somehow, joined to the wall as though my arm were growing out of it – or growing into it … I looked at the spot where flesh joined with plaster, stared at it uncomprehending. It was the exact spot Rufus's fingers had grasped.'[12] Pulling the arm towards her results in it being severed.

This horrific moment marks the most obvious way in which Butler asks the reader to consider how the past wounds and scars the present.

But she also draws attention to the intimate connection between the complex nature of racial identity and systems of business. Rufus turns out to be both a distant relative of Dana's and heir to his slave-owning father's plantation. Dana is thus taken back into the past so that she can save his life and ensure her own birth, while at the same time perpetuating that slave-owning class and an economic system of organised racism that provide part of the legacy of United States citizenship into which she will be born. Furthermore, Dana begins to travel back to nineteenth-century Maryland, and to experience the miscegenation that is part of the economic and social history of slavery and responsible for shaping her past, just when she moves into a new house with her white partner Kevin. After initially doubting Dana's time-travelling and putting her description of events down to some form of hallucination, Kevin is also transported back in time to Maryland. In this way, Butler uses both Dana's and Kevin's experiences of nineteenth-century United States slave and abolitionist culture as a way of having them understand the nature of their mixed-race relationship at the end of the twentieth century and the legacy of race of which it will need to take account.

If there are parallels, then, between past and present living conditions and relationships, one of the clearest is the way that work figures as a major theme for Butler in both historical moments. When Dana and Kevin first meet, Dana is working for a 'casual labor agency – we regulars called it a slave market' (K 52). Dana describes how it is, in fact, the 'opposite of slavery. The people who ran it couldn't have cared less whether or not you showed up to do the work they offered. They always had more job hunters than jobs anyway' (K 52). But this reversal is only true in one sense, since it is still those at the bottom of the economic ladder, or those marginalised in society, who rely on the wage slavery of the 'slave market':

> Waiting with you were winos trying to work themselves into a few more bottles, poor women with children trying to supplement their welfare checks, kids trying to get a first job, older people who'd lost one job too many, and usually a poor crazy old street lady who talked to herself constantly and who wasn't going to be hired no matter what because she only wore one shoe. (K 52)

The sort of work given to Dana and her fellow minimum-wage slaves was 'nearly always mindless' and it turned the people who performed it into what she describes as 'nonpeople' (K 53). The echoes of formal slavery here are clear in the way that economic exploitation and marginalisation lead to social invisibility and exclusion. But it is while working on one of these temporary assignments, at an auto-parts warehouse, that Dana meets Kevin and their mutual interest in writing brings them together. For Dana, writing is something she has to do when she can fit it into her schedule: 'I did the work, I went home, I ate, and then slept for a few hours, Finally I got up and wrote. At one or two in the morning, I was fully awake, fully alive, and busy working on my novel' (K 53). It is working routines of this kind that Dana finds and becomes a part of in her trips back to Maryland and which provide her with a way of forging friendships and coping strategies in the midst of the violent social structures of slavery. 'What's a slave for', she asks herself at one point, 'but to work? ... I have to make a place for myself here. That means work' (K 79). Working for Sarah in the cookhouse, Dana carries out all sorts of chores and sees how for women like Sarah social worth on the plantation is often determined by one's working abilities, and that along with social worth goes some small amount of social space: 'She's got her house', Sarah says about Margaret Weylin, the plantation owner's wife, 'and I got my kitchen' (K 94). When Margaret is away it is Sarah who allocates duties (K 144). When her trips back in time to Maryland become elongated, Dana has to work to pay for her keep and although not sold into slavery, she becomes part of a slavery workforce and thus experiences the way that work can signify differently depending on what one's work entails. Forced to do the washing at one point, Dana 'felt sweat on my face mingling with silent tears of frustration and anger' and concludes that 'slavery was a slow process of dulling' (K 183) although, when events on the plantation become too oppressive, Dana is 'almost glad to find myself put back to work' (K 210).

These ambivalent attitudes to work suggest the way in which it can signify in different ways even within a system of such embedded structural inequality as slavery. What needs to be considered, however, is that work, when set against the other markers of this structural inequality – murder, rape, beating, family break-up, the trading of black slaves – offers up a space where identity is not always totally prescribed by white plantation culture. Sarah and her daughter Carrie, for instance, turn the cookhouse into a place where not only 'Sometimes old people and children lounged', but a place where 'house servants or even field hands stealing a few moments of leisure' could hide out. And in this space, Dana listens to them talk 'to find out more about how they survived lives of slavery', admitting that 'Without knowing it, they prepared me to survive' (*K* 94).

There is a sense, then, that Butler creates a world of work in *Kindred* that is violent, brutal and unrewarding, but one that within it also contains gaps and pockets of air that allow people to breathe when working under conditions not of their own choosing. Short as these moments may be, they are significant for two reasons. First of all, they show the ways in which, rather than just a social and economic structure, slavery is a part of, and is experienced first of all as, a set of personal conditions with local variables that sometimes require creative responses. So, when Kevin travels back with Dana, and because of his colour sleeps not in servant quarters but in the main part of the house, Dana can assign herself jobs – getting the fire started, bringing water to his room – that give her 'legitimate reason for going in and out of Kevin's room at all hours' (*K* 92). Second, it is this notion of work as a site of creative negotiation that Butler builds into her depiction of Dana's working life in 1970s California.

After beginning her relationship with Kevin, Dana refuses to give up her work for the agency, even though Kevin has now sold his first novel and can afford to support her. 'The independence the agency gave me was shaky', she says, 'but it was real. It would hold me together until my novel was finished and I was ready to look for something more demanding. When that time came, I could walk away from the agency not owing anybody' (*K* 108–9). What is linked together here is a chain of events that is perhaps surprising, given Dana's earlier complaint that the temps with whom she worked became 'nonpeople'. In effect, from this position of marginalisation and invisibility, Dana forges not only some sense of independence, but also manages to use her time creatively in order to work on the writing which is both a way out of her position as agency worker in a 'slave-market' and also the means by which she can have a voice and emerge from the shadows of public invisibility. Thus, what is carried over from her time-travelling experience of work under slavery into a parallel world of wage slavery is the belief that work contains the gaps through which identity may emerge. Indeed, it is precisely her experience of work under slavery that informs her restructured sense of identity:

> I felt as though I were losing my place here in my own time. Rufus's time was a sharper, stronger reality. The work was harder, the smells and tastes were stronger, the danger was greater, the

pain was worse ... Rufus's time demanded things of me that had never been demanded before, and it could easily kill me if I did not meet its demands. That was a stark, powerful reality that the gentle conveniences and luxuries of this house, of *now*, could not touch. (*K* 191)

The impact of this experience is evident when Kevin asks Dana to act as his secretary, typing up his manuscripts. When she refuses a second time he is annoyed. When she refuses a third time he is so angry that for not doing 'him a little favour when he asked', he tells her she can leave (*K* 109). Later, Dana also tells how Kevin tries to get her 'to take care of his correspondence for him' (*K* 136). These refusals are part of the way Dana negotiates her identity in her relationship with Kevin through work: by setting limits on what she will and will not do, she establishes the kinds of personal boundaries denied to nineteenth-century slaves by violence and abuse.

If fictional narratives set in the future are often considered to be more urgently about the present, then the same can be said for *Kindred*. In this novel, the recovery of the past is not primarily an attempt to understand the past but a way of understanding and coping with the way in which the past organises the present. By saving Rufus's life on several occasions, Dana's relationship with the past is a very personal one. On only one occasion does *Kindred* gesture toward a narrative of national identity. This is near the end of the book when 'Kevin's friends came over on the Fourth of July and tried to get us to go to the Rose Bowl with them for the fireworks' (*K* 247). Dana does not want to go and Kevin will not go without her. Immediately after the friends have left, Dana is taken back to Maryland. This moment can be read as a way in which a narrative of national independence is rejected in favour of a narrative of personal acculturation and identity formation. The central place of slavery in nineteenth-century nation formation is a narrative superseded in *Kindred* by one that emphasises not a national connection to an economic and social structure, but – through Rufus – a personal connection that is then articulated and understood by way of a discourse of work rather than business systems and models of the nation. Butler's 'work' as the writer of *Kindred*, and Dana's 'work' as a character, reinstates the identity of those people whose identity was denied them because they were turned into nonpeople by the 'work' of slavery.

GISH JEN, *TYPICAL AMERICAN* (1991)

When Ralph Chang, the chief protagonist of *Typical American*, fails to renew his United States visa he imagines 'the deportation team arriving instantly, with snarling dogs, and ropes'[13] after being tipped off by someone from the university in New York where he is taking his postgraduate engineering degree. Trying to think of a way to overcome this problem, Ralph turns to the Chinese stories he heard as a child and a young adult but can only remember 'people smarter than he was' (*TA* 27). Forced to move several times to keep ahead of the letters from the Department of Immigration, Ralph becomes increasingly isolated while his New York friends 'became another lost family' (*TA* 32). Caught between cultures, both legally and culturally, Ralph, who has changed his name from Yifeng upon arriving in the United States, is stymied:

> So it was that Ralph felt not only his future to have failed, but with it his past, the twin engine that might have sustained him. He missed his home, missed having a place that was home. Home! And yet life there, no; it didn't begin to fill the measure of his hopes of life. It was no golden time ... He saw all of this now, with the terrible lucidity of a strained mind; and seeing it, wondered what there was to live for. (*TA* 33–4)

As a fugitive immigrant in 1947, Ralph's 'strained mind' is struggling to cope with the transnational experience of migration, and of not being able to inhabit that space of 'American' citizenship that inspired his parents to send him to the United States with 'his stomach burbling with fool hope' (*TA* 6).

African-American models of citizenship that challenge and confound a national model have more recently been matched by a critique of the Asian-American experience in the United States. Lisa Lowe, in her groundbreaking *Immigrant Acts*, begins her study of this experience from the position that 'Citizens inhabit the political space of the nation' and that 'through the terrain of national culture ... the individual subject is politically formed as the American citizen'.[14] But if the construction of a national culture – and its monuments, dreams and stereotypes – is meant to be the site through which, Lowe argues, the 'subject becomes, acts, and speaks itself as "American"',[15] then she conceives 'Asian American cultural productions as countersites to U.S. national memory and national culture'.[16] This is what Gish Jen's *Typical American* becomes once 'That splendour! That radiance!' (*TA* 7) that Ralph imagines he will feel on seeing the Golden Gate Bridge begins to fade: 'True, it wasn't the Statue of Liberty, but still in his mind its span glowed bright, an image of freedom, and hope' (*TA* 7). When his boat arrives in San Francisco harbour, however, he can hardly see the bridge for fog. And travelling to New York on the train through 'the whole holy American spectacle' he gets by 'without his looking up once' (*TA* 7). The gap between the expectation of 'America' and the moments of experiencing 'America' are the location for Lowe's Asian-American 'countersites'.

Driving this contention for Lowe is the fact that a national model of 'American' citizenship has, since the middle of the nineteenth century, struggled to come to terms with the Asian immigrant. In the realm of business and work, the Asian has been considered a particular threat. Chinese labourers during the nineteenth century were a source of anxiety for native and European white immigrants who feared they would be put out of work. But in wider terms too, American national culture has had to manage a situation all the way through the twentieth century whereby as a nation it has been fighting economically and militarily – Hawaii 1893, the Philippines 1898–1910, Japan 1941–45, Korea 1950–53, Vietnam 1962–75 – against Asian rivals, and at the same time trying to manage a racialised labour force within its domestic economy. Renewed economic rivalry during the 1970s and fears that the emerging 'tiger' economies of the Pacific Rim would undermine United States economic hegemony in the region all added to these anxieties.

The ways in which the nation-state has handled the perceived threat of contact with the Asian has included immigration exclusion acts and the legal prevention of Asian naturalisation. The repeal of such laws in the 1950s and '60s ushered in a new era of Asian experience in the United States, but for Lowe when the 'state legally transforms the Asian *alien* into the Asian American *citizen*, it institutionalizes the disavowal of the history of racialized exploitation and disenfranchisement through the promise of freedom in the political sphere' and in so doing only 'exacerbates the contradictions of the national project that promises the resolution of material inequalities through the political domain of equal representation'.[17] For second- and multiple-generation Asian Americans, the problems of immigration exclusion are replaced by the dilemmas of immigration inclusion. And this during a period when the United States has been fixated, as David Palumbo-Liu makes evident, with a vision of emphasising itself as a Pacific power and forging closer economic ties in the Pacific through 'a recognition of a common capitalist identity' shared with the Asian economies.[18]

The formation of immigrant and diasporic identities under such conditions is what concerns me during the remainder of this chapter. And for both Gish Jen and Chang-rae Lee it is the experience of work and business that play a key role in the negotiation of such identities. After contemplating what there is to live for, Ralph immediately mentions 'his new job' (TA 34). While there is a degree of irony in this suggestion, especially when the reader finds out that Ralph's job is to kill, clean and pluck chickens in the most squalid working conditions for the Chinese restaurant business, this element of the narrative allows the reader to see how Ralph's experience intersects with a story about work as the method by which one might be incorporated into national citizenship. Still a fugitive, Ralph actually forms part of that exploited racial labour market – although he may not articulate it in those terms – that is unable to fashion an acceptable identity within the 'American' national model through work. So Ralph is forced to turn to Pinkus, a college professor who has treated him sympathetically in the past. He appeals to Pinkus to help get him back into university to finish his PhD. But Pinkus's response only reinforces the kinds of exclusions that the Asian immigrant must endure. Pinkus characterises Chinese society as one based on dishonesty and marks his superiority over Ralph by pretending to have access to knowledge of 'national' characteristics that Ralph does not and lecturing him accordingly: 'I know, in China, everything's through the back door. You think I don't know? I have ears, I listen, I know. But China is China, this is America … You want to get somewhere, don't sneak around. And don't ask other people to sneak around for you' (TA 37).

Putting his trust in Pinkus, Ralph waits for a letter from the university and even imagines that in Pinkus he has found an ally, someone with whom – through work – he might share a fraternal identity:

Sometimes at work, he'd see Pinkus step out from behind the chicken crates, apologetic. He'd see Pinkus kneel down beside him, offer to help with the plucking.

No, Ralph would insist. No, no, no. You're a professor, this sort of work isn't for you.

But there was Pinkus, rolling up his sleeves, watching Ralph's hands. So show me. (TA 38)

Ralph takes an apartment near to Pinkus's house and even follows him around. But when he bumps into Pinkus one day, any hopes that Ralph may have had of forging a friendship with him are ripped apart by the sort of exclusionary racial history that Lowe sees marking Asian immigrant experience in the United States. 'Not only do I know who you are, I know what you are', Pinkus tells him, accusing him of being 'a liar' and 'a sneak': 'No more of this I'm a poor immigrant ... This is America you're in now. If you want to lie, you want to sneak around, you should go back to China. Here in America we have morals' (*TA* 40).

For Ralph, this encounter is a moment of complete disempowerment. Not only does he give up work, without seeing any way of resuming his education, but he is also forced to give up what Lowe describes as 'the reservoir of memory out of which the distinct forms and practices of Asian American culture itself emerge'.[19] Moving once more, Ralph loses contact with his last Chinese friend in the United States, Little Lou, and 'He lay waiting to see what happened. Anything could happen, this was America. He gave himself up to the country, and dreamt' (*TA* 42). Giving himself to 'America' is not a moment of racial assimilation or inclusion for Ralph, but a moment of despair. This is proved, I would suggest, by the fact that his 'deliverance' – the title of the succeeding chapter – is achieved by chance factors that come from outside of 'America': first, his sister Theresa, who has also moved to the United States, finds him on a park bench; and second, his fugitive status is resolved by the victory of the Communists in China – 'serendipity itself' (*TA* 58) – since many Chinese students were thrown into an illegitimate position. Sponsored by a deposed government, these students were now classified as 'No Status' (*TA* 58) and Ralph is able to join their ranks and re-enter college.

The first part of *Typical American*, then, marks the transition of Ralph's status from alien to permanent resident and ultimately – some nine years later – to citizen almost by default, and certainly not out of 'American' benevolence. What follows in the book is an account of the processes of assimilation connected with this access to citizenship. For Ralph, there are key stages on the way: finding a job (*TA* 120), celebrating 'Christmas in addition to Chinese New Year's', becoming 'regulars at Radio City Music Hall' and owning 'a Davy Crockett hat' (*TA* 123), and having 'English thoughts too ... There were things they did not know how to say in Chinese. The language of *outside the house* had seeped well inside – Cadillac, Pyrex, subway, Coney Island. Ringling Brothers and Barnum & Bailey Circus' (*TA*

123–4). Agreeing with his wife Helen, who came from China with Theresa, that their children should be 'American', Ralph decides to begin driving lessons: *'And what better way to* Americanize *the children than to buy a car!'* (*TA* 128). When Ralph achieves tenure in his academic job, there is a sense in which the word 'tenure' says much about how Ralph's work links him with 'American' land. Certainly the new house that Ralph, Helen and Theresa buy signals the importance of landowning tenure. The lawn they try to grow 'was more than just nature, just life. A lawn like this was America. It was the great blue American sky, beguiling the grass upward. It was the soil, so fresh, so robust. So much better quality than Chinese soil' (*TA* 159).

And yet despite these achievements, Ralph realises that there is still a further stage of success to get to and that this stage can only be reached through business. Shortly after being given a book about the power of positive thinking, Ralph meets Grover, a 'short, American-born, English-speaking businessman' (*TA* 86), whose generations of family have been in the United States so long that he does not know his Chinese home town, and who tells Ralph that 'in this country, the question to ask is: "So what do you do for a living"' (*TA* 105). A self-made millionaire, Grover persuades Ralph to give up his tenured position in academia to buy into a business store. Lulled by Grover's discourse of being self-made, Ralph sees the opportunity to follow in this path. Thinking about the modest business store,

> He saw past the present moment as though with a magic scope; through this special lens he saw an empire rise, grander and mightier than anything his father had commanded, even in his heyday. Ralph tingled with anticipation. Small doubts rained on him from time to time, but mostly he floated in hope, fabulous hope, a private ocean, gentle and green. (*TA* 193)

This 'private ocean' is one that isolates Ralph from Theresa, and his increasing attempts to imitate Grover force her to move out. The 'special lens' Ralph sees through is a lens that has been ground from hegemonic 'American' ideology. Rather than seeing himself as a member of a racial and ethnic group with whom he shares a linked experience, Ralph instead separates himself off from those people 'for whom America was a disappointment'. The 'special lens' puts him in a privileged position where 'he did not fear he would turn out like them; he only felt sorry that some people worked hard but proved unlucky ... his fortune was to live in the other America, the legendary America that was every wish come true' (*TA* 237).

To begin with, Ralph's business does well. Selling prodigious quantities of fried chicken – and here the reader is reminded of Ralph's old fugitive job – to people 'sick of pizza' (*TA* 239) allows Ralph to expand the store. Even when Grover is sent to prison for tax evasion, Ralph still has faith in his business. So much so that he too starts to falsify the accounts. And then the building that houses the store begins to crack. As I mentioned above, property ownership and 'tenure' are used by Jen to symbolise connection to national land in this novel. And when the reader finds that the building is cracking because it is built on a plot of land that covers an unstable pit, the intimation is that the business itself is built upon unstable ideological ground. Ralph discovers that Grover knew all about the land before letting him buy into the business. Ralph has to close the store and turn back to his family for support. With debts piling up, Ralph has no option but to sell the house with the lawn that signalled such a successful stage in his process of inclusion and assimilation. By the end of the novel, he has given up the 'special lens' of American exceptionalism: 'a man was as doomed here as he was in China ... He was not what he made up his mind to be. A man was the sum of his limits; freedom only made him see how much so. America was no America' (*TA* 295–6).

Typical American, then, offers a quite different version of the relationship between business and 'America' than the one offered elsewhere in the texts I have looked at so far. While the novel makes evident the ideological work done by the promise of financial success through business, and the way that this ideological work is carried out in tandem with the discourses of being 'self-made' and of 'positive thinking', what it finally suggests is that this ideology is damaged from its very origins, not just in its present-time manifestation. Remember that for white male literary culture it is the particular mode of post-war business formation – corporate, bureaucratic, multinational – that is disturbing and alienating. Ralph's business is a small store. If even here 'American' business is ruined by unstable foundations, then Jen is asking the reader to what extent Ralph can experience 'inclusion' in 'America' by way of the model of assimilation he follows. This model's ideological underpinnings, while they may seem – from China, and during Ralph's rise to United States citizenship – to offer hope and opportunity, are in fact the same national and 'American' underpinnings that have been responsible for Asian 'exclusion'. It is experiences such as Ralph's, then, that ruin the expectation of 'America' and that also prevent its ideological recovery.

CHANG-RAE LEE, *NATIVE SPEAKER* (1995)

If this situation is complex enough for a first-generation Asian immigrant like Ralph Chang, for a second-generation Asian American like Henry Park, the narrator of Chang-rae Lee's *Native Speaker*, the pitfalls of identity formation are even more problematic. While Henry's citizenship is never in question – Henry is automatically a national citizen – his acculturation positions him uncomfortably between national and diasporic cultures and the confusion that results is one more 'countersite' where 'immigration inclusion' projects an 'American' identity radically different to the one encountered elsewhere in post-war United States literature. While the title of Lee's novel unquestioningly describes Park as a native speaker, the question that remains unresolved is to which nation or continent 'native' refers: the United States or South Korea? 'America' or Asia?

Henry's confusion is dramatised through three key relationships in the novel: with his white, New England, middle-class wife, Lelia; with his immigrant father who moved to the United States from Korea in the 1960s, and with his employer Glimmer & Company, a surveillance firm for whom Henry works as a spy. Tim Engles has argued that Lelia is 'a representative, motivating figure of whiteness'[20] in the novel and that in his relationship with her, Henry 'reveals that he has tended to adopt unwittingly a middle-class white perspective on himself'.[21] However, when the novel opens, Henry is at a point of crisis because Lelia has left him to travel in Europe, pushing into his hand before doing so a list, Henry says, 'of who I was'.[22] Included in this list are uncomfortable references to his ethnic background that highlight the extent not to which Henry has accepted a white perspective on himself, but the extent to which Henry and Lelia's marriage has foundered as a result of their inability to live up to a white model of assimilation. When she uses phrases like 'illegal alien', 'emotional alien', 'Yellow peril', 'neo-American' and 'traitor' and 'spy' (*NS* 5), Lelia is describing Henry's personal faults in terms that are all too easily read as ethnic faults. What follows in the novel are Henry's attempts to flesh out the aphoristic nature of this list and to offer up his identity for examination, not through the mediating whiteness of Lelia, but in order to take account of the complicated web of cultural influences and expectations. Central to this process of examination is Henry's father's business success since moving to the United States – and the national values attached to this success – and Henry's own experience as a spy, particularly when working undercover with John Kwang.

For Henry's father, 'the world ... this very land, his chosen nation – operated on a determined set of procedures, certain rules of engagement' (*NS* 43). Mostly these revolved around money and family and Henry admits that he

> ... thought his life was all about money. He drew energy and pride from his ability to make it almost at will. He was some kind of human annuity. He had no real cleverness or secrets for good business; he simply refused to fail ... Knowing what every native loves to hear, he would have offered the classic immigrant story, casting himself as the heroic newcomer, self-sufficient, resourceful. (*NS* 46)

As Kenneth Millard has pointed out, this immigrant story is one way in which 'the erasure of his true history is the first sacrifice' of Henry's father's 'desire to become American'.[23] But Henry knows that this story is just that, a piece of fiction. He knows that his father was part of a Korean *ggeh* or money club and that the capital needed by local Korean businesses to get themselves economically established came through this club. Henry remembers the other businesses in Manhattan and the meetings and outings the businessmen and their families would go on. Henry's earliest memories, then, recognise the fissures between immigrant rhetoric and reality. Working in his father's store, Henry does not inherit his father's enthusiasm for business either. Rather than showing off his good English to customers, Henry sees that 'if I just kept speaking the language of our work the customers didn't seem to see me. I wasn't there. They didn't look at me. I was a comely shadow who didn't threaten them' (*NS* 49). This act of disappearing in the workplace is one that will become important in Henry's future career, once he has rejected the legacy that his father unfurls before him. Henry also sees that his father, 'like all successful immigrants before him gently and not so gently exploited his own' in business, paying them poor wages and justifying himself by arguing, 'This is way I learn business, this is way they learn business' (*NS* 50).

When business success begins to translate into disposable income, Henry's father, like his other Korean business friends, and like Ralph Chang in *Typical American*, buys a house in the suburbs. At this point,

Henry notices that his 'father and his friends got together less and less ... They all got busier and wealthier and lived farther and farther apart', and instead of maintaining the network established by the *ggeh* they 'joined their own neighbourhood pool and tennis clubs and were making drinking friends with Americans' (*NS* 47). It is in this world that Henry grows up and where he notices that his father 'never felt fully comfortable' (*NS* 48), and where he possesses none of the joy that marked the time when they lived in Queens (*NS* 47). It is in this suburban culture that Henry finds himself and his family not only displaced from the Korean community that supported them as new immigrants in the city, but also 'silent partners of the bordering WASPs and Jews, never rubbing them except with a smile, as if nothing could touch us or wreak anger or sadness upon us' (*NS* 48).

It is interesting to note the way that Henry uses 'us' in this section. Here the reader is given an insight into what it is that Henry inherits from his father even if he sees through the possibility of business as a means of establishing his identity as a Korean American. From his liminal position as an 'American' always marked by his Asian ancestry, Henry attempts to cope with what Millard describes as 'a fearful absence, a central inability to articulate a subjectivity which he feels is his own',[24] by becoming the 'amiable ... personable' character who possesses what he does as a 'result of a talent I have for making you feel good about yourself when you are with me' (*NS* 6). This other-directedness is part of a strategy of self-concealment, and what Henry also inherits from his father to bolster this concealment is a lack of emotional display. After his mother dies, Henry and his father eat dinner in restaurants instead of cooking: 'I remember how I sat with him in those restaurants, both of us eating without savor, unjoyous, and my wanting to show him that I could easily be as steely as he, my chin as rigid and unquivering as any of his displays, that I would tolerate no mysteries either, no shadowy wounds or scars of the heart' (*NS* 54).

All of this is excellent preparation for becoming a spy, 'the perfect vocation', Henry says, 'for the person I was, someone who could reside in his one place and take half-steps out whenever he wished. ... I found a sanction from our work, for I thought I had finally found my truest place in the culture' (*NS* 118). An outsider because of his ethnicity, Henry uses this status to be an observer of 'American' culture. Indeed, the business for which Henry works does not require its employees to be the sort of spies who are also patriots. Working for 'multinational corporations, bureaus of foreign governments, individuals of resource and connection', Glimmer & Company 'deal in people' (NS 16) in a recognisably transnational climate. Which people one deals with is determined by ethnicity: 'Each of us engaged our own kind, more or less. Foreign workers, immigrants, first-generationals, neo-Americans. I worked with Koreans, Pete with Japanese' (NS 16).

The problem for Henry, however, is that his work is 'entirely personal' (NS 6), requiring that he take on roles which are mapped out in detailed stories (or 'legends') of who he is meant to be and which he must successfully memorise in order to embark upon 'intricate and open-ended conspiracies' (NS 16). By playing these Asian roles, though, Henry starts to have revealed to him the grounds of his own confused Asian-American identity that thus far he has been able to keep at arm's length through the emotional detachment he inherits from his father. In one assignment with a Filipino psychoanalyst, Dr Luzan, Henry finds himself 'inexplicably ... stringing the legend back upon myself ... freely talking about my life, suddenly breaching the confidences of my father and my mother and my wife' (NS 20). Such encounters suggest the instability of the coping strategy Henry has devised. 'I had always thought that I could be anyone, perhaps several anyones at once', Henry says (NS 118), but his experience with Luzan suggests otherwise.

Similarly, Henry's main assignment during the course of the novel raises questions not just about Henry's ethnic identity but about contemporary ethnic identities in the United States more generally. Sent to spy on John Kwang, a Korean mayoral candidate for New York, Henry becomes increasingly close to him. Working on the campaign team Henry impersonates Kwang when the team choreograph his movements on the streets (NS 85). Later, Henry talks about the 'ready connections' he has to him: 'We were of different stripes, like any two people, though taken together you might say that one was an outlying version of the other ... I don't exactly know what he saw in me. Maybe a someone we Koreans were becoming, the latest brand of an American. That I was from the future' (NS 129). And when Henry visits the parents of Eduardo, a fellow campaign worker killed by a bomb attack on Kwang's headquarters, Eduardo's father mistakes him for Kwang himself (NS 241). Henry is once again, not just in these moments, but in his growing admiration and support for Kwang and for his politics, allowing the boundary between his work and non-work identities to become confused. What Henry finds appealing about Kwang is precisely his political attempts to overcome the simple oppositions of 'American' and ethnic 'American'; the oppositions Glimmer & Company rely upon for allocating work assignments. Kwang sets himself the task of forging a post-ethnic politics that goes beyond simple ethnic politics and appeals not just to Koreans but to

> ... Indians, Vietnamese, Haitians, Colombians, Nigerians, these brown and yellow whatevers, whoevers, countless unheard nobodies, each offering to the marketplace their gross of kimchee, lichee, plantain, black bean, soy milk, coconut milk, ginger, grouper, ahi, yello curry, cuchifrito, jalpeño, their everything, selling anything to each other and to themselves, every day of the year, and every minute. (*NS* 77)

It is through this kind of political agenda, according to Henry, where Kwang can 'think of America as a part of him, maybe even his, and this for me was the crucial leap of his character, deep flaw, or not, the leap of his identity no one in our work would find valuable but me' (*NS* 196). To gather political support, Kwang organises a *ggeh* of his own, one whose network crosses ethnic boundaries. It is the breaking of ethnic divisions – through business and the marketplace in this instance – without making race or ethnicity disappear (by drawing, that is, on traditional ethnic forms of engagement) that separates Kwang and Henry from a discourse of 'America' that has at its core the myth of the melting pot. Were this not the case then political opposition to Kwang's campaign would not be necessary. Instead, there is another spy under cover in the campaign team and Kwang has him shot when he finds out. As Kwang's campaign collapses, news about the *ggeh* becomes public. It is the state, in the form of the Immigration and Naturalization Service who has also been spying on Kwang (*NS* 305).

The defeat of this post-ethnic political possibility at the hands of the nation-state makes Henry more cynical about the hope of overcoming the opposition between Asian and American; of what David Palumbo-Liu has written about as that schizophrenic identity produced in the transnational climate where 'discontinuous "assimilation" ... puts into crisis the notion of nationhood and citizenship' and where there is a 'fundamental splitting apart of social and political subjectivity'.[25] Henry suggests that 'what I have done with my life is the darkest version' of what his father only dreamed of: 'to enter a place and tender the native language with body and tongue and have no one turn and point to the door' (*NS* 310). And yet still it is not enough. Henry may protest that he is 'as American as anyone', but he now knows that he 'can never stop considering the pitch and drift of … forlorn boats on the sea, the movements that must be endless, promising nothing to their numbers within, headlong voyages scaled in a lyric of search' (*NS* 310–11).

It is through working as a spy, then, work for which his Korean parentage, upbringing and background has fitted him, that Henry approaches 'America' in *Native Speaker*. What he finds is a terrain of ethnic and racial difference where his own identity is constantly buffeted on the one hand by the demands and expectations of a nation incapable of imagining what it might be like to think of race in other than denominational terms, and, on the other, by an immigrant assimilationist logic that Henry picks up from his father and which produces what Henry describes as an 'always honourable-seeming absence' that may be 'my assimilation … the long-sought sweetness' (*NS* 188). While there is what might be considered as guarded optimism at the end of the book – as Henry and Lelia are reunited and Henry helps Lelia in her job as a language teacher – this does little, however, to override the sense of pessimism produced by the death of Mitt, Henry and Lelia's son. In Mitt there is a character who might signal towards a post-ethnic future. According to Henry, 'he could mimic the finest gradations in our English and Korean' and 'imagine, if ever briefly, that this was our truest world, rich with disparate melodies' (*NS* 223). This promise, however, is starkly dismantled not only by the childish horseplay which kills him, but by Lelia's acute remark that 'Maybe the world wasn't ready for him' (*NS* 120).

6
Queer Profits and Losses

If the intellectual challenges inspired by the turns to gender, race and ethnicity during and after the 1970s have so occupied the American Studies community that the field itself has changed substantially as a result, then it is hard to attribute similar effects to a renewed critical attention to sexuality. While literary and cultural critics from outside of American Studies – Eve Kosofsky Sedgwick, Judith Butler, Jonathan Dollimore, Leo Bersani and Lee Edelman – have taken up Michel Foucault's legacy and helped forge potent queer theoretical discourses, all too often these remain ignored or diluted in books and collections aimed at the American Studies community.[1]

Bryce Traister has identified one particularly damaging way in which gay/lesbian/queer studies has been watered down in the American Studies field in the form of the new masculinity studies which, he argues, has seen 'a restoration of the representations of men – produced by men and analyzed for the most part by men – to the center of academic cultural criticism'.[2] While such masculinity studies have emphasised the constructed and contingent nature of an American male identity perpetually in crisis, they have also, according to Traister, appropriated the critical discourses from which these ideas derive not to 'produce anti-foundational and alterable accounts of gendered identity', but 'a picture of American hetero-masculinity that is surprisingly unchanging and fixed'.[3] At the same time, such studies overlook women and feminist texts and marginalise the ways in which women are oppressed by men. In terms of sexuality, where Sedgwick insisted on a 'continuum between homosocial and homosexual – a continuum whose visibility, for men, *in our society*, is radically disrupted' (my emphasis),[4] it should also be added that new masculinity studies often rely upon a notion that this radical disruption is true for *all* American societies at *all* moments and thus ignore the possibility of alternative formations of sexualised identities.

The way that Traister emphasises the 'American' dimension to the rise of this new field of study should alert us to a national investment in masculinity. This link – and more specifically the link between heterosexual masculinity and nation – dominated Cold War rhetoric about male homosexuality. Taking the case of Walter Jenkins, Lyndon Johnson's chief of staff, who was arrested in 1964 and charged with performing 'indecent acts' with a Hungarian-born man in a public toilet, Lee Edelman demonstrates how the demonising of homosexuality after the war relied upon the promotion of an idea of gay male sexuality as an 'alien presence' that was unnatural precisely because it was un-American and resulted 'from the entanglement with Foreign Countries – and foreign nationals – during the war'.[5] Homosexuality was national treachery almost by definition. For Alan Sinfield, Cold War psychological attempts to justify the nuclear family and condemn homosexuality as dysfunctional, made it 'only a small step to the thought that anyone who did not fit in was implicitly queer'.[6] This dysfunctionality exercised official discourses because the nation needed to be as sound as possible to defend itself against the threat of communism. Popular Freudian psychoanalysis and, following in the wake of the Kinsey Report, notions of homosexual latency also worked to interrogate the script of male sexuality and produce a situation whereby homosexuality was un-American because it threatened the values of the manly man.

Such homophobic discourses meshed quite easily with the kinds of anti-corporate rhetoric of those writers I looked at in the first part of this book. The clearest example of this is Sloan Wilson's depiction of Ralph Hopkins in *The Man in the Gray Flannel Suit*. Hopkins is quite clearly situated within a discourse of Cold War latency that does more than just suggest his homosexuality. There is his marriage of convenience, the rumours about him being queer that are planted early on in the novel,[7] his description as the son of an 'ineffectual man' and a strong mother, and the sessions of psychoanalysis that lead him to believe the analyst's diagnosis that he has a guilt complex inspired by a fear of homosexuality.[8] Wilson thus constructs his questioning of the corporation's national loyalty by establishing that at the very top of the corporation is a man who, in Cold War terms, was deemed to be un-American. For Wilson and for other male writers during this period, it was increasingly difficult to imagine the corporation in heterosexual and masculine terms since the offices housing corporations were feminised by the influx of women during the Second World War and their remaining in their jobs once the war finished.

The literary repetition of this formula whereby male heterosexuality is incompatible with both corporate and national identity means that sexuality lies at the very heart of this book. But while the regulatory grid of Cold War homophobia clearly shapes the way that sexualities were experienced during this period, there are other narratives of post-war sexuality which need to be considered. As Robert Corber points out, while homosexuality during the Cold War may have been 'understood as a form of psychopathology that undermined the nation's defenses against Communism', the politicisation of homosexuality by discourses of national security during this period also meant that homosexual subjectivities were politicised with important consequences:

> Many gay male writers treated homosexuality as a subversive form of identity that had the potential to disrupt the system of representation underpinning the Cold War consensus. Their explicit treatment of gay male experience contributed to the dismantling of the signifying practices that naturalized the production of gender and sexual identity in the postwar period.[9]

Corber situates this development alongside, but separates it from, the gay and lesbian civil rights movements that became increasingly visible during the 1950s and '60s. What distinguishes the kind of response in which Corber is interested is the way it relies not upon an identarian model of homosexuality – a minority group whose problems could be solved by assimilation into the liberal polity – but that looked ahead instead to 'the end of "the homosexual" as a category of individual'.[10]

Here Corber is clearly drawing upon queer theoretical discourses whose intention has been – like the activist group Queer Nation – to, as Joseph Bristow puts it, 'expand the vocabulary used to name and know styles of sexuality'.[11] The intention here is to move beyond a restrictive identity politics in order to register the impact of different forms of sexual behaviour and lifestyle that question or undermine a heteronormative grid too reliant on the simple opposition of terms like male/female, man/woman, masculine/feminine and heterosexual/homosexual. Because of the ways in which treatments of business and the workplace have been integral to fashioning not only a sense of nation but also a sexualised sense of nation, what I want to turn to in this chapter are ways in which writers have conceptualised business and work as locations through and against which sexual identities may be undermined and questioned. If corporate business and work was so antipathetic to straight white male culture, what opportunity has it offered for Corber's 'dismantling of the signifying practices that naturalized the production of gender and sexual identity'?

CARSON McCULLERS, *THE BALLAD OF THE SAD CAFÉ* (1951)

All too often, critical attention to the fiction of Carson McCullers has only managed to erase the complexities of sexuality at the very moment of invoking sexuality as a theme in her work. In one of the most recent considerations of *The Ballad of the Sad Café*, for instance, McCullers's short novel, first published along with a collection of short stories in 1951, is treated as a synecdoche of the author's whole body of work because it conveys the 'perception that unspeakable isolation is the fundamental human condition'.[12] Steering a course towards this conclusion via Freudian and Lacanian psychoanalysis, the terms masculine and feminine are addressed, as is the fact that they often fail in this story to equate with male and female. But in seeking to identify the fight between Miss Amelia and Marvin Macy as a 'reenactment of the primal scene',[13] McCullers's representations of gender and sexuality are quickly regulated by the critic so that they conform to a heterosexual matrix of male/female: 'There can be only one outcome. Both McCullers's subtext and the psychoanalytic narrative propose that all love is in some way an attempt to reenact the first love, and this mother–child relationship must give way to the law. The imaginary must give way to the symbolic; the mother must give way to the father.'[14]

Such critical interpretations repeat the very real way in which non-heterosexual opportunities have not only been closed off for many American citizens in the post-war period but also violently policed. But one only needs to consider how often McCullers uses the word 'queer' in *The Ballad of the Sad Café* to recognise that this is a novel whose regime of representation offers a much more fluid account of sexual subjectivities. Gregory Woods has suggested that the word queer 'is the lexical bridge between late nineteenth-century decadents' reverence for the *strange* and the mid-twentieth century epithet for all that is homosexual, used as both insult and self-affirmation'.[15] Taking up the importance of this term in McCullers's work, Rachel Adams suggests that 'queer refers loosely to acts and desires that cannot be described as heterosexual'[16] and that McCullers uses the word queer 'to pose persistently messy obstacles to any systematic codification of behaviour or desire'.[17] This is all very different from the 'one outcome' suggested by universalising psychoanalytical approaches and allows a different novella to emerge.

Business is central to the very existence of the town in which McCullers sets *The Ballad of the Sad Café*. A factory town where work is dominated by a cotton-mill, it is against this bleak backdrop that we first see Miss Amelia whose face is described as 'sexless and white'.[18] 'Sexless' here can have at least two, not unrelated, connotations, of course: one who does not engage in sexual contact, but also one who does not have ascribed to them a biological male or female sex. What the novella provides for the reader can be seen as an account of how Amelia ends up in this 'sexless' position, living in the boarded-up house that once accommodated two different types of business: a store and a café. The location of Amelia's 'sexless' body is also, then, the location of businesses that Amelia has run profitably and successfully at one time but which have altered in nature and profitability in line with Amelia's desirous relationships with the hunchback Lymon Willis and her 'strange and dangerous … queer marriage' (*TBOTSC* 9) to Marvin Macy.

Codified in explicitly masculine terms – 'She was a dark, tall woman with bones and muscles like a man. Her hair was cut short and brushed back from the forehead, and there was about her sunburned face a tense, haggard quality' (*TBOTSC* 8) – the world of business seems to offer Amelia the opportunity to be a 'man' of trade and opens up a way for her to deal not in personal relationships but in objects. Ill at ease with people, 'With all things which could be made by the hands Miss Amelia prospered' (*TBOTSC* 9). With her store, an alcohol still in the swamp, and her medical skills, Amelia is 'the richest woman for miles around' (*TBOTSC* 9), although the only gap in her skills as a physician are exposed by those patients who 'came with a female complaint' and for whom 'she could do nothing' (*TBOTSC* 23). Amelia, then, a six-foot-two-inch woman who cannot help with female complaints and looks like a man while also occupying a patriarchal position in business, after being 'raised motherless by her father' (*TBOTSC* 20) is a blur of mixed gender and sex attributes. McCullers clearly emphasises this blurring of Amelia's body and character by falling back on words like 'queer' (*TBOTSC* 9, 20) and 'contrary' (*TBOTSC* 20) with which to describe her, but the real treatments of Amelia's character are to be found at those times when she loses or forgets her uneasiness with people and forges relationships, however temporary and fragile.

The arrival of Lymon Willis in town claiming to be Amelia's distant relative is one such instance. Unmoved by his telling of his story, Amelia listens in silence to the four-foot hunchback with 'crooked little legs ... great warped chest and the hump that sat on his shoulders' (*TBOTSC* 11) until he begins to cry. Accused of being a 'regular Morris Finestein' – a label used by town inhabitants 'if a man were prissy in any way, or if a man ever wept' (*TBOTSC* 14) – Amelia goes over to him, touches his hump and then offers him a free drink. Such an act of generosity is unknown to the onlookers: 'Miss Amelia could seldom be persuaded to sell her liquor on credit, and for her to give so much as a drop away free was almost unknown' (*TBOTSC* 14). The way in which Amelia's homemade liquor is described thereafter gives some sense of how this gesture to Lymon can be read. What is stressed is the liquor's transformative capacity. Possessing 'a special quality of its own', the liquor causes 'Things that have gone unnoticed, thoughts that have been harboured far back in the dark mind' to be 'suddenly recognized and comprehended' (*TBOTSC* 15). This moment, when Amelia touches Lymon's hump and gives him free liquor, signals the beginning of the process which will see Amelia's store transformed into a café. It also sees the beginning of Amelia and Lymon's relationship which will transform Amelia from the solitary person she has been up until this point into Lymon's partner.

There is clearly something in Lymon's freakishness and his effeminacy, then, that prompts Amelia to suspend her normal business procedures. Given what I have already written about the queerness and contrariness of McCullers's description of Amelia, it is worth going back to Rachel Adams at this point because she suggests that 'freaks ... are beings who make all kinds of queer tendencies visible on the body's surfaces'.[19] Amelia's touching of Lymon's hump would indicate that it is this physical attribute which is central to her acceptance of him and that she feels in it a freakishness which she knows herself: she is cross-eyed as well as exceptionally tall. If, as Adams suggests, 'the deviant body is both the cause of anguish and self-loathing' but also 'the inspiration for her [McCullers's] characters' struggles to imagine other possibilities' of queer sex and gender configuration, then what can be seen in the forging of a partnership between freakish butch Amelia and freakish femme Lymon is one version of these 'other possibilities'.

What is important to note in this shift is the way that Amelia's identity, which is shaped by, and in turn shapes, her business priorities, feeds back to affect the nature of her business. Business and identity are engaged in a mutually dependent relationship, whereas one of the things that was immediately noticeable in the first part of this book was the way in which white male writers, while alert to the negative effects of business upon them, steadfastly resisted – with the exception of Douglas Coupland in *Microserfs* – the possibility of business or work-oriented reinvention and turned instead to recovery narratives of 'America'. McCullers's story of a small southern town steadfastly resists this temptation.

The transformation of Amelia's store into café also facilitates a new atmosphere of pleasure to which the townsfolk are unused. The café implies qualities of 'fellowship, the satisfactions of the belly, and a certain gaiety and grace of behaviour' (*TBOTSC* 29). Amelia has about her 'the lonesome look of the lover' (*TBOTSC* 30) and over the next few years as the café is established she becomes less 'quick to cheat her fellow man and to exact cruel payments', and even wears a dress on Sundays (*TBOTSC* 31). It is clear to everyone that Amelia loves Lymon and that this love has affected not only what business she does, but the way that she performs her business too.

What pushes Amelia into her 'sexless' position in the boarded-up building that once housed her store and café is the return to the town of her husband Marvin Macy. Before looking at the erotic triangle that develops between Amelia, Lymon and Marvin, and which destroys the relationship between Amelia and Lymon, it is worth remembering how Amelia's marriage to Marvin has already raised the issue of queer love and business. A rapist who 'degraded and shamed' young girls before deciding that Amelia, the 'solitary gangling queer-eyed girl', was the one he desired (*TBOTSC* 34–5), Marvin might be expected to take part in the 'traffic in women' that Gayle Rubin and later Eve Sedgwick have argued ensures that women pass 'between men' in the institution of marriage.[20] Instead, in Amelia and Marvin's 'queer' marriage, Amelia refuses the position as object of exchange and herself treats the marriage like a business transaction: 'It is said that on the way [from the marriage ceremony] Miss Amelia began to talk about some deal she had worked up with a farmer over a load of kindling wood. In fact, she treated her groom in exactly the same manner she would have used with some customer who had come into the store to buy a pint from her' (*TBOTSC* 38).

On their wedding night, Amelia comes down from the marital bedroom after just half an hour and begins working and puts the present that Marvin has bought her up for sale in the store (*TBOTSC*

39). When the marriage ends shortly afterwards, it is Marvin who signs over all his possessions to Amelia (*TBOTSC* 40).

Amelia assumes the patriarchal position, then, in this failed relationship and all economic value from the marriage flows to her. During her successful non-marital relationship with Lymon, however, she loses this role. Not only does Lymon prompt the change in the nature of her business, but 'queerly enough … it was the hunchback who was most responsible for the great popularity of the café. Things were never so gay as when he was around' (*TBOTSC* 49). In terms laid out by McCullers, Lymon's ability to inspire Amelia's affection turns her into 'lover' and Lymon into her 'beloved', where 'these two come from different countries' (*TBOTSC* 33). Preparing the reader for what will follow, McCullers writes that 'Almost everyone wants to be the lover. And the curt truth is that, in a deep secret way, the state of being beloved is intolerable to many' (*TBOTSC* 34). This alienation at the heart of romance makes Amelia's position unstable once her love object, Lymon, moves from position of 'beloved' to 'lover', which he does when Marvin returns to town. It is Lymon's attachment to Marvin, the way he smiles at him 'with an entreaty that was near to desperation' (*TBOTSC* 59), the way that he always wants to follow him around, that signals that Lymon has found his own 'beloved'.

The performance of, and resolution to, this erotic triangle provides one more example of the way in which McCullers queers gender and sex relations and connects them to business in this novella. The erotic triangles of which Sedgwick writes, where two males codified as men fight for one female codified as a woman, rely upon two structures of sexual oppression – heterosexual marriage and homophobia – in order to maintain patriarchal power and the homosocial male–male relations that stand at its core. McCullers's erotic triangle is both similar and quite different. In one respect it is a triangle of two codified men and one codified woman, but, as I showed earlier, one of the men – Amelia – is not male, and the woman – Lymon – is not female. The tension that structures the triangle thus cannot easily be folded back into a heteronormative grid of desire. The sex–gender disparity of the characters means that heterosexual marriage is not an outcome that will successfully resolve the tension.

This tension between the three characters reaches its climax when Lymon comes to the aid of Marvin, just as he is being beaten in a fight with Amelia. The superhuman leap that sees Lymon defeat Amelia leads to Marvin and Lymon leaving town, although not before attacking Amelia once more, this time in a way which can be read as an attack upon the transformed identity which she created out of the café and its 'beloved' inspiration. Marvin and Lymon 'carved terrible words on the café tables ... poured a gallon of sorghum syrup all over the kitchen floor and smashed the jars of preserves' and they 'completely wrecked the still' (*TBOTSC* 81). By destroying the café business upon which Amelia founded her transformed 'queer' and 'contrary' identity, Marvin and Lymon also damage that identity itself, leaving Amelia 'sexless' – in both senses of the word – in the boarded-up store.

McCullers's story, then, envisages a community where business and economics are closely connected to a sense of gendered and sexed identity, and if it opens up the possibility of queer business and working identities through Amelia's relationship with the freakish Lymon, it also recognises the ways in which such possibilities may be fleeting and foreclosed, or, as Rachel Adams puts it, 'not ... fully realized within a shifting social atmosphere'.[21] But it is just this sense of the shifting nature not only of one's social environment but of one's responses to and position in this environment that makes *The Ballad of the Sad Café* less a fiction of a fixed and unchangeable nature of gender identity, or of a homosexual identity that might form the basis of a politicised gay and lesbian movement, than of that process of acculturation through which queer sexualities both are produced and themselves produce. In a national climate mostly inimical to the fostering of such sexualities, McCullers turns to this localised narrative to register her feelings.

WILLIAM BURROUGHS, *NAKED LUNCH* (1959)

The grandson of the inventor of the Burroughs Adding Machine and founder of the Burroughs Corporation, William Burroughs was born into a business family wealthy enough to fund his writing career and nomadic lifestyle. Whether this puts him in a better position than others to assess the relationship between business and 'American' identity is difficult to say, but Burroughs certainly articulates a vision of the relationship between the nation, the nation-state and homo-sexuality that sees capitalism and its manifestation in 'American' business as an incredibly powerful force in *Naked Lunch* and in his many other novels.

Although not reducible to one phrase, the vast and confusing number of events that fill *Naked Lunch*, may be more manageably collected and condensed by way of one of the book's most telling phrases: the 'algebra of need'. In *Naked Lunch* the desire for commodities in 'American' mass culture is metonymically reduced to the desire for 'junk', or drugs. Junk fulfils the role of perfect business commodity because there is 'no sales talk necessary': 'The client will crawl through a sewer and beg to buy ... The junk merchant does not sell his product to the consumer, he sells the consumer to his product. He does not improve and simplify his merchandise. He degrades and simplifies the client. He pays his staff in junk.'[22]

Merchandise of this kind creates addicts out of its users who are linked in the 'pyramid of junk' where people feed on those below them, and at the bottom of which lies the 'addict in the street' (*NL* 7). This is the position in which William Lee, the narrator for parts of *Naked Lunch*, finds himself, and it is with his escaping arrest that the novel opens. According to the rationale of *Naked Lunch*, however, arrest and rehabilitation is something that will only lead to the collapse of the junk pyramid and this is precisely why, therefore, the United States does not practise such rehabilitation: '*The addict in the street who must have junk to live is the one irreplaceable factor in the junk equation*. When there are no more addicts to buy junk there will be no more junk traffic' (*NL* 9).

In many ways, what Burroughs creates in *Naked Lunch* is a systemic vision of America that is dominated by, and relies upon, the business of junk, with the street addict occupying the lowest level and the state occupying the summit point of control. When he then goes on to write about the 'junk virus' (*NL* 9), he is reiterating the systemic nature of this state of affairs and gesturing to the way in which 'American' experience is driving global experience, since viruses do not respect national borders. In this scenario, junk becomes less an object to be consumed than an agent invading and controlling the bodies of its host, a viral agent that is anthropomorphically represented in the novel by other agents of junk conspiracy, most notably the doctors like Dr Benway, Dr Fingers Schafer, Dr Berger, and the German doctor in the 'Joselito' section (*NL* 48–52). These characters, agents for the political parties of Interzone – the Liquefactionists, the Senders and the Divisionists, all of whom are addicted to control – put into practice the medicalised version of control that impinged not just upon the junk addict but, from the 1930s through into the 1970s, on the male homosexual too. In Burroughs's own account of the novel to Allen Ginsberg, he explains that the junk virus 'only passes from man to man or woman to woman, which is why Benway is turning out homosexuals on assembly-line basis'.[23]

Regulating sexuality is part of Benway's method. Boasting about his ability to modify behaviour and personality, he explains at one point that 'You can make a square heterosex citizen queer ... that is, reinforce and second his rejection of normally latent homosexual trends – at the same time depriving him of cunt and subjecting him to homosex stimulation' (*NL* 35), while Berger displays a 'cured homosexual' in one of his television broadcasts whose face has a look of 'Blank stupidity' and who is led out of the studio 'nodding and smiling' (NL 114). This 'turning out homosexuals' is Burroughs' critique of the manner in which state-funded medicine tried to regulate and 'cure' homosexual behaviour in the post-war period by way of electric shock therapy, psychoanalysis and hormone replacement treatment. But Jamie Russell is alert to the way in which this generalised objection to the state manipulation and regulation of homosexual identity also relied on a working model that Burroughs objected to just as ferociously.

Russell draws attention to the way in which the words 'queer' and 'fag' signify in Burroughs's fiction and correspondence, with 'queer' regularly standing in for the good, masculine homosexual man, while 'fag' is used to denote the bad, effeminate homosexual man that Burroughs hated. Such a hatred of effeminate homosexual men registers, according to Russell, Burroughs' dissatisfaction with the way that the effeminate model of homosexuality was used by the state in order to justify its regulatory practices. So much so that the pre-eminence in the narrative of doctors and psychiatrists means that *Naked Lunch* 'explicitly links schizophrenia with the state's deployment of the effeminate paradigm of homosexuality'.[24] Rather than seeing effeminate homosexuality as a mode of behaviour self-consciously adopted by homosexual men, Burroughs is unable to separate such effeminacy from the state's reliance on such a model. What Burroughs wants to protect or resurrect more than anything else is the idea of an identity that is authentic or original, which for him meant masculine. Unwilling to creatively entangle the gender–sex oppositions of male/man/masculine with female/woman/feminine, in *Naked Lunch*, 'the role of effeminacy ... is transformed into the defining characteristic of the individual who loses, by default, all opportunity of returning to his original masculine state'.[25]

The business of junk and the control of the addict also incorporates, then, the control of sexuality and, most pertinently to Burroughs – who both underwent psychoanalysis and was one of the subjects on whom Kinsey based his study of American sexuality – homosexuality.

But it would seem that it is the issue of control that overrides Burroughs' attention to homosexuality. One of the most famous passages in *Naked Lunch* is Benway's account of 'the man who taught his asshole to talk' (*NL* 110). The fact that it is Benway's story automatically makes the story part of those official and regulatory state-medical discourses on sexuality. But furthermore, the story itself is one of appropriation. While the man initially uses his new-found skill on the stage, eventually the asshole becomes independent, taking over the man's body as the mouth is covered over by what Benway calls 'un-D.T., Undifferentiated Tissue' (*NL* 110). The inversion that has taken place here invites a reading which suggests a link with the kind of gender inversion on which the state-sponsored effeminate model of male homosexuality relies. Russell hints at this when he suggests that 'the fag is the asshole that has learned to talk' and that the Talking Asshole passage demonstrates 'a relinquishing of sovereignty to the "feminine" anus'.[26] But the talking anus also signals such an inversion by way of a logic that links femininity with passivity and the anus as the passive receptor of a vigorous masculine activity and penetration. Burroughs's reliance on this paradigm in order to denigrate effeminate homosexuality is a risky strategy. In the talking asshole passage, mimicry leads to appropriation. Following this example through into a wider cultural domain, Burroughs seems to be suggesting that effeminate homosexual men and their female mimicking style represent a threat to an authentic masculine – queer or otherwise – identity. This then sounds rhetorically very close to the kinds of Cold War homophobia about which Burroughs was so critical. Whereas Russell argues that 'Autonomous control of the self becomes the key to Burroughs' queer project',[27] I would want to suggest that the phrases 'Autonomous control of the self' and 'queer project' stand in uneasy – even oxymoronic – juxtaposition if one understands 'queer' to mean the undermining of a heteronormative grid that is over-reliant on the simple opposition of terms like male/female, man/woman, heterosexual/homosexual and masculine/feminine. Not only that but Burroughs actually repeats the violence of Cold War homophobia by identifying and marking out effeminate queer men and that he does so by way of a paradigm familiar to the writers in first part of this book: American business – here in the guise of the junk pyramid – as that which erases individual male identity and thus betrays the possibility of self-government.

When Burroughs suggests that 'Junk is the mold of monopoly and possession' (*NL* 8), he is quite explicitly linking business and the control of the individual. But by incorporating drugs as the junk product *par excellence*, he is also injecting a discourse of addiction that Timothy Melley argues is similar to 'other postwar discourses of agency' in the way that it 'is governed by a refusal to abandon the assumptions of possessive individualism'.[28] The way in which Burroughs represents characters addicted to junk – as grotesque bodies always on the very physical limits of disintegration into cellular fluids or metamorphosing into insects and other non-human forms – signals the way in which addiction to junk not only makes one self-reliant on others, but the way in which one's body becomes dedicated to the job of finding and ingesting junk. The Catch-22 of addiction is that to gain control over their body, the addict must come off junk, only then to face the withdrawal that takes them into the grotesque world of collapsing bodies and a situation that can only be remedied by junk. Melley points out that this representational logic relies upon a separation of self and body such that 'control is a property, parceled out *either* to oneself or to one's environment but never a mixture of the two'.[29] From what I have said above it is clear that Burroughs believes such control should reside entirely in one's own hands.

If Gregory Woods is right and Burroughs was 'a Western writer all along',[30] then it may be that what makes him so is not the way he eroticises relationships of difference or sexual possibility that occur on frontiers, but the way that he deploys a rhetoric of masculine individuality which, while it has inspired both hetero- and homoerotic depictions of frontier life, produces very different effects depending on how it positions sexuality in relation to gender codifications. Burroughs's hatred of effeminate men and the thoroughgoing way in which he utilises the archetype of masculine individuality in *Naked Lunch*, at the level of his discursive strategy if not at the level of character, and at the expense of differently gendered modes of queer subjectivity and lifestyle, is testament to the damaging legacy such dreams of the West have bequeathed. As with William Gibson's reinvention of the cowboy on a new technological frontier in *Neuromancer*, so it is that Burroughs's frontier reinscribes a national rhetoric rather than questions it.

ARMISTEAD MAUPIN, *TALES OF THE CITY* (1978), *MORE TALES OF THE CITY* (1980), *FURTHER TALES OF THE CITY* (1982)

The systemic vision of Burroughs' *Naked Lunch* is far removed from the vision presented in the *Tales of the City* dramas produced by

Armistead Maupin over the course of six novels between 1978 and 1990. Collectively, these novels amount to a city saga that, while recognising the place of San Francisco in a national culture – as a city, that is, whose difference from other locations attracts people from outside California – also patiently reports the local qualities of life in the city. The publication history of the series almost demanded such attention to local detail. Originally serialised in the *San Francisco Chronicle* starting in 1976, the stories were written for an audience familiar with Barbary Lane, Montgomery Street, the Castro, and Haight Ashbury and who would also recognise the bars and clubs as well as the business and socialite figures Maupin incorporated into his stories. Not that this local dimension stopped the national and international success of Maupin's tales of personal and sexual excitement, disappointment and development.

While business and work may not appear central to the ebbs and flows of these personal experiences, they do constitute an important element in the novels for two reasons. First, they help produce the local texture of the stories. The first novel in the series, *Tales of the City*, opens with Mary Ann Singleton leaving her job as a secretary in Cleveland, Ohio. When she calls home, her mother, in an effort to make her return to Cleveland, tells her 'the office is just falling apart with you gone. They don't get many good secretaries at Lassiter Fertilizers.'[31] Reminders like this of the parochial nature of her former life only make Mary Ann even more determined to stay and find a life for herself in the decidedly un-parochial San Francisco and, after finding a room in Anna Madrigal's house, the first thing Mary Ann does is sign up with an employment agency so that she can afford to stay. In the later novels, particularly *Further Tales of the City* and *Sure of You*, Mary Ann's burgeoning television career and the problems it creates for her relationship with Brian becomes one of the central plot elements. As well as utilising work in this way, Maupin uses business and work to establish class and status hierarchies amongst his array of characters. While Beauchamp Day, Edgar Halcyon, Edgar's daughter DeDe and his wife Frannie, are all connected at various points to the more central characters who live at 28 Barbary Lane – Michael Tolliver, Mary Ann, Anna Madrigal, Brian Hawkins and Mona Ramsey – they live in a world of business and money unknown to these latter characters, who instead struggle to establish their careers in the early books of the series. Brian is a lawyer turned waiter, Michael does very little until he starts his 'Green-collar Gay' job at a garden nursery, Mona gets fired from Edgar Halcyon's ad agency, and Anna Madrigal seems to live off her room rentals.

The second and perhaps more important way in which Maupin uses the themes of business and work is to make a link between the world of consumption in which these characters live and work and the issue of sexuality. When Mary Ann turns up for her first job interview at an office supply company, she is met by Earl Creech whose innuendoes about taking working trips – 'If you're not ... you know ... uptight' – Mary Ann does not know how to deal with. When she tells him she *is* uptight, he sends her on her way (*TOTC* 25). She learns from her mistake on her next try, however. Mona gets her an interview for a job at Halcyon Communications and Mary Ann puts on a confident display which is anything but uptight:

> 'You're not planning to run back to Cleveland, are you?'
> 'Sir?'
> 'You're staying put?'
> 'Yes, sir. I love San Francisco.'
> 'They all say that.'
> 'In my case, it happens to be the truth.'
> Halcyon's huge white eyebrows leaped. 'Are you that sassy with your parents, young lady?'
> Mary Ann deadpanned. 'Why do you think I can't go back to Cleveland?'
> It was risky, but it worked. (*TOTC* 27–8)

Mary Ann learns quickly that she needs to display the right attitude. She has moved into a culture where identity – including sexual identity – has become part of the more general cultural process of consumption and commodification. It is no coincidence that Halcyon Communications is an advertising agency. One of Mona's most pressing projects is a campaign for pantyhose. Responding to the link she identifies between consumption and identity, her approach is to emphasise the sexiness of the garment and its lifestyle qualities for women. She tells the client that the 'youth image is important ... The cotton crotch is young, vibrant, hip. The cotton crotch is for with-it women on the go' (*TOTC* 82). When she shows the client what sort of campaign she has in mind she reveals on her storyboard 'a young woman with a Dorothy Hamill haircut hanging off the side of a cable car. The copy read: "Under my clothes, I like to feel Adorable"' (*TOTC* 82–3). Unfortunately for Mona, the client is more interested in the hygienic qualities of the crotch and she is fired for objecting.

Writing about the 1990s, Dennis Allen has suggested that 'identity categories must now be understood not as the inevitable outcome of individual (sexual) desire but rather as the insertion of that desire into a differentiated structure of social signs that defines identities through consumption'.[32] But it would seem that such a structure whereby sexuality is commodified in order that it may be consumed is evident to Michael too in San Francisco during the 1970s. 'There's a nasty epidemic of heterosexuality afoot', he tells Mona at one point. 'I know lots of gay guys who're sneaking off to the Sutro Baths to get it on with women ... everything gets old after a while' (TOTC 78). Sexual experience it seems is selected more like pantyhose than it is determined by some identarian logic. Maupin clearly plays on the confusion this can lead to for comedic effect – such as when Brian goes to the baths to pick up women but chooses one who wants him only if he admits to being gay – but he also alertly dramatises that process whereby the gay scene and gay districts of San Francisco themselves start to become commodified to the extent that they bring in tourists. Michael tells Mona about a lunchtime visit to Hamburger Mary's:

> There I was ... eating a bean sprout salad and wondering if my new Sear work boots looked *too* new, when this couple waltzed in and took a seat in the middle of a heavy biker contingent ... A guy and his wife, slumming. Radical chic, vintage 1976. She was wearing a David Bowie T-shirt to show where her sympathies lay, and he was looking *grossly* uncomfortable in a Grodins sports ensemble. I mean, five years ago you could have caught these turkeys down in the Filmore, chowing down on chitlins and black-eyed peas with the Brothers and Sisters. Now they're into faggots. They want *desperately* to relate to perverts. (TOTC 108)

If the commodification and consumption of sexuality in this contemporary period highlight the way in which business and work feed back to affect desire, it may even be the case that business and work have played a central role in the determination of sexual identity going all the way back to the nineteenth century. John D'Emilio has argued that the development of gay and lesbian urban subcultures – primitive versions of what San Francisco has become since the Second World War – was a result of the free labour market of United States capitalism which not only 'allowed individuals to survive beyond the confines of the family'[33] but also enabled 'some men and women to organize a personal life around their erotic/emotional attraction to their own sex'.[34] The opportunity to find work away from one's home and family, as many of the characters do in the *Tales of the City* series, testifies to the continued importance of just such a process. Michael's letters to his mother and father and Mary Ann's telephone calls to her parents register this idea that sexed and gendered identities are often re-formed in new locations.

This is not always a comfortable experience, however. Mary Ann, as much as she likes San Francisco, is also partly alienated by the very emphasis upon identity-as-consumption that she finds there. She makes her mind up that she will return to Cleveland, complaining to Michael that 'there's no stability here. Everything's too easy. Nobody sticks with anybody or anything, because there's always just a little bit better waiting around the corner ... I want to live somewhere where you don't have to apologize for serving instant coffee ... People in Cleveland aren't "into" anything' (*TOTC* 112). Just in time, her mother calls, and luckily for Mary Ann it is Michael who answers. As her mother pesters her about strange men answering the phone, Mary Ann hears all the reasons she wanted to leave Cleveland in the first place and blurts out, 'Mom, Michael is a homosexual ... He likes *boys*, got it? I know you've heard of it. They've got it on TV now' (*TOTC* 113).

Television, the ultimate space of consumption, now even does homosexuality and, at the beginning of *Further Tales of the City*, the reader finds Mary Ann presenting her own show in the world of consumption that once nearly drove her away from San Francisco. But it is Michael's career change which is perhaps more compelling and provides an insight into the way that sexual identity and business and work are important to one another. Michael finds that 'the fruits of his labors' as manager at God's Green Earth nursery are 'aesthetic, spiritual, physical and even sexual', and not just because 'a number of men in the city found nothing quite so erotic as the sight of someone's first name stitched crudely across the front of a pair of faded green overalls'.[35] While the construction of homosexuality as 'unnatural' in homophobic discourses has in part led to attempts to recover male–male sexual contact in natural settings, both in the United States and elsewhere, Michael's work allows him to connect to a world of nature in a way that has been central to gay reimaginings specifically of the 'American' West. While Burroughs conceptualises the West as that place where masculinity may be free from women and the feminine, for other writers what has been important about the West and the frontier is that, like the industrial city and like San Francisco, it is a space where one can be free from the institution of the heterosexual family. As Gregory Woods points out, the figure of the cowboy 'occupies a crucial position in American gay culture, in terms of both styles and ideals'.[36]

Accordingly, Michael combines his green-collar gay career with trips to Devil's Herd, San Francisco's most popular gay country-and-western bar, where he remarks ironically that what he 'liked most about the saloon was its authenticity: the twangy down-home band … the horse collars dangling from the ceiling, the folksy Annie Oakley dykes shouting "yahoo" from the bar' (*FTOTC* 30). As a member of the San Francisco Gay Men's Chorus he also goes off for weekends 'to the wilds of Northern California' where 'the western motif was in evidence everywhere' (*FTOTC* 37). And then there is a trip to the National Gay Rodeo in Reno where Michael is disappointed to find very few real cowboys and only signs of 'clone encroachment' (*FTOTC* 152). While Michael himself cultivates his masculine physical image, the West to which he feels drawn is not one which excludes women or the feminine. Returning from the chorus trip, Michael and his boss Ned, along with six of their friends, spot a just-married couple. While the bridegroom recognises what kind of men they are and mouths 'fags', the bride tells them her and her husband's song. As the gay chorus begins singing, Maupin writes that 'The Andrews sisters were never lovelier' (*FTOTC* 39). All the way through Maupin's series, Michael is also closely attached to both Mona Ramsey and Mary Ann, providing support for and seeking support from, them both.

What is so noticeably different about the queer landscape of Maupin's stories and Burroughs's dystopian vision in *Naked Lunch*, is the way that Maupin reclaims the discourse of 'family' and, rather than concentrating on systems of oppression, fashions a space between oppressions in which his ensemble of mixed gender and sexuality characters can cope in the world. At the head of this 'makeshift family'[37] stands Anna Madrigal, beneficent landlady, who 'would counsel them, scold them and listen unflinchingly to their tales of amatory disaster' and who was 'the true mother of them all' (*MTOTC* 9). Using the word 'true' here, Maupin is making a distinction between biological and non-biological parenting in a way that suggests Anna's non-biological mothering has become more important to the members of her family. Since, in the later books in the series, the previous tenants of 28 Barbary Lane seem to stay in contact with her more regularly than their biological parents this would appear to be the case. But Maupin is also drawing attention to the fact that being a mother is not restricted to biological females. When the reader discovers Anna Madrigal is a chosen name, and that it has been chosen because it is an anagram of 'A GIRL AND A MAN' and that Anna is a male-to-female transsexual, then the heteronormative grid aligning biological sex, gender attribution and sexual classification looks increasingly inappropriate to the family of which Anna Madrigal is matriarch.

Maupin's stories, then, can be seen to write an anti-national narrative in which work becomes one more way in which characters negotiate their contact with the oppressive discourses of business, work and sexuality in their contemporary commodified variants. It is testament to the skill of Maupin's writing that while unsettling the sex/gender grid of heteronormativity, he does so without denying the importance of identification with sexual subcultures. Michael, for all he notices the slippages of identity that occur as sexuality becomes commodified, remains staunchly defensive of his identity as a gay man. He is, he tells his lover Jon, a 'perfect Kinsey six' (*TOTC* 102) and remains so to the end of the series.

LESLIE FEINBERG, *STONE BUTCH BLUES* (1993)

It is on the complex boundaries of the heteronormative grid of gender and sexuality that Jess Goldberg finds herself in Leslie Feinberg's semi-autobiographical novel, *Stone Butch Blues*. Growing up, Jess recognises that she 'didn't look like any of the girls or women … in the Sears catalog'[38] and has to face constant taunts and questions about whether she is a boy or a girl. Biologically female but resolutely unfeminine, Jess is subjected to the normalising demands of her parents who not only take her to hospital to undergo medical tests but also send her to charm school in a final effort to resolve what they consider to be the discrepancy between biological sex and Jess's gender attributes. For Jess, however, 'Charm school finally taught me once and for all that I wasn't pretty, wasn't feminine, and would never be graceful' (*SBB* 23).

These attempts to resolve what is perceived as the misalignment of Jess's sex and gender represent a normalising ideological force that tries to work through conditioning. But at high school, Jess is subjected to the violent corollary of such a process when she is gang-raped by members of the football team. The supposed damage that her masculine appearance does to the idea of being a woman and to the heterosexual males who consider themselves the rightful owners of masculinity, is 'corrected' by them putting her in that subordinated position where male and masculine identity might be reunited and the gap that Jess opens up forcefully closed down.

What Feinberg demonstrates in these early parts of her novel is how the environments of the heterosexual family and the school prove inimical to Jess's development. What Feinberg then goes on to articulate, however, is the way in which it is the world of work, in addition to the transgender bar scene, that goes some way towards providing environments that might offer more viable alternatives. 'When I was fifteen years old', Jess says, 'I got an after-school job. That changed everything' (SBB 25). The job as a typesetter introduces her to an entirely different world of adult work where she finds tolerances to which so far she has not had access. From one of her co-workers, Gloria, she discovers the existence of cross-dressing bars, and when she first visits Tifka's she sees a world that 'released tears I'd held back for many years: strong, burly women, wearing ties and suit coats ... They were the handsomest women I'd ever seen. Some of them were wrapped in slow motion dances with women in tight dresses and high heels who touched them tenderly. Just watching made me ache with need' (SBB 27–8).

In order to save enough money to move out of her parents' house, Jess then starts 'Working like crazy' (SBB 39). It is Jess's labour and the independence beyond the family that work brings, that allows her to not only access but also to become a full-time member of this 'he-she' subculture. And it is the nature of the factory jobs Jess takes that also allow her to work alongside other butches: 'It was heaven', she says of working alongside nine butches at a bindery (SBB 81).

In Feinberg's novel, then, doing the kind of factory work that is predominantly reserved for men enables Jess to consolidate a butch identity. Rather than the systems of business within which these factories operate, it is the conditions as Jess and her fellow butches experience them that are of central concern. Here the whole process of unionisation becomes important for facilitating and maintaining circumstances that allow butches to stay in the workplace. Jess knows that it is better to work in a unionised environment, such as in the steel or automotive industries: 'The strength of the unions in those heavy industries had won liveable wages and decent benefits' she says (SBB 75). But it is not just about wages. Being a butch in a predominantly male working environment still means one is exposed to the kinds of violent intolerances that Jess has suffered elsewhere. However, with 'union protection, all the butches agreed, a he-she could carve out a niche, and begin earning valuable seniority' (SBB 75). So while it may be 'heaven' in the bindery, Jess soon finds that without a union she is unable to break through the discriminatory wage structure that has kept men and women – however butch – on different grades and stopped them achieving the seniority which would secure a butch identity in the workplace. When a steel plant advertises for women workers, Jess is eager to leave her bindery job and she explains herself to one of her fellow workers in terms that make explicit the connection between work and her 'he-she' identity: 'All we got is the clothes we wear, the bikes we ride, and where we work, you know? You can ride a Honda and work in a bindery or you can ride a Harley and work at the steel plant' (SBB 100). The job at the steel plant, however, turns out to offer only false hope and Jess is forced back into a series of temporary, non-unionised jobs that place her in a vulnerable situation: while she relies on the workplace to help construct her butch identity, without unionised employment she cannot consolidate that identity over any length of time.

Such a situation may in part be responsible for Jess's increasing dissatisfaction with the 'he-she' life she leads. When she starts work in a cannery, she sees her future lover, the femme Theresa, 'working on a machine, coring apples' (SBB 119) and the two of them are soon living together. This part of the novel is set in the late 1960s and the increasing visibility of a politicised feminism leads to Jess and Theresa having to defend their sex/gender positions against accusations that on the one hand Theresa has been brainwashed because of her ultra-femininity, while on the other that Jess is a male chauvinist because of her masculine gender performance. Theresa justifies her love for Jess by telling her 'I'm not with a fake man, I'm with a real butch' (SBB 139), but when she also tells Jess 'You're a woman', Jess protests otherwise: 'No I'm not ... I'm a he-she. That's different' (SBB 147). The reason it is different is that for Jess, being a 'he-she' with a female lover is not the same as being a lesbian. She wants to distinguish herself from the 'Saturday night butches', for whom a butch identity is a fleeting lifestyle choice quickly discarded, and to emphasise the lasting importance of the 'he' side of the 'he-she' identity. Ultimately for Jess this means hormone therapy, mastectomy and passing as a man. Theresa's refusal to support her through it, or to accept her if she follows this course of action leads to them splitting up.

One of the consequences of Jess's medical treatment is that it becomes possible for her to pass as a man at work. At one plant where she works for several months, she says, 'I was considered one of the guys' (*SBB* 200). But while this hard-won position allows her to fulfil her desire to be a 'he', the disadvantages soon become apparent: 'At first, everything was fun. The world stopped feeling like a gauntlet I had to run through. But very quickly I discovered that passing didn't just mean slipping below the surface, it meant being buried alive. I was still me on the inside ... but I was no longer me on the outside' (*SBB* 173).

What Jess finds is that by passing she eliminates many important aspects of her identity: 'As far as the world was concerned, I was born the day I began to pass. I have no past, no loved ones, no memories, no me' (*SBB* 213). The hormone and medical treatment has altered her appearance to such an extent that what is no longer visible on her public body is what she describes as 'the contrasts of my gender' (*SBB* 222). This compelling phrase suggests two things: first, that it is the very ambiguity of Jess's identity that has constituted her identity as a child and as an adult and, second, that her decision to pass as a man has separated her from this ambiguity. Before stopping taking hormones and moving to New York, she sums up the debilitating effects of choosing to pass as a man as follows: 'I didn't get to explore being a he-she ... I simply became a he – a man without a past. Who was I now – woman or man? That question could never be answered as long as those were the only choices' (*SBB* 222).

It is to the world of work that Jess then returns in order to establish the next stage in her search for a strategy that will allow her to cope with a sex/gender grid that has only woman and man as its options. Putting aside something from each pay cheque she receives, eventually she realises that she has turned her apartment into a 'home' (*SBB* 236–7). After feeling as though she had disappeared and become a 'ghost' while passing as a man, this moment is crucial in the way that it then presages her return to a public world from which she has always felt excluded. She gets a job as a typesetter again and tracks down information about her aunt who had been an organiser for the International Ladies Garment Workers. She also finds the Stonewall Bar where the riots began, and then finds herself taking the stage at a gay and lesbian rally and chronicling her experiences to a supportive audience. When she is approached to take up a role as a union organiser herself, one can see that Feinberg is meshing together work and sexuality in such a way as to emphasise that only by eliminating discriminatory practices in the workplace is it possible to create a working culture where queer men and women can sell their labour in order to achieve the kinds of 'home' in which they will feel comfortable. That her own work is part and parcel of this process, Jess makes clear too: 'At work, when everyone else is at lunch, I've been typesetting all the history I've found, trying to make it look as important as it feels to me' (*SBB* 271).

Feinberg's novel, then, clearly represents in Jess a character for whom the oppositions of male/female, man/woman, masculine/feminine do not line up neatly underneath one another. That there is a national dimension to this situation becomes clear to her when, while passing as a man, she realises that she cannot leave the United States. She has no valid identification as a man and, as she says, 'Getting identification required identification' (*SBB* 175). It is at this moment that Jess confronts the way in which, along with its other institutions and structures, the nation-state legitimates that situation whereby there is only a choice between 'woman and man' and that once a decision is made it is fixed and irreversible in the eyes of the state. Jess spends her life in environments where that dichotomy is both ruthlessly policed and violently enforced, often by state agents – Jess is raped by the police (*SBB* 62–3) – but also in environments where it is suspended, however temporarily: in bar culture, when Jess is passing. While it may not necessarily be the case that the suspension of the 'woman and man' binary leads to a suspension of the nation-state in its legal capacity or the nation in its ideological capacity, what such a suspension does is to perhaps prompt a question: what form would a nation take that did not rely on the choice between 'woman and man'?

It seems to me that through her representation of work as an integral component in the construction of Jess's identity, Feinberg has taken us as far away as it is possible to get from the recovery narratives that dominated white male literary culture's dealings with business that I looked at in the first part of this book. Rather than asking what has happened to the nation and where has it gone and how can we reclaim it as it is ever more tainted by the machinations of corporate business, Feinberg, together with Carson McCullers and Armistead Maupin, asks questions about how the intervention of queer discourses and queer experiences of acculturation change the very contours of the nation about which she is thinking.

Notes

INTRODUCTION

1. Calvin Coolidge, 'The Press Under a Free Government', Address before the American Society of Newspaper Editors Washington, DC, 17 January 1925 <http://www.calvin-coolidge.org/pages/history/speeches/aspres/250117.html> (28 April 2003).
2. Benjamin Franklin, 'The Way to Wealth', in Nina Baym et al. (eds), *The Norton Anthology of American Literature*, Vol. 1, 4th edition (New York and London: W.W. Norton & Company), p. 443.
3. J. Hector St. Jean de Crèvecoeur, *Letters from an American Farmer*, in Baym et al. (eds), *The Norton Anthology of American Literature*, Vol. 1, p. 658.
4. Booker T. Washington, *Up From Slavery: An Autobiography* (New York: Doubleday & Company, 1901), p. 126.
5. Richard Godden, *Fictions of Capital: The American Novel from James to Mailer* (Cambridge: Cambridge University Press, 1990), p. 6.
6. Emily Stipes Watt, *The Businessman in American Literature* (Athens: University of Georgia Press, 1982), p. 150. Watt has good things to say only about Ken Kesey's *Sometimes a Great Notion*, Stanley Elkin's *A Bad Man* and *The Franchiser*, and James Dickey's *Deliverance*.
7. Henry David Thoreau, *Walden, or Life in the Woods*, in Baym et al. (eds), *The Norton Anthology of American Literature*, Vol. 1, p. 1722.
8. Arthur Miller, *Death of a Salesman* (Harmondsworth: Penguin, 1962 [1949]), p. 8.
9. Timothy Melley, *Empire of Conspiracy: The Culture of Paranoia in Postwar America* (Ithaca, NY and London: Cornell University Press, 2000), p. vii.
10. Dwight D. Eisenhower, 'Farewell Address' <http://www.eisenhower.utexas.edu/farewell.htm> (7 May 2003).
11. Joseph Heller, *Catch-22* (London: Vintage, 1994 [1961]), p. 337.
12. Watt, *The Businessman in American Literature*, p. 151.
13. Sinclair Lewis, *Babbitt* (London: Vintage, 1994 [1922]), p. 179.
14. Naomi Klein, *No Logo* (London: Flamingo, 2000), p. 441.
15. Donald J. Boudreaux, 'Self-Government' <http://www.libertyhaven.com/politicsandcurrentevents/biggovernment/selfgov.shtml> (28 April 2003).
16. Jonathan Freedman, 'The Affect of the Market: Economic and Racial Exchange in *The Searchers*', *American Literary History*, Vol. 12, No. 3 (2000), pp. 585–6.
17. Dana Nelson, *National Manhood: Capitalist Citizenship and the Imagined Fraternity of White Men* (Durham, NC and London: Duke University Press, 1998).
18. Margaret L. Hedstrom, 'Beyond Feminisation: Clerical Workers in the United States from the 1920s through the 1960s', in Gregory Anderson (ed.), *The White-Blouse Revolution: Female Office Workers Since 1870* (Manchester and New York: Manchester University Press, 1988), p. 147.

See also Angel Kwolek-Folland, *Engendering Business: Men and Women in the Corporate Office, 1870–1930* (Baltimore, MD: Johns Hopkins University Press, 1994) and Fiona McNally, *Women for Hire: A Study of the Female Office Worker* (London: Macmillan, 1979).

19. E. Anthony Rotundo, *American Manhood: Transformations in Masculinity from the Revolution to the Modern Era* (New York: Basic Books, 1993), especially pp. 167–93 and 194–221. For ways in which the heterosexual/homosexual hierarchy is threatened but ultimately secured in the office see Graham Thompson, '"Dead Letters ... Dead Men": The Rhetoric of the Office in Melville's "Bartleby, the Scrivener"', *Journal of American Studies*, Vol. 34, No. 3 (December 2000), pp. 395–411; Graham Thompson, '"And that paint is a thing that will bear looking into": The Business of Sexuality in *The Rise of Silas Lapham*', *American Literary Realism*, Vol. 34, No. 1 (Fall 2000), pp. 1–20.

20. Roger Bell, *Last Among Equals: Hawaiian Statehood and American Politics* (Honolulu: University of Hawaii Press, 1984), p. 24.

21. John Carlos Rowe, *Literary Culture and U.S. Imperialism: From The Revolution to World War II* (Oxford and New York: Oxford University Press, 2000), p. 7.

22. Rowe, *Literary Culture and U.S. Imperialism*, p. 3.

23. Thomas Jefferson, 'Letter to James Madison', 27 April 1809 <http://www.loc.gov/exhibits/jefferson/149.html> (28 April 2003).

24. George Washington, 'Farewell Address' <http://usinfo.state.gov/usa/infousa/facts/democrac/49.htm> (28 April 2003).

25. *Harper's Weekly*, 18 November 1899.

26. Bill Clinton, 'Remarks by President Clinton for the 50th Anniversary of the Marshall Plan' <http://www.useu.be/DOCS/sumu4.html> (25 July 2001).

27. Andrew Carnegie, 'Americanism versus Imperialism – I', *North American Review*, Vol. 168, Issue 506 (1899), pp. 1–13 and 'Americanism versus Imperialism – II', *North American Review*, Vol. 168, Issue 508 (1899), pp. 362–72.

28. Carnegie, 'Americanism versus Imperialism – I', p. 9.

29. Carnegie, 'Americanism versus Imperialism – I', p. 10.

30. Carnegie, 'Americanism versus Imperialism – I', p. 10.

31. Carnegie, 'Americanism versus Imperialism – II', p. 370.

32. Carl Shurz, '"Manifest Destiny"', *Harper's New Monthly Magazine*, Vol. 87, Issue 521 (1893), p. 746.

33. Lorrin A. Thurston, 'The Sandwich Islands. I. – The Advantages of Annexation', *North American Review*, Vol. 156, Issue 436 (1893), p. 279.

34. John L. Stevens, 'The Hawaiian Situation: II – A Plea for Annexation', *North American Review*, Vol. 157, Issue 445 (1893), p. 743.

35. George Ticknor Curtis, 'The Sandwich Islands. II. – Is it Constitutional?', *North American Review*, Vol. 156, Issue 436 (1893), p. 284.

36. Amy Kaplan, 'Imperial Triangles: Mark Twain's Foreign Affairs', *Modern Fiction Studies*, Vol. 43, No. 1 (1997), p. 241.

37. Rowe, *Literary Culture and U.S. Imperialism*, pp. 121–39.

38. Wai-Chee Dimock, *Empire for Liberty: Melville and the Poetics of Individualism* (Princeton, NJ: Princeton University Press, 1989), p. 8.

39. Dimock, *Empire for Liberty*, p. 20.
40. See William H. Whyte, *The Organization Man* (1956); Vance Packard, *The Hidden Persuaders* (1957); David Riesman, *The Lonely Crowd* (1950).
41. Paul Gilroy, *The Black Atlantic: Modernity and Double Consciousness* (Cambridge, MA: Harvard University Press, 1993).
42. Freedman, 'The Affect of the Market', p. 587.
43. Thorstein Veblen, *The Theory of the Leisure Class* (New York: Dover, 1994 [1899]), p. 8.
44. *The American Heritage® Dictionary of the English Language*, 4th edition (2000), <http://www.bartleby.com/61/61/A0046100.html> (31 July 2001).
45. Granger Babcock, '"What's the Secret?": Willy Loman as Desiring Machine', *American Drama*, Vol. 2, No. 1 (1992), p. 67.
46. Paul Giles, *Transatlantic Insurrections: British Culture and the Formulation of American Literature, 1730–1860* (Philadelphia: University of Pennsylvania Press, 2001), p. 1.
47. Gene Wise, '"Paradigm Dramas" in American Studies: A Cultural and Institutional History of the Movement', in Lucy Maddox (ed.), *Locating American Studies: The Evolution of a Discipline* (Baltimore, MD and London: The Johns Hopkins University Press, 1999), pp. 173–4. In the introduction to a recent collection of essays, Donald Pease and Robyn Wiegman deal with some of the conceptual problems of Wise's temporal structure. See Donald E. Pease and Robyn Wiegman (eds), *The Futures of American Studies* (Durham, NC and London: Duke University Press, 2002), pp. 1–42. Notwithstanding these criticisms, Wise's essay still provides a useful working introduction the history of the subject in the United States.
48. Wise, '"Paradigm Dramas"', pp. 179–80.
49. Tremaine McDowell, *American Studies* (Minneapolis: University of Minnesota Press, 1948), p. 33.
50. McDowell, *American Studies*, p. 90.
51. McDowell, *American Studies*, p. 93.
52. Wise, '"Paradigm Dramas"', pp. 181–2.
53. C. E. Ayres, 'The Industrial Way of Life', *American Quarterly*, Vol. 1, No. 4 (1949), pp. 291–301, p. 291.
54. Ayres, 'The Industrial Way of Life', p. 293.
55. Richard Pells, *Not Like Us: How Europeans Have Loved, Hated and Transformed American Culture Since World War II* (New York: Basic Books, 1997), pp. 33–4.
56. Julianne Burton-Carajal, '"Surprise Package": Looking Southward with Disney', in Eric Smoodin (ed.), *Disney Discourse: Producing the Magic Kingdom* (New York and London: Routledge, 1994), pp. 131–47. The three films Disney produced were *South of the Border with Disney* (1941), *Saludos Amigos* (1943), and *The Three Caballeros* (1945).
57. Pells, *Not Like Us*, pp. 100–1.
58. Neil Jumonville, *Henry Steele Commager: Midcentury Liberalism and the History of the Present* (Chapel Hill and London: University of North Carolina Press, 1999), pp. 94–5.
59. Pells, *Not Like Us*, p. 111; p. 65.

CHAPTER 1

1. Perry Miller, *Errand in the Wilderness* (Cambridge, MA and London: Harvard University Press, 1993 [1956]), p. vii.
2. Miller, *Errand into the Wilderness*, p. ix.
3. Amy Kaplan, '"Left Alone with America": The Absence of Empire in the Study of American Culture', in Amy Kaplan and Donald Pease (eds), *Cultures of United States Imperialism* (Durham, NC and London: Duke University Press), p. 4.
4. Michel Foucault, *The History of Sexuality Volume 1: An Introduction* (Harmondsworth: Penguin, 1990), p. 55.
5. Kaplan, '"Left Alone with America"', p. 14. Michael J. Hogan in *Cross of Iron: Harry S. Truman and the Origins of the National Security State 1945–1954* (Cambridge: Cambridge University Press, 1998), has written about the ways in which the political culture of the United States after the Second World War was dominated by similar centrifugal and centripetal forces. Opposed to those who articulated a new ideology of national security and global obligation was a faction who defended the longstanding political values of isolationism and anti-statism.
6. Arthur Miller, *Death of a Salesman* (Harmondsworth: Penguin, 1962 [1949]), p. 7. This text is subsequently referred to as *DOAS*; citations appear in parentheses.
7. See Gayle Austin, 'The Exchange of Women and Male Homosocial Desire in Arthur Miller's *Death of a Salesman* and LH's *Another Part of the Forest*', in June Schlueter (ed.), *Feminist Rereadings of Modern American Drama* (Rutherford, NJ: Fairleigh Dickinson University Press, 1989), pp. 59–66; Kay Stanton, 'Women and the American Dream of a Salesman', in Schlueter (ed.), *Feminist Rereadings*, pp. 67–102; Granger Babcock, '"What's the Secret?": Willy Loman as Desiring Machine', *American Drama*, Vol. 2, No. 1 (1992), pp. 59–83; Paul Blumberg, 'Sociology and Social Literature: Work Alienation in the Plays of Arthur Miller', *American Quarterly*, Vol. 21, No. 2 (1969), pp. 291–310; Richard T. Brucher, 'Willy Loman and the *Soul of a New Machine*: Technology and the Common Man', *Journal of American Studies*, Vol. 17, No. 3 (1983), pp. 325–36.
8. Harold Bloom (ed.), *Willy Loman* (New York and Philadelphia: Chelsea House Publishers, 1991), pp. 1–4.
9. Brenda Murphy, 'Willy Loman: Icon of Business Culture', *Michigan Quarterly Review*, Vol. 37, No. 4 (1998), pp. 755–66.
10. Arthur Ganz, *Realms of the Self: Variations on a Theme in Modern Drama* (New York: New York University Press, 1980), p. 127.
11. Jeremy Hawthorn, 'Sales and Solidarity', in Bloom (ed.), *Willy Loman*, p. 96.
12. Babcock, '"What's the Secret?"', p. 67.
13. Arthur Miller, *Timebends* (London: Methuen, 1987), p. 62.
14. Miller, *Timebends*, p. 203.
15. Miller, *Timebends*, p. 223.
16. Revenue was raised for military expenditure by a combination of increased personal and corporate taxation, and the imposition of an excess-profits tax. The Revenue Act of 1942 actually set exemption levels below the

level of average earnings, thus significantly increasing the number of working-class wage-earners who paid tax. See Michael Edelstein, 'War and the American Economy in the Twentieth Century', in Stanley L. Engerman and Robert E. Gallman (eds), *The Cambridge Economic History of the United States Volume III: The Twentieth Century* (Cambridge: Cambridge University Press, 2000), pp. 357–66.

17. David Ryan, *US Foreign Policy in World History* (London and New York: Routledge, 2000), p. 101.

18. Nigel Leigh, *Radical Fictions and the Novels of Norman Mailer* (London: Macmillan, 1990), p. 7.

19. Quoted in Hogan, *Cross of Iron*, p. 150.

20. Richard Godden, *Fictions of Capital: The American Novel from James to Mailer* (Cambridge: Cambridge University Press, 1990), p. 174.

21. For more on this see Christopher Dandeker, *Surveillance, Power and Modernity* (Cambridge: Polity, 1990).

22. Norman Mailer, *The Naked and the Dead* (London: Flamingo, 1993 [1949]), p. 56. This text is subsequently referred to as *TNATD*; citations appear in parentheses.

23. Sean McCann, 'The Imperiled Republic: Norman Mailer and the Poetics of Anti-Liberalism', *English Literary History*, Vol. 67, No. 1 (2000), p. 295.

24. McCann, 'The Imperiled Republic', p. 303.

25. McCann, 'The Imperiled Republic', pp. 305–6.

26. Michael Roper, *Masculinity and the British Organization Man since 1945* (Oxford: Oxford University Press, 1994), p. 49. Roper argues that in Britain, because of the legacy of family capitalism, the managerial revolution occurred much more slowly and that as a result business organisation didn't restructure itself so as to maintain competitive advantage.

27. For the fullest account of this process, see Alfred D. Chandler, *The Visible Hand: The Managerial Revolution in America* (Cambridge, MA and London: Harvard University Press, 1977).

28. Michael Crozier, *The World of the Office Worker* (London and Chicago: The University of Chicago Press, 1971 [1965]), p. 1.

29. Sinclair Lewis, *Babbitt* (London: Vintage, 1994 [1922]), p. 180.

30. Vance Packard, *The Status Seekers* (Harmondsworth: Penguin, 1961 [1957]), p. 106.

31. Sloan Wilson, *The Man in the Gray Flannel Suit* (New York: Simon and Schuster, 1955), p. 29, p. 26. This text is subsequently referred to as *TMITGFS*; citations appear in parentheses.

32. William H. Whyte, *The Organization Man* (Harmondsworth: Penguin, 1960 [1956]), p. 372.

33. Whyte, *The Organization Man*, p. 22.

34. See Catherina Jurca, 'The Sanctimonious Suburbanite: Sloan Wilson's *The Man in the Gray Flannel Suit*', *American Literary History*, Vol. 11, No. 1 (1999), pp. 82–106.

35. Joseph Heller, *Catch-22* (London: Vintage, 1994 [1961]), p. 302. This text is subsequently referred to as *C22*; citations appear in parentheses.

36. Heller quoted in Thomas Blues, 'The Moral Structure of *Catch-22*', *Studies in the Novel*, Vol. 31, No. 1 (1971), p. 64.

37. Brian Way, 'Formal Experiment and Social Discontent: Joseph Heller's *Catch-22*', *Journal of American Studies*, Vol. 2, No. 2 (1968), p. 259.
38. Timothy Melley, *Empire of Conspiracy: The Culture of Paranoia in Postwar America* (Ithaca and London: Cornell University Press, 2000), pp. 66–7.
39. Melley, *Empire of Conspiracy*, p. 68.

CHAPTER 2

1. See Donald Pease, 'New Americanists: Revisionist Interventions into the Canon', *boundary 2*, Vol. 17, No. 1 (1990), pp. 1–37.
2. Bruce Kuklick, 'Myth and Symbol in American Studies', *American Quarterly*, Vol. 24, No. 4 (1972), pp. 435–50.
3. Gene Wise, '"Paradigm Dramas" in American Studies: A Cultural and Institutional History of the Movement', in Lucy Maddox (ed.), *Locating American Studies: The Evolution of a Discipline* (Baltimore, MD and London: The Johns Hopkins University Press, 1999), p. 185.
4. Frederick Buell, *National Culture and the New Global System* (Baltimore, MD and London: The Johns Hopkins University Press, 1994), p. 144.
5. Buell, *National Culture*, p. 146.
6. Immanuel Wallerstein, *The Modern World System* (New York: Academic Press, 1974).
7. Buell, *National Culture*, p. 136.
8. John Barth, 'The Literature of Exhaustion', *The Atlantic*, Vol. 220, No. 2 (1967), pp. 29–34.
9. Thomas Pynchon, *The Crying of Lot 49* (Harmondsworth: Penguin, 1974 [1966]), p. 38; p. 31. This text is subsequently referred to as *COL49*; citations appear in parentheses.
10. Malcolm Bradbury, *The Modern American Novel* (Oxford: Oxford University Press, 1984 [1983]), p. 177.
11. Brian McHale, *Postmodernist Fiction* (London: Routledge, 1989 [1987]), pp. 21–5.
12. McHale, *Postmodernist Fiction*, p. 10.
13. Pierre-Yves Petillon, 'A Re-cognition of the Errand into the Wilderness', in Patrick O'Donnell (ed.), *New Essays on* The Crying of Lot 49 (Cambridge: Cambridge University Press, 1991), p. 140.
14. Timothy Melley, *Empire of Conspiracy: The Culture of Paranoia in Postwar America* (Ithaca, NY and London: Cornell University Press, 2000), p. 42.
15. Thomas H. Schaub, *Pynchon: The Voice of Ambiguity* (Urbana, Chicago: University of Illinois Press, 1981), p. 28.
16. Petillon, 'A Re-cognition of the Errand into the Wilderness', p. 154.
17. Thomas Pynchon, 'A Journey into the Mind of Watts', 12 June 1966, <http://www.nytimes.com/books/97/05/18/reviews/pynchon-watts.html>, (29 April 2003).
18. Petillon, 'A Re-cognition of the Errand into the Wilderness', p. 155.
19. William Gaddis, *JR* (Harmondsworth: Penguin, 1993 [1975]), p. 18. This text is subsequently referred to as *JR*; citations appear in parentheses.
20. Thomas LeClair, 'William Gaddis, *JR*, & the Art of Excess', *Modern Fiction Studies*, Vol. 27, No. 4 (1981–82), p. 588.

21. LeClair, 'William Gaddis', p. 597.
22. Joel Dana Black, 'The Paper Empires and Empirical Fictions of William Gaddis', *The Reviews of Contemporary Fiction*, Vol. 2, No. 2 (1982), p. 22.
23. Stephen Weisenburger, 'Contra Naturam?: Usury in William Gaddis' *JR*', *Genre*, Vol. 13 (1980), p. 94.
24. Weisenburger, 'Contra Naturam?', p. 106.
25. Christopher J. Knight, *Hints and Guesses: William Gaddis's Fiction of Longing* (Madison: University of Wisconsin Press, 1997), p. 84.
26. Quoted in Stephen Moore, *William Gaddis* (Boston: Twayne Publishers, 1989), p. 13.
27. Leslie Fiedler, *Love and Death in the American Novel* (New York: Criterion, 1960).
28. Moore, *William Gaddis*, p. 136.
29. Quoted in Moore, *William Gaddis*, p. 8.
30. Moore, *William Gaddis*, p. 88.
31. See Moore, *William Gaddis*, pp. 88–99.
32. Moore, *William Gaddis*, p. 137.
33. Gregory Comnes, *The Ethics of Indeterminacy in the Novels of William Gaddis* (Gainesville: University Press of Florida, 1994), p. 97.
34. LeClair, 'William Gaddis', p. 600.
35. Joseph Heller, *Something Happened* (New York: Alfred A. Knopf, 1974), p. 527. This text is subsequently referred to as *SH*; citations appear in parentheses.
36. Lindsey Tucker, 'Entropy and Information Theory in Heller's *Something Happened*', *Contemporary Literature*, Vol. 25, No. 3 (1984), pp. 323–40.
37. Lois Tyson, 'Joseph Heller's *Something Happened*: The Commodification of Consciousness and the Postmodern Flight from Inwardness', *CEA Critic*, Vol. 54, No. 2 (1992), p. 38.
38. Tyson, 'Joseph Heller's *Something Happened*', p. 39.
39. I am grateful for this information to Stephen Moore's excellent website on William Gaddis, available at <http://www.williamgaddis.org>.

CHAPTER 3

1. Gene Wise, '"Paradigm Dramas" in American Studies: A Cultural and Institutional History of the Movement', in Lucy Maddox (ed.), *Locating American Studies: The Evolution of a Discipline* (Baltimore, MD and London: The Johns Hopkins University Press, 1999), p. 205.
2. Wise, '"Paradigm Dramas"', p. 198. Italics in the original.
3. Donald Pease, 'National Narratives, Postnational Narration', *Modern Fiction Studies*, Vol. 43, No. 1 (1997), p. 1.
4. Pease, 'National Narratives', p. 4; p. 7.
5. Dinesh D'Souza, *Illiberal Education: the Politics of Race and Sex on Campus* (New York and Oxford: Maxwell Macmillan International, 1991); Allan Bloom, *The Closing of the American Mind* (New York: Simon and Schuster, 1987); Richard Bernstein, *Dictatorship of Virtue: Multiculturalism and the Battle for America's Future* (New York: Knopf, 1994); Arthur Schlesinger, Jr, *Disuniting of America* (New York and London: Norton, 1992). For a

defence of multicultural developments in United States education, see
Gerald Graff, *Beyond the Culture Wars: How Teaching the Conflicts Can
Revitalize American Education* (New York and London: Norton, 1992);
Lawrence Levine's *Opening of the American Mind: Canons, Culture and
History* (Boston: Beacon, 1998); John K. Wilson, *The Myth of Political
Correctness: The Conservative Attack on Higher Education* (Durham, NC:
Duke University Press, 1995); Michael Bérubé, *Public Access: Literary Theory
and American Cultural Politics* (New York: Verso, 1996).

6. Donald Pease, 'From American Studies to Cultural Studies: Paradigms
   and Paradoxes', *European Journal of American Culture*, Vol. 19, No. 1 (1999),
   p. 8.
7. Frederick Buell, 'Nationalist Postnationalism: Globalist Discourse in
   Contemporary American Culture', *American Quarterly*, Vol. 50, No. 3
   (1998), p. 550.
8. Buell, 'Nationalist Postnationalism', p. 551.
9. Buell, 'Nationalist Postnationalism', p. 553.
10. Buell, 'Nationalist Postnationalism', pp. 559–60.
11. David Mamet, *American Buffalo* (London: Methuen, 1984 [1975]), pp. 74–5.
    This text is subsequently referred to as *AB*; citations appear in parentheses.
12. C. W. E. Bigsby, *David Mamet* (London and New York: Methuen, 1985),
    p. 78.
13. Leslie Kane (ed.), *David Mamet in Conversation* (Ann Arbor: The University
    of Michigan Press, 2001), p. 47.
14. Ralph Waldo Emerson, 'The Poet', in Nina Baym et al. (eds), *The Norton
    Anthology of American Literature*, Vol. 1, 4th edition (New York and London:
    W.W. Norton & Company), p. 1086.
15. Herman Melville, 'Hawthorne and His Mosses', in Baym et al. (eds), *The
    Norton Anthology of American Literature*, p. 2207.
16. Quoted in Bigsby, *David Mamet*, p. 11.
17. Nina Baym, 'Melodramas of Beset Manhood: How Theories of American
    Fiction Exclude Women Authors', in Maddox (ed.), *Locating American
    Studies*, p. 222.
18. Steven Price, 'Negative Creation: The Detective Story in *Glengarry Glen
    Ross*', in Leslie Kane (ed.), *David Mamet's* Glengarry Glen Ross*: Text and
    Performance* (New York and London: Garland Publishing, 2000 [1996]),
    p. 4.
19. Price, 'Negative Creation', p. 5.
20. Price, 'Negative Creation', p. 8.
21. David Mamet, *Glengarry Glen Ross* (London: Methuen, 1984), p. 57. This
    text is subsequently referred to as *GGR*; citations appear in parentheses.
22. Price, 'Negative Creation', p. 5.
23. Baym, 'Melodramas of Beset Manhood', p. 221.
24. Fredric Jameson, 'Postmodernism and Consumer Capitalism', in Hal
    Foster (ed.), *Postmodern Culture* (London and Concord, MA: Pluto Press,
    1985 [1982]), p. 125.
25. Jameson, 'Postmodernism and Consumer Capitalism', p. 125.
26. The exception is a chase sequence. See Bret Easton Ellis, *American Psycho*
    (London: Picador, 1991), pp. 350–1. This text is subsequently referred to
    as *AP*; citations appear in parentheses.

27. Jameson, 'Postmodernism and Consumer Capitalism', p. 114.
28. Philip E. Simmons, *Deep Surfaces: Mass Culture and History in Postmodern American Fiction* (Athens: University of Georgia Press, 1997), p. 20.
29. Simmons, *Deep Surfaces*, p. 41.
30. John Carlos Rowe, *Literary Culture and U.S. Imperialism: From the Revolution to World War II* (Oxford and New York: Oxford University Press, 2000), p. 297.
31. Buell, 'Nationalist Postnationalism', p. 564.
32. Buell, 'Nationalist Postnationalism', p. 564.
33. David Brande, 'The Business of Cyberpunk: Symbolic Economy and Ideology in William Gibson', *Configurations*, Vol. 2, No. 3 (1994), p. 509.
34. William Gibson, *Neuromancer* (London: Voyager Classics, 2001 [1984]), p. 12. This text is subsequently referred to as *NM*; citations appear in parentheses.
35. Brande, 'The Business of Cyberpunk', p. 511.
36. Brande, 'The Business of Cyberpunk', pp. 530–1.
37. Catherine Casey, *Work, Self and Society After Industrialism* (London and New York: Routledge, 1995), pp. 138–82.
38. Brande, 'The Business of Cyberpunk', p. 535.
39. Richard Slotkin, *Gunfighter Nation: The Myth of the Frontier in Twentieth-Century America* (New York: Harper Perennial, 1993 [1992]).
40. Buell, 'Nationalist Postnationalism', p. 565.
41. Buell, 'Nationalist Postnationalism', p. 565.
42. Buell, 'Nationalist Postnationalism', p. 565.
43. Fred Pfeil, *Another Tale to Tell: Politics and Narrative in Postmodern Culture* (New York: Verso, 1990), pp. 97–125.
44. Nick Heffernan, *Capital, Class and Technology in Contemporary American Culture* (London and Sterling, VA: Pluto Press, 2000), p. 90.
45. Douglas Coupland, *Generation X* (London: Abacus 1997 [1991]), p. 26. This text is subsequently referred to as *GX*; citations appear in parentheses.
46. Heffernan, *Capital, Class and Technology*, p. 91.
47. Heffernan, *Capital, Class and Technology*, p. 92.
48. Heffernan, *Capital, Class and Technology*, p. 95.
49. Heffernan, *Capital, Class and Technology*, p. 99.
50. Buell, 'Nationalist Postnationalism', p. 565; p. 567.
51. Paul E. Ceruzzi, *A History of Modern Computing* (Cambridge, MA: MIT Press, 2000), p. 79.
52. Douglas Coupland, *Microserfs* (London: Flamingo, 1995), p. 23. This text is subsequently referred to as *MS*; citations appear in parentheses.
53. Bill Gates, *The Road Ahead* (Harmondsworth: Penguin, 1996, revised edition).
54. Arthur Kroker, 'Virtual Capitalism', in Stanley Aranowitz, Barbara Martinsons and Michael Menser (eds), *Technoscience and Cyberculture* (New York and London: Routledge, 1996), p. 168.
55. Kroker, 'Virtual Capitalism', p. 178.
56. Peter Stoneley, 'Rewriting the Gold Rush: Twain, Harte and Homosociality', *Journal of American Studies*, Vol. 30, No. 2 (1996), p. 189.
57. Po Bronson, *The Nudist on the Late Shift: And Other Tales from Silicon Valley* (London: Secker & Warburg, 1999), p. xvii.

CHAPTER 4

1. John Carlos Rowe, *Literary Culture and U.S. Imperialism: From the Revolution to World War II* (Oxford and New York: Oxford University Press, 2000), p. 3.
2. Michael Spindler, *Veblen and Modern America: Revolutionary Iconoclast* (London and Sterling, VA: Pluto Press, 2002), pp. 26–32.
3. Spindler, *Veblen and Modern America*, pp. 31–2.
4. Spindler, *Veblen and Modern America*, p. 41.
5. Shelley Streeby, *American Sensations: Class, Empire, and the Production of Popular Culture* (Berkeley, Los Angeles and London: University of California Press, 2002), p. 84.
6. Amy Kaplan, 'Manifest Domesticity', *American Literature*, Vol. 70, No. 3 (1998), p. 582.
7. Kaplan, 'Manifest Domesticity', p. 585.
8. Kaplan, 'Manifest Domesticity', p. 584.
9. Paul Giles, 'Virtual Eden: *Lolita*, Pornography, and the Perversion of American Studies', *Journal of American Studies*, Vol. 34, No. 1 (2000), p. 41.
10. Giles, 'Virtual Eden', p. 51
11. Giles, 'Virtual Eden', p. 65.
12. Ayn Rand, *Atlas Shrugged* (Harmondsworth: Signet, 1992 [1957]), p. 1075. This text is subsequently referred to as *AS*; citations appear in parentheses.
13. Ayn Rand, *The Fountainhead* (London: Harper Collins, 1994 [1947]), pp. 7–8. This text is subsequently referred to as *TF*; citations appear in parentheses.
14. William H. Whyte, *The Organization Man* (Harmondsworth: Penguin, 1960 [1956]), p. 8.
15. Sacvan Bercovitch, *The American Jeremiad* (Madison: The University of Wisconsin Press, 1978).
16. Leonard Peikoff, 'It Is Time to Declare War', *Washington Post*, 20 September 2001.
17. Joyce Carol Oates, *Expensive People* (Virago: London, 1999 [1968]), p. 32. This text is subsequently referred to as *EP*; citations appear in parentheses.
18. Kaplan, 'Manifest Domesticity', p. 582.
19. Kathy Acker, *Empire of the Senseless* (Picador: London (1989 [1988]), p. 3. This text is subsequently referred to as *EOTS*; citations appear in parentheses.
20. Brian McHale, *Constructing Postmodernism* (Routledge: London, 1992), p. 234.
21. Donna Haraway, *Simians, Cyborgs and Women: The Reinvention of Nature* (Routledge: New York, 1991), p. 150.
22. Haraway, *Simians, Cyborgs and Women*, p. 149.
23. Michel Foucault, 'Of Other Spaces', *Diacritics*, Vol. 16, No. 1 (1986), p. 27.

CHAPTER 5

1. Gene Wise, '"Paradigm Dramas" in American Studies: A Cultural and Institutional History of the Movement', in Lucy Maddox (ed.), *Locating*

American Studies: The Evolution of a Discipline (Baltimore and London: The Johns Hopkins University Press, 1999), p. 187.

2. John Carlos Rowe (ed.), *Post-Nationalist American Studies* (Berkeley, Los Angeles and London: University of California Press, 2000), p. 12.
3. Deborah Shnookal and Mirta Muniz (eds), *Jose Marti Reader: Writings on the Americas* (Melbourne: Ocean Press, 1999), pp. 111–20.
4. Janice Radway, 'What's in a Name? Presidential Address to the American Studies Association, 20 November, 1998', *American Quarterly*, Vol. 51, No. 1 (1999), p. 2.
5. David Kazanjian, 'Race, Nation, Equality: Olaudah Equiano's *Interesting Narrative* and a Genealogy of U.S. Mercantilism', in Rowe (ed.), *Post-Nationalist American Studies*, p. 131.
6. Kazanjian, 'Race, Nation, Equality', p. 148.
7. Kazanjian, 'Race, Nation, Equality', p. 151.
8. Ralph Ellison, *Invisible Man* (London: Penguin Books, 2001 [1952]), p. xxvi. This text is subsequently referred to as *IM*; citations appear in parentheses.
9. See Frantz Fanon, *Black Skin, White Masks*, translated by Charles Lam Markmann (London: Pluto, 1986 [1951]) and bell hooks, *Black Looks: Race and Representation* (Boston, MA: South End Press, 1992); *Art on my Mind: Visual Politics* (New York: New Press, 1995).
10. J. Edgar Hoover, *Masters of Deceit: The Story of Communism in America* (London: Dent, 1958), p. 81.
11. Vance Packard, *The Hidden Persuaders* (Harmondsworth: Penguin, 1961 [1957]), p. 11.
12. Octavia Butler, *Kindred* (London: The Women's Press, 1995 [1979]), p. 261. This text is subsequently referred to as *K*; citations appear in parentheses.
13. Gish Jen, *Typical American* (London: Granta, 1998 [1991]), p. 27. This text is subsequently referred to as *TA*; citations appear in parentheses.
14. Lisa Lowe, *Immigrant Acts: On Asian American Cultural Politics* (Durham, NC: Duke University Press, 1996), p. 2.
15. Lowe, *Immigrant Acts*, p. 3.
16. Lowe, *Immigrant Acts*, p. 4.
17. Lowe, *Immigrant Acts*, p. 10.
18. David Palumbo-Liu, *Asian/American: Historical Crossings of a Racial Frontier* (Stanford, CA: Stanford University Press, 1999), p. 341.
19. Lowe, *Immigrant Acts*, p. 29.
20. Tim Engles, '"Visions of me in the whitest raw light": Assimilation and Doxic Whiteness in Chang-rae Lee's *Native Speaker*', *Hitting Critical Mass*, Vol. 4, No. 2 (1997), p. 27.
21. Engles, '"Visions of me in the whitest raw light"', p. 28.
22. Chang-rae Lee, *Native Speaker* (London: Granta, 1998 [1995]), p. 1. This text is subsequently referred to as *NS*; citations appear in parentheses.
23. Kenneth Millard, *Contemporary American Fiction: An Introduction to American Fiction since 1970* (Oxford: Oxford University Press, 2000), p. 164.
24. Millard, *Contemporary American Fiction*, p. 166.
25. Palumbo-Liu, *Asian/American*, p. 320–1.

CHAPTER 6

1. Even the most recent attempts to represent the emerging field of postnational American Studies fall short here. Of the 23 essays in Donald E. Pease and Robyn Wiegman (eds), *The Futures of American Studies* (Durham, NC and London: Duke University Press, 2002) only one foregrounds the issue of sexuality. John Carlos Rowe's collection, *Post-Nationalist American Studies* (Berkeley, Los Angeles and London: University of California Press, 2000) ignores sexuality entirely.
2. Bryce Traister, 'Academic Viagra: The Rise of American Masculinity Studies', *American Quarterly*, Vol. 52, No. 2 (2000), p. 276.
3. Traister, 'Academic Viagra', p. 276.
4. Eve Kosofsky Sedgwick, *Between Men: English Literature and Male Homosocial Desire* (New York: Columbia University Press, 1985), pp. 1–2.
5. Lee Edelman, *Homographesis: Essays in Gay Literary and Cultural Theory* (New York and London: Routledge, 1994), p. 158.
6. Alan Sinfield, *Cultural Politics – Queer Reading* (London: Routledge, 1994), p. 42.
7. Sloan Wilson, *The Man in the Gray Flannel Suit* (New York: Simon and Schuster, 1955), p. 29.
8. Wilson, *The Man in the Gray Flannel Suit*, p. 156.
9. Robert J. Corber, *Homosexuality in Cold War America: Resistance and the Crisis of Masculinity* (Durham, NC and London: Duke University Press, 1997), p. 3.
10. Corber, *Homosexuality in Cold War America*, p. 4.
11. Joseph Bristow, *Sexuality* (London and New York: Routledge, 1997), p. 216.
12. Doreen Fowler, 'Carson McCullers's Primal Scenes: *The Ballad of the Sad Café*', *Critique: Studies in Contemporary Fiction*, Vol. 43, No. 3 (2002), p. 260.
13. Fowler, 'Carson McCullers's Primal Scenes', p. 266.
14. Fowler, 'Carson McCullers's Primal Scenes', p. 268.
15. Gregory Woods, *A History of Gay Literature: The Male Tradition* (New Haven, CT and London: Yale University Press, 1998), p. 13.
16. Rachel Adams, *Sideshow U.S.A: Freaks and the American Cultural Imagination* (Chicago and London: University of Chicago Press, 2001), p. 90.
17. Adams, *Sideshow U.S.A*, p. 93.
18. Carson McCullers, *The Ballad of the Sad Café* (Harmondsworth: Penguin, 1979 [1951]), p. 7. This text is subsequently referred to as *TBOTSC*; citations appear in parentheses.
19. Adams, *Sideshow U.S.A*, p. 90.
20. See Gayle Rubin, 'The Traffic in Women: Notes on the "Political Economy" of Sex', in Rayna R. Reiter (ed.), *Toward an Anthropology of Women* (New York: Monthly Review Press, 1975) and Sedgwick, *Between Men*.
21. Adams, *Sideshow U.S.A*, p. 91.
22. William Burroughs, *Naked Lunch* (London: Flamingo, 1993 [1959]), p. 8. This text is subsequently referred to as *NL*; citations appear in parentheses.
23. Quoted in Jamie Russell, *Queer Burroughs* (London: Palgrave, 2001), p. 44.
24. Russell, *Queer Burroughs*, p. 44.
25. Russell, *Queer Burroughs*, p. 47.
26. Russell, *Queer Burroughs*, p. 49.

27. Russell, *Queer Burroughs*, p. 50.
28. Timothy Melley, *Empire of Conspiracy: The Culture of Paranoia in Postwar America* (Ithaca, NY and London: Cornell University Press, 2000), p. 163.
29. Melley, *Empire of Conspiracy*, p. 168.
30. Woods, A *History of Gay Literature*, p. 161.
31. Armistead Maupin, *Tales of the City* (London: Black Swan, 1990 [1978]), p. 7. This text is subsequently referred to as *TOTC*; citations appear in parentheses.
32. Dennis Allen, 'Lesbian and Gay Studies: A Consumer's Guide', in Thomas Foster, Carol Siegel and Ellen E. Berry (eds), *The Gay 90s: Disciplinary and Interdisciplinary Formations in Queer Studies* (New York and London: New York University Press, 1997), p. 24.
33. John D'Emilio, *Making Trouble: Essays on Gay History, Politics, and the University* (New York: Routledge, 1992), p. 9.
34. D'Emilio, *Making Trouble*, p. 7.
35. Armistead Maupin, *Further Tales of the City* (Corgi: London, 1987 [1982]), pp. 11–12. This text is subsequently referred to as *FTOTC*; citations appear in parentheses.
36. Woods, A *History of Gay Literature*, p. 162.
37. Armistead Maupin, *More Tales of the City* (Black Swan: London, 1990 [1980]), p. 8. This text is subsequently referred to as *MTOTC*; citations appear in parentheses.
38. Leslie Feinberg, *Stone Butch Blues* (New York: Firebrand Books, 1993), p. 20. This text is subsequently referred to as *SBB*; citations appear in parentheses.

Index